Churches, Temples, and Financial Crimes

Fausto Martin De Sanctis

Churches, Temples, and Financial Crimes

A Judicial Perspective of the Abuse of Faith

Springer

Fausto Martin De Sanctis
Tribunal Regional Federal 3rd Region
São Paulo, Brazil

ISBN 978-3-319-15680-4 ISBN 978-3-319-15681-1 (eBook)
DOI 10.1007/978-3-319-15681-1

Library of Congress Control Number: 2015933515

Springer Cham Heidelberg New York Dordrecht London

Printed on acid-free paper

Springer International Publishing AG Switzerland is part of Springer Science+Business Media (www.springer.com)

Acknowledgments

I acknowledge, with gratitude, the help that I have received from my friends and all of the civil servants in my chambers at the Federal Appellate Court in São Paulo, especially Noemia Maria Ferreira Fonseca, José Antonio Monteiro, Tatyanne Costa, and Rafael Gomes Dias.

I would like to thank Hana Nagdimov, Welmoed Spahr, Olivier Duverger, Norberto Bonavita, and Helio Egydio de Matos Nogueira for their invaluable support.

I am also thankful to Rebecca Szucs for her excellent work editing this book.

I am particularly grateful to my sons Thomaz and Theodoro for their patience and understanding during my writing and their constant motivation and support.

Finally, I would like to express my respect for the churches and temples that promote love, reason, and living in harmony with creation and the creator.

Contents

About the Author

Fausto Martin De Sanctis holds a Doctorate in Criminal Law from the University of São Paulo's School of Law (USP) and an advanced degree in Civil Procedure from the Federal University of Brasilia (UnB) in Brazil. He was a Public Defender in São Paulo from 1989 to 1990 and a State Court Judge, also in São Paulo, from 1990 to 1991, until he was appointed to the Federal Courts.

He is currently a Federal Appellate Judge in Brazil's Federal Court for the Third Region, with jurisdiction over the states of São Paulo and Mato Grosso do Sul. He is also the Deputy Director of the Federal Judicial School and a member of the Portuguese Language Law Jurists Community (CJLP). Since 2013, he has been an Advisory Council Member for the Brazil–U.S. Legal and Judicial Studies Program at American University Washington College of Law.

Judge De Sanctis was selected to handle a specialized federal court created in Brazil to exclusively hear complex cases involving financial crimes and money laundering offenses. He is a world-renowned expert on this topic and has been invited to participate in programs and conferences both in Brazil and internationally.

From April 2 to September 28, 2012, Judge De Sanctis was a fellow at Federal Judicial Center in Washington, DC.

His publications include, among others:

Books:

Football, Gambling, and Money Laundering: A Global Criminal Justice Perspective. Cham, Heidelberg, New York, Dordrecht, London: Springer, 2014;
Criminal Law – General Rules (*Direito Penal – Parte Geral*). São Paulo, Método, Rio de Janeiro: Forense, 2014;
Money Laundering Through Art: A Criminal Justice Perspective. Cham, Heidelberg, New York, Dordrecht, London: Springer, 2013;
Money Laundering Through Gambling and Soccer: Analysis and Proposals (*Lavagem de Dinheiro. Jogos de Azar e Futebol. Análise e Proposições*). Curitiba: Editora Juruá, 2010;
Criminal Liability of Corporations and Modern Criminal Methods (*Responsabilidade Penal das Corporações e Criminalidade Moderna*). São Paulo: Saraiva, 2009;
Organized Crime and the Disposal of Seized Assets: Money Laundering, Plea Bargains, and Social Responsibility (*Crime Organizado e Destinação de Bens Apreendidos. Lavagem de Dinheiro, Delação Premiada e Responsabilidade Social*). São Paulo: Saraiva, 2009;
The Fight Against Money Laundering: Theory and Practice (*Combate à Lavagem de Dinheiro, Teoria e Prática*). Campinas: Millennium, 2008;
Criminal Tax Law: Highlights (*Direito Penal Tributário: Aspectos Relevantes*). Campinas: Bookseller, 2006;
Criminality in the National Financial System: Criminal Law and Protection of Brazil's National Financial System (*Punibilidade no Sistema Financeiro Nacional: Tipos Penais que Tutelam o Sistema Financeiro Nacional*). Campinas: Millennium, 2003;
Criminal Liability of Corporations (*Responsabilidade Penal da Pessoa Jurídica*), São Paulo: Saraiva, 1999.

Articles and Book Chapters:

"Criminal Liability of Corporations" ("Responsabilidade Penal das Corporações"). In *A Book in Honor of Miguel Reale Junior* (*Livro Homenagem a Miguel Reale Junior*). Rio de Janeiro: GZ, 2014;
"Popular Action. Using Habeas Corpus in the Context of Financial Crimes" ("Ação Popular: A Utilização do Habeas Corpus na Dinâmica dos Crimes Financeiros"). In *Popular Action* (*Ação Popular*). São Paulo: Saraiva, 2013;
"Coherent and Functional Criminal Law" ("Direito Penal Coerente e Funcional"). São Paulo: Revista dos Tribunais, Vol. 919, 2012;
"Telephone Tapping and Fundamental Rights" ("Interceptações Telefônicas e Direitos Fundamentais"). In *A Tribute to Afrânio Silva Jardim: Writings and Studies* (*Tributo a Afrânio Silva Jardim: Escritos e Estudos*). Rio de Janeiro: Lúmen Júris, 2011;
"The Constitution and Freedoms" ("Constituição e Regime das Liberdades"). São Paulo: Revista dos Tribunais, 2009;
"Human Trafficking: The Crime and Victim Consent" ("Tráfico Internacional de Pessoas: Tipo Penal e o Consentimento do Ofendido"). In *Women and Criminal Law* (*Mulher e Direito Penal*). Rio de Janeiro: Forense, 2007;

"Crimes Against the National Financial System: A Precursor to Money Laundering" ("Crimes Contra o Sistema Financerio Nacional como Antecedentes de Lavagem de Valores"). In *Money Laundering - Commentary on the Law by Judges at Specialized Courts, In Honor of Gilson Dipp* (*Lavagem de Dinheiro – Comentários à Lei pelos Juízes das Varas Especializadas. Homenagem ao Ministro Gilson Dipp*). Porto Alegre: Livraria do Advogado, 2007;

Judge De Sanctis has also written a number of articles published in newspapers and magazines specializing in law and economics.

Chapter 1
Introduction

To find out how easy it is to commit fraud in the name of God, a law firm in São Paulo, Brazil, adopted measures to create a fake church. They verified that there are no theological or doctrinal requirements to register a church with the state, nor is there a minimum number of followers. All that was required was filing one document in the National Register of Legal Entities. With this single registration, the "church" was allowed to open bank accounts, hold several financial investments, purchase and sell property, and engage in other economic transactions, all while benefitting from tax exempt status. The "church" could designate personal property for exemption from municipal taxes, and its leaders were even exempt from compulsory military service.[1]

"Religious life manifests itself on two conceptually distinct levels: on an individual level, where individuals seek to shape their beliefs and actions with respect to their own conceptions of spiritual precepts, and on a communal level, where individuals holding shared beliefs develop and exercise those beliefs as a group. One of the key features distinguishing the two categories is the expansionist nature of the former: unlike individual religion, corporate religion seeks to recruit converts to its views of God and the world."[2]

Churches and temples occupy a unique place in human culture. For a long time they have been one of the most hospitable institutions in a legally constituted society. Churches have such a strong influence on human behavior that, in the words of Jon Meacham, churches "give the best chance to keep violence down, discourage out-of-wedlock births, encourage the healthy upbringing of children, and imbue a sense of work and responsibility that would help end poverty."[3] Although churches and temples should have a protected right to govern and manage their own affairs

---

[1] DALLARI, Dalmo. Fraudes em nome de Deus. Observatório da Imprensa, caderno da cidadania, http://observatoriodaimprensa.com.br/news/view/fraudes_em_nome_de_deus, Mar. 16, 2010.

[2] See SMITH, Michael E. The Special Place of Religion in the Constitution. 1983 Sup. Ct. Rev. 83, 90.

[3] MEACHAM, Jon. The Gospel Truth. Washington Monthly, Dec. 25, 1993, p. 8.

F.M. De Sanctis, *Churches, Temples, and Financial Crimes*,
DOI 10.1007/978-3-319-15681-1_1

spreading religious doctrine, they must also keep their moral and legal obligations. Unfortunately, churches and temples are increasingly being used to commit crimes, notably fraud, embezzlement, tax evasion, and money laundering.[4]

The fact that religious institutions enjoy significant autonomy and constitutional protection from state interference makes it especially difficult for law enforcement to detect their illegal activities, particularly in the area of financial crimes. Churches and temples should be required to submit to the state's law enforcement interests, like verification of the destination of donations to and from churches and temples, in a way that does not impair the institutions' beliefs, operations, and development.

The purpose of this book is to provide an understanding of the weaknesses present in the management of churches and temples, as well as the deficiencies in the legal system. The book seeks to dispel the many mysteries surrounding financial crimes, especially money laundering, by inquiring into the scale of the problem and examining legislative and institutional loopholes that give power and mobility to organized crime. After sketching the landscape of this interesting topic, the book suggests effective proposals for improving the assessment, investigation, and prosecution of financial crimes. Considerations will be presented in an effort to further the study of methods likely to add transparency to business dealings and thereby inhibit or curtail unlawful activity.

This book is divided into eight chapters. The first and current chapter introduces the topic. Chap. 2 addresses the concept of religious freedom, with particular attention paid to constitutional protections and tax immunities for churches in the United States and Brazil. Chap. 3 discusses the legal nature and government regulation of religious organizations. Chap. 4 outlines several criminal cases and investigations that involve financial crimes carried out by and through religious institutions. International religious activities and legal cooperation for repatriation of assets are analyzed in Chap. 5. Payments using illegal and disguised instruments, and the misuse of churches, temples, NGOs, trusts, associations, and foundations are addressed in Chap. 6. Chap. 7 offers conclusions clarifying how the prevention of financial crimes applies to the religious organizations. The final chapter (Chap. 8) presents national and international proposals for improving the war against financial crimes within churches and temples.

This book will show the importance of guaranteeing religious freedom without allowing such freedom to be abused for illegal purposes. Although this work may, at a glance, appear to cover the entire subject, this is actually far from the case. The book does, however, aim at achieving a logical and practical "completeness" in describing a sensitive and virtually unknown world in which religion is used to commit serious crimes.

---

[4] See CANDELORO, Ana Paula P., MARTINS DE RIZZO, Maria Balbina, PINHO, Vinicius. *Compliance 360°: Riscos, Estratégias, Conflitos e Vaidades no Mundo Corporativo*. São Paulo: Trevisan Editora Universitária, 2012, pp. 388–99.

Bibliography

CANDELORO, Ana Paula P., MARTINS DE RIZZO, Maria Balbina, PINHO, Vinicius. Compliance 360°: Riscos, Estratégias, Conflitos e Vaidades no Mundo Corporativo. São Paulo: Trevisan Editora Universitária, 2012.

DALLARI, Dalmo. Fraudes em nome de Deus. Observatório da Imprensa, caderno da cidadania, http://observatoriodaimprensa.com.br/news/view/fraudes_em_nome_de_deus, Mar. 16, 2010.

MEACHAM, Jon. The Gospel Truth. Washington Monthly, Dec. 25, 1993.

SMITH, Michael E. The Special Place of Religion in the Constitution, 1983 Sup. Ct. Rev. 83.

Chapter 2
Religious Freedom

2.1 Defining the Concept of Religion: Mega-Churches and Mega-Temples

What is religion? An institution's self-identification as "religious" is typically not questioned. Indeed, any definition of religion by the state runs the risk of violating the Establishment Clause.[1] It is necessary to look to non-legal fields for assistance when formulating a legal definition of religion, avoiding attempts to define religion by reference only to the entities in which the adherent believes, which may collapse into disputes about the unverifiable.

The traditional image of God and religion is being subsumed by a potent force of materialistic progress and alternative scientific paradigms for defining the facts of world. With exploding cultural and religious diversity in the world, especially in the United States and Brazil, courts face an increasingly varied and complicated religious environment. So much seems to be included "under the umbrella of religion that little is left over – and if everything qualifies as a religion, then the term, itself, stops being very useful anymore."[2] That is why some flexibility and careful consideration are needed.

Courts must develop an understanding of religion to be applied in cases presented before them. They cannot avoid defining religion and the definition should be express, even though it will never be perfect. The plurality of the understandings of religion can be apparent and it is important that its definition be applied in a consistent manner.

---

[1] Developments in the Law – Religion and the State, 100 Harvard Law Review 1606, 1623 (1986–1987).

[2] USMAN, Jeffrey Omar. Defining Religion: The Struggle to Define Religion Under the First Amendment and the Contributions and Insights of Other Disciplines of Study Including Theology, Psychology, Sociology, the Arts, and Anthropology. 83 North Dakota Law Review 123 (2007) (quoting Austin Cline, Religion as Faith and Ultimate Concern, http://atheism.about.com/od/aboutreligion/a/UltimateConcern.htm).

F.M. De Sanctis, *Churches, Temples, and Financial Crimes*,
DOI 10.1007/978-3-319-15681-1_2

"Religion exists both in the cultural sense as well as the ritual sense. It is about a community of like-minded people who identify with each other in ways other than what they are doing when they are praying. Religion is an aspect, sometimes a defining aspect, of culture. However, it is different from other forms of culture because religious adherents believe that their system of beliefs has a divine origin: they believe God decided what the rules are, and these rules are more fixed than fluid."[3]

In some way there is "a consensus that, first, a religion's essential nature is not simply private experience; second, religion cannot be unqualifiedly identified either with the irrational and emotive or with the rational and conceptual; third, religion is not identical with morality; and fourth, religion needs not to be theistic."[4]

The U.S. Supreme Court first attempted to define religion substantively in 1890, in *Davis v. Beason*, stating "The term 'religion' has reference to one's views of his relations to his Creator, and to the obligations they impose of reverence for his being and character, and of obedience to his will."[5] In its 1961 decision in *Torcaso v. Watkins*, a unanimous Supreme Court invalidated a provision of the Maryland Declaration of Rights that required public officials to declare a belief in God prior to taking office.[6] The Court, per Justice Black, held that neither the state nor the federal government may "aid those religions based on a belief in the existence of God as against those religions founded on different beliefs."[7]

The U.S. Internal Revenue Service, in its Tax Guide for Churches and Religious Organizations, states that it generally uses a combination of factors in analyzing the facts and circumstances to determine if an organization is a church for federal tax purposes.

It is hard to clarify the definitional ambiguity, but there is some need to adopt a clear standard of what constitutes a church or a temple, including one that can be applied to electronic or virtual ministries. It is important to draw a line to elucidate how it is possible that churches and temples are religious organizations, but not all religious organizations are churches or temples.[8]

A particularly potent source of conflict in church-state relations is the treatment of new or emerging religions. Many of these faiths, loosely grouped together under the label "cults," have been especially troubling to observers of religion and religious freedom, both for their own behavior and for the way they have been treated.[9]

---

[3] ARZT, Donna E., CHON, Margaret. Walking While Muslim. 68 Law & Contemporary Problems 215 (2004–2005).

[4] Developments in the Law – Religion and the State. 100 Harvard Law Review 1606, 1624 (1986–1987).

[5] 133 U.S. 333, 342 (1890).

[6] 367 U.S. 488 (1961).

[7] See Developments in the Law – Religion and the State, 100 Harvard Law Review 1606, 1624 (1986–1987).

[8] See DEAN, Jacob E. Do You Have That New Church App For A Clearer And Broader Definition of Church Under The Internal Revenue Code. 46 Creighton L. Rev. 173.

[9] HORWITZ, Paul. Scientology in Court: A Comparative Analysis and Some Thoughts on Selected Issues in Law and Religion. 47 DePaul Law Review 1 (Fall 1997).

Mega-churches have ushered in a new form of religious observance distinct from the style of observance commonly associated with a traditional church. They are not only houses for services and prayer, but also one-stop shops for congregants. Their amenities range from sports arenas and gymnasiums to day care centers and entire apartment complexes.[10]

Mega-churches and mega-temples are continuously expanding their worship and services to new cities. They usually have a unique worship style that includes one dominant male pastor, motivational speeches, and an innovative use of uplifting songs.[11] Part church, part civic community, they function like small towns. They have the ability to devote their activities, labor, and funds to influence legislation and directly lobby policy makers. The adverse effects that these establishments impose on those who reside nearby have prompted justifiable concern among some communities. Yet the religious aspects of mega-churches, like the functioning of any other church, are protected by law because they are still considered eleemosynary institutions, regardless of the amount of money that they make. Churches that function as commercial organizations should not be warranted the same protection as traditional churches if, for example, they offer gym memberships, bookstores, and franchises. These aspects do not fit the definition of eleemosynary and should not have the same level of protection that is granted to the church itself. The services provided should be considered commercial and private, not religious. Yet the presumption is still that they have eleemosynary status if the religious benefits provided are similar to those provided by typical churches. In this case, the protection of the law should be granted as it is granted to any church or charitable organization.

New religious movements raise questions of ultimate values and, in some degree or another, cannot be evaluated in terms common to all citizens. If a religion is based on beliefs whose source is beyond common comprehension, it makes principled challenges to the status quo. New religious movements may claim the right to enjoy the privileges accorded to churches in non-separationist societies as well as the right to be judged with suspicion.

The vagueness of the term "religion" leads to a broad definition that can make tax-exempt status easily ascertainable. Tax exemption, of course, does not subsidize churches, but permits them to operate freely without having financial burdens placed on them by the government. The protection afforded to the sanctity of the relationship between a church and its members promotes the principle of autonomy by recognizing the true inter-independence that defines the appropriate relationship between church and state. It is helpful to verify how churches and temples, Congress, courts, and the IRS might apply these concepts. Moral and religious issues are at stake, which include some degree of direct and indirect lobbying, and can result in pejorative and immediate calls for the revocation of a church's tax-exempt status.[12]

---

[10] See WELCH, Heather M. The Religious Land Use and Institutionalized Persons Act and Mega-Churches: Demonstrating the Limits of Religious Land Use Exemptions in Federal Legislation. 39 University of Baltimore Law Rev. 255 (2010).

[11] *Id.*

[12] See ANDERSEN, David M. Political Silence at Church: The Empty Threat of Removing Tax-Exempt Status for Insubstantial Attempts To Influence Legislation. 2006 B. Y. U. L. Rev 115.

It is important that the government requires, through the IRS, formal recognition of the status of churches or temples as exempt to qualify for tax benefits, with clear criteria that distinguishes churches and religious organizations.

Some argue that any taxation of churches is unconstitutional.[13] At the opposite extreme, there are those who claim that the tax-exempt status of churches is an unconstitutional establishment of religion.[14]

Given the short-comings of proposed definitions, it is difficult to ascertain a single or even multi-factor analysis to arrive at an acceptable definition of religion. For example, a stricter and clearer definition may be required in order to avoid the adoption of a "Temple of Marijuana" as a church. Similarly, it is difficult to delineate whether a school should be judged independently from the church, and whether it is a religious institution for purposes of obtaining tax exemption.

In a preliminary and simple search using the Aurélio Portuguese dictionary, one can find the following as the first and main definition of religion: "Belief in the existence of one or many supernatural forces, considered as the creator(s) of the Universe and that, as such, should be worshipped and obeyed."[15] This is the main definition provided, and all other definitions presented by this dictionary use the first conception of a belief in a supernatural entity. The term "religion" ("religião," in Portuguese), according to the dictionary, comes from the Latin word *religione*, which has uncertain etymology. In the work of Cicero, the word refers to *relegere*, which encompasses the meanings of "recover," "read again," "revise," and "revisit." Some Christian authors, on the other hand, connect the meaning of *religione* to the verb *religare*, which means "connecting again."[16]

One could, considering such meanings, identify a common denominator between those multiple semantic contents: all of them refer to the resumption of something that has been lost, or from which one has been—or still is—distant. This is what the constant presence of the prefix "re" suggests—be it in "religion" or *religione* or any other of the historically preceding terms. This conception is especially acceptable when one takes into consideration the western religious experience, which influenced greatly the development of linguistic and social concepts of the western civilization and was founded on the organized spirituality of Christianity. It is well known that this religious system has its beliefs centered in Jesus Christ, who, according to Christian teachings, is the Messiah, sent to historical reality to redeem human beings and unite them once again with God—who is, according to such beliefs, the Lord and origin of the universe. Therefore, one could assume that religion—especially its western conception—has, as a presupposition, the view that there is one or more supernatural entities with whom one tries to relate.

---

[13] GOODWIN, Glenn. Would Caesar Tax God? The Constitutionality of the Governmental Taxation of Churches. 35 Drake L. Rev. 383, 403–04 (1986).

[14] For instance, William A. DOHAHUE (in ANDERSEN, David M. Political Silence at Church: The Empty Threat of Removing Tax-Exempt Status for Insubstantial Attempts To Influence Legislation. 2006 B. Y. U. L. Rev 115.

[15] FERREIRA, A. B. H. *Novo Dicionário Eletrônico Aurélio versão 6.0.1*. 4ª Ed. [S.l.]: 2009.

[16] HARPER, D. Religion. In: *Online EtymologyDictionary*. http://www.etymonline.com/index.php?allowed_in_frame=0&search=religion&searchmode=none, accessed Aug. 21, 2013.

Sociologically, the view of Durkheim, who analyzed the theme of religion in his work *Les formes elementáires de la vie religieuse* (The Elementary Forms of Religious Life), is a very useful one. The author identifies religion as a social fact consisting of a unified system of beliefs and practices related to sacred elements, around which a moral community forms and accepts them as venerable. For Durkheim, sacred is everything that is considered apart—or even forsaken—from the ordinary life. For that reason, the concept of the sociologist can be considered broader, covering not only systems related to supernatural elements, but also immanent elements, such as simple objects and beings, like a pebble, trees, animals, and many other things.[17]

This discussion about the amplitude of the term "religion" was the subject of a judgment by the Supreme Federal Court of Brazil (*Supremo Tribunal Federal*), when the Court had to rule on Extreme Appeal (*Recurso Extraordinário*) No. 562.351/RS. On that occasion, the justices looked into the questions regarding the definition of "religion," "worship," and "temple" in order to decide whether tax immunity should be applied to entities related to the Freemasonry. The prevailing thesis was the one presented by Justice Ricardo Lewandowski, who concluded that tax immunity should not be applied to Masonic activity. In this decision, the justice adopted a broad conception by which "temples of any denomination" (*templos de qualquer culto*) refers to religious entities themselves and not only to the places where the acts of worship take place. Still, the justice explained that there was a need to interpret immunities restrictively, differently from constitutional freedoms, in a way that the Freemasonry could not be considered immune because it does not consist of a religion, nor does it present any kind of religious worship. Thus, considering that the goal of the constitutional norm in question consists of the protection of religious freedom and assuming that Freemasonry is not a religion, it was ruled that the constitutional immunity was inapplicable in that case.[18]

There was, however, a diverging voice in the Court. Justice Marco Aurélio, disagreeing with Lewandowski, affirmed that immunities, as means of protection of freedoms, should be interpreted in a broad way, differently from exemptions (*isenções*). Justice Aurélio noted that the Constitution only mentions the word "worship" (*culto*) and not the word "religion." He thus concluded that only the term "worship" (*culto*) was necessary in order to configure the application of tax immunity. He also claimed that there were undisputable religious elements in Freemasonry, including the expression of faith in common values and even in a supernatural being, the so-called Great Architect of the Universe. Finally, he employed a comparative law analysis, showing how Freemasonry is registered as a civil religion in other places. For those reasons, outvoted Justice Aurélio ruled in favor of the extraordinary appeal.

---

[17] DURKHEIM, E. *The Elementary Forms of the Religious Life*. Translated by Joseph Ward Swain. London: George Allen & Unwin Ltd., 1915. p. 47.

[18] Extraordinary Appeal, Brazilian Supreme Court (Recurso Extraordinário No. 562.351-RS, STF, 1ª Turma, Rel. Ricardo Lewandowski). Sept. 4, 2012, in http://www.stf.jus.br/portal/principal/principal.asp, accessed Aug. 27, 2013.

Thus, the exercise of defining religion may have some weight in determining how a new religious movement is treated in a legal system, despite the long tradition of tolerance for religious faiths. Considering cultural and historical context is important not only for our understanding of how a state will define freedom of religion, but also for the formation of legal and rhetorical strategies to protect this freedom.[19]

Applying the definition of religion in a consistent manner requires being cautious, but not frightened to a point where courts retreat to such vague definitions that the term loses its meaning.

2.2 Civil Religion

Civil religion is a shared public set of beliefs, symbols, and rituals indicating a popularly accepted religious legitimation of political authority. According to Professor Robert Bellah, "every nation exhibits public rituals and discourse that constitute an identifiable form of religion paralleling ordinary religion."[20] Both the Brazilian and American governments have "received popular legitimation by the invocation of a suprapolitical sovereignty, 'a God who stands above the nation and whose ends are standards by which to judge the nation and indeed only in terms of which the nation's existence is justified.'"[21]

The rhetoric of strict separation of church and state has obscured the many ways in which the state is inherently religious.

The phenomenon of civil religion raises questions about the assumed neutrality of government in its treatment of religions. There is a risk of expansion of the regulatory state, increasing the points of contact between churches/temples and government. Yet the need for highly limited government powers, leaving individuals and groups free to shape their own destinies, remains.

Helping religious education could be considered a violation of the Constitution and a breakdown of the separation between church and state. Nevertheless, it is necessary to distinguish between secular and sacred subjects in education—tax aid to religious schools is not the same as tax aid to the church or temple itself. Complete separation is the best for the state and for religion, but the educational curriculum of some religious bodies can be verified to uphold the principle of separation.[22]

---

[19] HORWITZ, Paul. Scientology in Court: A Comparative Analysis and Some Thoughts on Selected Issues in Law and Religion. 47 DePaul Law Review 32 (Fall 1997).

[20] See Developments in the Law – Religion and the State, 100 Harvard Law Review 1606, 1620 (1986–1987) (citing R. BELLAH, Civil Religion in America, in *Beyond Belief: Essays on Religion in a Post-Traditional* World 20, 168 (1970)).

[21] Developments in the Law – Religion and the State: Complex Interaction Between Religion and Government, 100 Harv. L. Rev. 1612, 1620 (1987).

[22] See KONVITZ, Milton R. in a similar perspective, but defending the refusal of public aid to parochial schools. Separation of Church and State: The First Freedom, 14 Law & Contemporary Problems 44 (1949).

2.3 Religious Freedom in the U.S. Constitutional Order

The First Amendment to the United States Constitution, adopted on December 15, 1791, as one of the ten amendments that comprise the Bill of Rights, prohibits the making of any law respecting an establishment of religion, impeding the free exercise of religion, abridging the freedom of speech, infringing on the freedom of press, interfering with the right to peaceably assemble, or prohibiting the petitioning for a governmental redress of grievances. Originally, the First Amendment applied only to the federal government, but the 1947 U.S. Supreme Court decision in *Everson v. Board of Education* incorporated the Establishment Clause, making it applicable to the states.

The Establishment Clause of the First Amendment means that neither a state nor the federal government can set up a church or pass laws that aid one religion, aid all religions, or prefer one religion over another. No tax in any amount, large or small, can be levied to support any religious activity or institution.[23]

The U.S. Supreme Court, in its first major free exercise case, rejected the suggestion that the Free Exercise Clause created exemptions from generally applicable laws. In 1878, in the case of *Reynolds v. United States*, the Court limited the scope of First Amendment protection by weighing conflicts between laws of general applicability and religious practices in favor of laws of general applicability. Reynolds, the petitioner, challenged a federal statute that prohibited plural marriages, a practice he engaged in as a requirement of his religious faith and church. Although the law required imprisonment of Reynolds for obeying a command of his religion, the Court upheld the law, reasoning that "laws are made for the government of actions, and while they cannot interfere with mere religious belief and opinions, they may with practices." Beginning in 1963, the Court's interpretation of the Free Exercise Clause shifted in favor of religious conduct. In *Sherbert v. Verner*, the Court departed from *Reynolds* and adopted a strict scrutiny test for exercise cases. Any government act that significantly burdened religiously-motivated conduct was presumptively unconstitutional and government-imposed burdens were valid only where the state could establish a compelling government interest.[24]

On November 6, 2013, the U.S. Supreme Court heard oral arguments in *Town of Greece v. Galloway*, the first legislative prayer case that the Court has taken in more than three decades.[25] *Greece* focuses on whether a small town in upstate New York

[23] The U.S. Supreme Court extended the establishment clause to the states and recited separationist dicta that would seem to prohibit any aid to religion (*Everton v. Board of Education*, 330 U.S. 1, 15–16 (1947)).

[24] In WELCH, Heather M. The Religious Land Use and Institutionalized Persons Act and Mega-Churches: Demonstrating the Limits of Religious Land Use Exemptions in Federal Legislation. 39 University of Baltimore L. Rev. 255 (2010).

[25] Two town residents, after asking the board to change its practice several times, filed a lawsuit against the town board in 2008 because they were offended by the "town board's alignment with Christianity through the board's persistent presentation of Christian prayers." In their complaint, they argued that this "sends the message to non-Christians that they are unwelcome at Board meetings and that the Board does not represent non-Christians' concerns." (Complaint at 5, *Galloway v. Town of Greece*, 732 F. Supp. 2d 195 (W.D.N.Y. 2010)).

acted unconstitutionally in allowing only Christian clergy to open official town meetings with sectarian prayer. The outcome of this case could have major implications for the future of religion in the public sphere in America. The case could determine whether religious liberty in the United States remains strong or is seriously limited. *Greece* is just one of many religious liberty cases winding their way through the federal courts today, on issues ranging from the role of religion in same-sex marriage to protests of contraceptive coverage in the Affordable Care Act. The decisions in each of these cases will either strengthen and broaden religious liberty or limit and weaken it.

Sandhya Bathija stated that the "last time the U.S. Supreme court explored the topic of legislative prayer at public meetings was in *Marsh v. Chambers* in 1983. That case examined whether it was constitutional for the Nebraska Legislature to open each legislative day with a prayer offered by a chaplain paid by the state. A majority of the Court said the practice was constitutional and not a violation of the First Amendment." The Supreme Court pointed to the country's long history and tradition of opening public and legislative meetings with prayer. In 1989, however, the Supreme Court (in *Allegheny v. American Civil Liberties Union*) ruled unconstitutional a nativity scene on government-owned property. The Court explained: "However history may affect the constitutionality of nonsectarian references to religion by the government, history cannot legitimate practices that demonstrate the government's allegiance to a particular sect or creed."[26] Although legislative prayer is part of the country's history, the Supreme Court made clear that public bodies do not have blanket permission to open meetings with sectarian prayers because doing so would align the government with a particular religion. So the government cannot endorse or favor a particular religious view.

Typically, in analyzing the free exercise clause of the First Amendment to the U.S. Constitution, commentators focus on individual religious exercise and belief. "The right of conscientious objection—the free exercise right that protects individual religious practice when the commands of the state conflict with the demands of religion—figures prominently in their work. Religious organizations are usually dismissed as being mere aggregations of individuals holding common beliefs and thus significant only in that they represent the free exercise concerns of their individual members. In the past [forty] years, however, religious organizations themselves have begun to challenge government regulation under the free exercise clause, both as representatives of their members and on their own behalf."[27]

As Laurence Tribe has noted, the constitutional guarantee of free exercise cannot be concerned merely with the protection of individuals: "Worship and practice both are commonly mediated through structures of social interactions; each would wither if such structures could be easily ruptured by government. . . . So it follows that the autonomy of religious entities, both congregational and hierarchical, is not simply

[26] See *Greece v. Galloway: Why We Should Care About Legislative Prayer.* Center for American Progress publication. Oct. 1, 2013, p. 2.

[27] Developments in the Law – Religion and the State, 100 Harvard Law Review 1740, 1741–42 (May 1987).

one of several doctrines supporting the religion clauses of the Constitution. It follows that such autonomy lies at the very core of religion's place in the Constitution's scheme."[28]

The freedom of conscience cannot be served by protecting only individual free exercise rights. To protect the individual's freedom of conscience from substantial government intrusion, "society must protect the social structure or zone in which that freedom of conscience is exercised. By joining a religious organization and agreeing to the responsibilities that group membership entails, an individual engages in perhaps the most fundamental exercise of religion protected by the first amendment."[29]

The U.S. Supreme Court has decided the following cases related to religious liberty[30]:

01. **Tax Exemptions** – Upheld property tax levies on land owned by and adjacent to a church but not used or needed for its convenient enjoyment (*Gibbons v. District of Columbia*, 116 U.S. 404 (1886));

02. **Church Property** – Vow of poverty and communal ownership of property is not contrary to public policy (*St. Benedict Order v. Steinhauser*, 234 U.S. 640 (1914)); Civil courts may resolve church property disputes as long as they do not involve inquiry into church doctrine (*Maryland & Virginia Churches v. Sharpsburg Church*, 396 U.S. 367 (1970));

03. **Exemption from Military Service** – Exemption of clergy, theology students, and pacifist sects from combat service is constitutional (*Selective Draft Law Cases, Arver v. United States*, 245 U.S. 366 (1918));

04. **Naturalization Qualifications** – Refusal to bear arms in defense of the United States is a valid reason to bar naturalization as a U.S. citizen (*United States v. Bland*, 283 U.S. 636 (1931));

05. **Distribution of Religious Literature** – Ordinance making it unlawful to distribute handbills on sidewalk, street, or any other public place is unconstitutional (*Schneider v. State of New Jersey*, 308 U.S. 147 (1939); *Jamison v. State of Texas*, 318 U.S. 413 (1943));

06. **Breach of the Peace** – State may not unduly suppress communication of religious views under guise of conserving public peace, or deciding what is a legitimate "religion" for solicitation purposes. Free exercise clause expressly applied to states through the Fourteenth Amendment (*Cantwell v. Connecticut*, 310 U.S. 296 (1940));

07. **Saluting Flag** – An education board requirement that students salute the national flag in daily school exercises as a condition of attending free public

---

[28] TRIBE, Laurence Henry. *Church and State in the Constitution*, in Government Intervention in Religious Affairs 31, 32–33 (D. Kelley ed. 1982).

[29] Developments in the Law – Religion and the State, 100 Harvard Law Review 1606, 1748 (1986–1987).

[30] See ESBECK, Carl H. Table of United States Supreme Court Decisions Relating to Religious Liberty 1789 – 1994, Religious Liberty. Journal of Law & Religion, 10 J. L. & Religion 573 (1993–1994).

school is not violative of due process (*Minersville School District v. Gobitis*, 310 U.S. 586 (1940)); to salute flag and recite pledge is invalid as applied to Jehovah's Witnesses because it denies "freedom of speech" and "freedom of belief" (*West Virginia State Board of Education v. Barnette*, 319 U.S. 624 (1943));

08. Flat License Tax – The mere fact that religious literature is sold by itinerant preachers rather than donated does not transform evangelism into a "commercial enterprise" (*Murdock v. Pennsylvania*, 319 U.S. 105 (1943));

09. Religious Fraud – Truth of a religious belief may not be subject to the scrutiny of a jury, but sincerity may (*United States v. Ballard*, 322 U.S. 78 (1944));

10. Censorship – State law permitting censorship of films that are "sacrilegious" is unconstitutional (*Joseph Burstyn, Inc. v. Wilson*, 343 U.S. 495 (1952));

11. Public Meetings – Ordinance leaving no discretion to officials granting permits for conducting religious meetings in public park is constitutional (*Poulos v. New Hampshire*, 345 U.S. 395 (1953));

12. Sunday Closing Law – Sunday closing law does not violate the establishment clause (*Two Guys from Harrison Allentown, Inc. v. McGinley*, 366 U.S. 582 (1961));

13. Public Office Oaths – Declaration of belief in existence of God as a requirement to hold public office is unconstitutional (*Torcaso v. Watkins*, 367 U.S. 488 (1961));

14. Bible Reading – Disallowed practice of daily classroom devotional Bible recitation (*Abington School District v. Schempp*, 374 U.S. 203 (1963)); Reading of Bible and recitation of Lord's Prayer in public school is unconstitutional (*Chamberlin v. Public Instruction Board*, 377 U.S. 402 (1964));

15. Unemployment Compensation Benefits – Refusal to accept employment due to religious beliefs does not disqualify claimant for unemployment compensation (*Sherbert v. Verner*, 374 U.S. 398 (1963)); refusal to award unemployment compensation benefits to claimant who was discharged when she refused to work on her Sabbath violated the Constitution (*Hobbie v. Unemployment Appeals Commission of Florida*, 480 U.S. 136 (1987));

16. Evolution – Disallowed prohibition on teaching theory of evolution (*Epperson v. Arkansas*, 393 U.S. 97 (1968));

17. Medical Care – Blood transfusions may be administered to children over religious objections (*Jehovah's Witnesses v. King County Hospital*, 390 U.S. 598 (1968));

18. Employment – Rejected free exercise claim of a Sabbatarian (*Dewey v. Reynolds Metals Co.*, 402 U.S. 6898 (1971));

19. Prisoner Rights – Reasonable opportunities to exercise religion must be afforded to prison inmates (*Cruz v. Beto*, 405 U.S. 319 (1972));

20. Pacifism and Taxes – Conscientious objection to payment of war taxes does not excuse withholding tax payments (*United States v. American Friends Service Committee*, 419 U.S. 7 (1974));

21. Abortion and Religion – Upheld congressional restrictions on Medicaid-funded abortions (*Harris v. McRae*, 448 U.S. 297 (1980));

22. **Charitable Solicitation Law** – Disallowed state law that required only certain religious organizations to make reports (*Larson v. Valente*, 456 U.S. 228 (1982));
23. **Legislative Prayer** – Upheld state practice of hiring chaplain and offering prayers in the legislature (*Marsh v. Chambers*, 463 U.S. 783 (1983));
24. **Nativity Scene** – Upheld government practice of displaying nativity scene as part of a holiday display (*Lynch v. Donnelly*, 465 U.S. 668 (1984)); Christmas nativity scene permitted in village park (*Scarsdale v. McCreary*, 471 U.S. 83 (1985));
25. **Sabbath Laws** – Disallowed state law guaranteeing private sector employees right not to work on one's Sabbath (*Estate of Thorton v. Caldor, Inc.*, 472 U.S. 402 (1985));
26. **Driver's License Photograph** – Law requiring that applicant submit to having color photograph taken for affixing on license unconstitutionally burdened applicant's free exercise of her sincerely held religious beliefs (*Jensen v. Quaring*, 472 U.S. 478 (1985));
27. **Moment of Silence** – Disallowed state law requiring moment of silence for prayer or meditation in public schools (*Wallace v. Jaffree*, 472 U.S. 38 (1985));
28. **Creationism** – Disallowed state law requiring teaching of creation if evolution is taught (*Edwards v. Aguillard*, 482 U.S. 578 (1987));
29. **Equal Access** – Struck down school policy that denied use of facilities to church as viewpoint discrimination (*Lamb's Chapel v. Center Moriches Union Free School Dist.*, 508 U.S. 384 (1993));
30. **Ritual Sacrifice of Animals** – Municipal ordinance regulating ritual sacrifice of animals violates free exercise clause (*Church of The Lukumi Babalu Aye, Inc. v. Hialeah*, 508 U.S. 520 (1993));
31. **Delegation of Civil Power** – Creation of a public school district coterminous with boundaries of a religious sect's village enclave violates establishment clause (*Bd. of Educ. of Kiryas Joel Village Sch. Dist. v. Grumet*, 512 U.S. 687 (1994));
32. **Business Owners and Healthcare** – Business owners can object on religious grounds to a provision of the Affordable Care Act that requires closely held private companies to provide health insurance that covers birth control (*Burwell v. Hobby Lobby Stores, Inc.*, 134 S. Ct. 2751 (2014)).

2.4 U.S. Tax Immunity and Exemptions for Religious Organizations

The term "church" is found, but not specifically defined, in the U.S. Internal Revenue Code (IRC). It is not used by all faiths, but in its generic sense it is a place of worship including, for example, mosques and synagogues. Because special tax rules apply to churches and temples, it is important to distinguish churches and temples from other religious organizations. Religious organizations that are not churches or temples typically include nondenominational ministries, interdenominational and ecumenical organizations, and other entities whose principal purpose is the study or advancement of religion. Both churches and religious organizations may be legally organized in a variety of ways under state law, such as unincorporated associations, nonprofit corporations, corporations sole, and charitable trusts.[31]

Churches or temples and religious organizations, like many other charitable organizations, qualify for exemption from federal income tax under IRC section 501(c)(3) and are generally eligible to receive tax-deductible contributions. To qualify for tax-exempt status, such an organization must meet the following requirements: the organization must be organized and operated exclusively for religious, educational, scientific, or other charitable purposes; net earnings may not inure to the benefit of any private individual or shareholder; attempting to influence legislation may not be a substantial part of its activity; the organization may not intervene in political campaigns; and the organization's purposes and activities may not be illegal or violate fundamental public policy.

Religious institutions that meet the requirements of IRC section 501(c)(3) are automatically considered tax exempt and are not required to apply for recognition of tax-exempt status from the IRS. Although there is no requirement to do so, many churches seek recognition to ensure their members and contributors that the church is recognized as exempt and qualifies for related tax benefits. For example, contributors to a church that has been recognized as tax exempt would know that their contributions generally are tax-deductible.

Unlike churches and temples, religious organizations that wish to be tax exempt generally must apply to the IRS for tax-exempt status unless their annual gross receipts do not normally exceed $5,000.

According to the U.S. Tax Guide for Churches and Religious Organizations, every tax-exempt organization, including churches, should have an employer identification number (EIN), whether or not the organization has any employees. There are many circumstances for which an EIN is necessary. For example, a church needs an EIN when it opens a bank account, in order to be listed as a subordinate in a group ruling, and if it files returns with the IRS.

Under IRC section 501(c)(3), organizations, including churches and religious organizations, are absolutely prohibited from directly or indirectly participating in, or intervening in, any political campaign on behalf of (or in opposition to) any candidate for elective public office. However, churches and religious organizations may invite political candidates to speak at their events without jeopardizing their tax-exempt status.

IRC section 501(c)(3) places two restrictions on the political speech and activities of tax-exempt organizations. "The first is a more limited restriction mandating that 'no substantial part of [a 501(a)(3) organization's] activities' may consist of 'carrying on propaganda, or otherwise attempting, to influence legislation.'

[31] See Tax Guide For Churches and Religious Organizations. Internal Revenue Service, http://www.irs.gov/pub/irs-pdf/p1828.pdf, p. 3, accessed on Dec. 5, 2014.

The second restriction mandates that 501(c)(3) organizations may 'not participate in, or intervene in (including the publishing or distributing of statements), any political campaign on behalf of (or in opposition to) any candidate for public office.' These two restrictions have caused great concern to parties on both sides of the issue—some arguing that the restrictions do not go far enough to separate churches from the political arena and others arguing that these restrictions are an unconstitutional burden on religion."[32] David M. Andersen explains that "to this day, the IRS has never revoked the tax-exempt status of a church solely for having a substantial amount of its activities dedicated to influencing legislation. Nonetheless, groups opposed to the political activity by churches continue to threaten religious entities with revocation of tax-exempt status for speaking out on social policy issues and urging members to take action in support of church positions."[33]

Congress has afforded churches significant tax benefits that are not available to other traditional non-profit organizations. Foremost among these benefits is the fact that churches automatically qualify for tax-exempt status under 501(c)(3). As a result, the tax code does not require them to apply for and obtain formal recognition of their tax-exempt status. Churches are subject to less stringent annual reporting and filing requirements than other non-profit organizations.

This is a fairly recent trend, however, in that churches were added to IRC section 501(c)(3) just 60 years ago, in 1954. The addition was an attempt to silence the church and eliminate the significant influence the church had always had in shaping public policy. This "favor" to churches came with consequent restrictions placed upon their ability to speak out on the vital issues of the day. If a 501(c)(3) church openly organizes in opposition to anything that the government declares "legal," even if the church considers it immoral (e.g., abortion, homosexuality, same-sex marriage, etc.), this will jeopardize the church's tax-exempt status.

"Churches and religious organizations, like all exempt organizations under IRC section 501(c)(3), are prohibited from engaging in activities that result in inurement of the church's or organization's income or assets to insiders (i.e., persons having a personal and private interest in the activities of organization). Insiders could include the minister, church board members, officers, and in certain circumstances, employees. Examples of prohibited inurement include the payment of dividends, the payment of unreasonable compensation to insiders, and transferring property to insiders for less than fair market value. The prohibition against inurement to insiders is absolute. . . . An IRC section 501(c)(3) organization's activities must be directed exclusively toward charitable, educational, religious, or other exempt purposes. Such an organization's activities may not serve the private interests of any individual or organization. Rather, beneficiaries of an organization's activities must be recognized objects of charity (such as the poor or the distressed) or the community at large (for example, through the conduct of religious services or the promotion of religion). Private benefit is different from inurement to insiders. Private benefit may

[32] In ANDERSEN, David M. Political Silence at Church: The Empty Threat of Removing Tax-Exempt Status for Insubstantial Attempts to Influence Legislation. 2006 B.Y.U.L. Rev. 115.

[33] *Id.*

occur even if the persons benefited are not insiders. Also, private benefit must be substantial in order to jeopardize tax-exempt status."[34]

This kind of restriction does not exist in Brazil. There is no political speech restriction on religious organizations in Brazil. The United States and Brazil are similar, however, in that both countries have afforded churches and temples significant tax benefits that are not available to other traditional non-profit organizations. Among these benefits is the fact that they automatically qualify for tax-exempt status and are not required to apply for or obtain formal recognition.

In the United States, churches and religious organizations, like other tax-exempt organizations, may engage in income-producing activities unrelated to their tax-exempt purposes, as long as the unrelated activities are not a substantial part of the organization's activities. The net income from such activities is subject to the Unrelated Business Income Tax (UBIT) if the following three conditions are met: the activity constitutes a trade or business; the trade or business is regularly carried out; and the trade or business is not substantially related to the organization's exempt purpose. The exceptions to the UBIT are: "substantially all of the work in operating the trade or business is performed by volunteers; the activity is conducted by the organization primarily for the convenience of its members; or the trade or business involves the selling of merchandise substantially all of which was donated." In general, rents from real property, royalties, capital gains, and interest and dividends are not subject to the UBIT unless financed with borrowed money. Examples of unrelated business activities include advertising (income from the sale of advertising space), gaming (pull-tabs, raffles, bingo games), sale of merchandise and publications, rental income (unless there is debt outstanding), and parking lot fees if the parking lot is used by church members and visitors while attending church services.[35]

All tax-exempt organizations, including churches and religious organizations (regardless of whether tax-exempt status has been officially recognized by the IRS), are required to maintain accounting books and other records necessary to justify their claim for exemption in the event of an audit. Tax-deductible contributions to some organizations, nonetheless, are used to support luxury lifestyles, taking advantage of religious and a tax-exempt status in order to provide personal benefits to the individuals who run them.

The charitable nature of an institution is not sufficient reason in and of itself to grant it immunity from liability.[36] In the modern world there is no factual justification for granting immunities to charities that are really large-scale business organizations. "Several jurisdictions limit the immunity of charitable organizations to cases involving beneficiaries of the charity as opposed to strangers, on the theory that the beneficiary, apparently acting out of reciprocal generosity, implicitly waives

[34] Tax Guide For Churches and Religious Organizations. Internal Revenue Service, http://www.irs.gov/pub/irs-pdf/p1828.pdf, p. 5, accessed on Dec. 5, 2014.

[35] *Id.* pp. 16–17.

[36] See *Mullikin v. Jewish Hospital Ass'n of Louisville*, 348 S.W. 2d 930 (Ky 1961).

his right to redress when he accepts the benefits of the charity." The case illustrated by *Springer v. Federated Church of Reno* revealed the difficulty in distinguishing between a beneficiary and a stranger. In this case, the Supreme Court of the U.S. state of Nevada found that a church member received spiritual benefit by reason of her membership and thus was a beneficiary of the church and as a beneficiary of a charitable institution she could not sue for injuries resulting from the allegedly negligent construction of church steps.[37]

In this sense, Thomas M. French and Jon Abels deem that "none of the arguments advanced historically in support of charitable immunity have validity when viewed in the light of the present status and characteristics of modern charitable institutions."[38]

In *Flagiello v. Pennsylvania*,[39] Justice Musmanno of the Supreme Court of the U.S. state of Pennsylvania stated in 1965: "Whatever the law may have been regarding charitable institutions in the past, it does not meet the conditions of today. Charitable enterprises are no longer housed in ramshackle wooden structures. They are not mere storm shelters to succor the traveler and temporarily refuge those stricken in a common disaster."

In its landmark decision in *Walz v. Tax Commission*, the U.S. Supreme Court generally upheld the constitutionality of tax exemptions for religious organizations, stating that "Adherents of particular faiths and individual churches frequently take strong positions on public issues including . . . vigorous advocacy of legal or constitutional positions. Of course, churches as much as secular bodies and private citizens have that right."[40] "In *Regan v. Taxation with Representation*, the Court upheld the IRS's denial of tax-exempt status to a newly organized nonprofit corporation solely because a substantial part of its intended activities would consist of attempts to influence legislation. Focusing on tax-exempt status as a 'form of subsidy', the Court held tightly to two important principles: (1) the First Amendment does not require the government to subsidize lobbying and (2) 'a legislature's decision not to subsidize the exercise of a fundamental right does not infringe the right.' Based on this subsidy framework, the Court concluded that the lobbying restrictions neither created an unconstitutional burden of free speech rights under the First Amendment nor violated equal protection under the Fifth Amendment."[41]

There is a need for lawmakers to clarify the extent to which churches or temples may engage in lobbying efforts and what activities constitute attempts to influence legislation. According to David M. Andersen, "the purpose of applying the lobbying

---

[37] *Springer v. Federated Church of Reno*, 71 Nev. 177, 283 P.2d 1071 (1955).

[38] In FRENCH, Thomas M. and ABELS, Jon. Recent Decisions. Indiana Legal Forum. *Harris v. Y.W.C.A. of Terre Haute Ind.*: Abolition of Charitable Immunity in Indiana. 2 Ind. Legal F. 378 (1968–1969).

[39] In *Flagiello v. Pennsylvania*, 208 A.2d 193 (1965).

[40] *Walz v. Tax Commission of City of New York*, 397 U.S. 664 (1970).

[41] See ANDERSEN, David M. Political Silence at Church: The Empty Threat of Removing Tax-Exempt Status for Insubstantial Attempts to Influence Legislation. 2006 B.Y.U.L. Rev. 115 (quoting *Regan v. Taxation With Representation of Washington*, 461 U.S. 540 (1983)).

restrictions to churches has never been to prevent religious beliefs from influencing public policy, but rather to ferret out those organizations that would abuse their tax-exempt status to promote a purely nonreligious political agenda under the guise of religion. Accordingly, the law must recognize the rights of churches and church leaders to teach members about important policy issues and urge members to apply their religious beliefs by participating in the political process."[42]

Tax-deductible contributions to some organizations cannot be used to support luxury lifestyles, taking advantage of religious and a tax-exempt status in order to provide personal benefits to the individuals who run them (e.g., extravagant spending, such as buying a private jet, driving wealthy automobiles, or having high-level properties).

2.5 Religious Freedom in the Brazilian Constitutional Order

Protection of religious freedom is also expressed through the Constitution of the Federal Republic of Brazil, in Article 5, Part VI, which states that freedom of conscience and of belief are unalienable rights, securing religious acts of worship as well as its places of practice and liturgies. It is important, from the beginning, to demonstrate that the distinction between freedom of conscience and freedom of belief denotes the insertion, in the grounds of protection, of the non-believer, that is, the one who claims to have no faith at all (being identified as an atheist, agnostic, or any other denomination). That was the lesson of Pontes de Miranda, the well-known Brazilian jurst, when he treated this distinction by analyzing it in the light of the 1967 Brazilian Constitution.[43]

According to José Afonso da Silva, religious freedom comprises three forms of expression: (1) freedom of belief, (2) freedom of worship, and (3) freedom of religious organization.[44] The author posits that the first freedom, the freedom of belief, refers to the constitutional right to adhere to any religion, to change from one religion to another, and to not to adhere to any religion. So, this facet of religious freedom encompasses everyone, protecting believers and non-believers.

The second of the freedoms is freedom of worship. The definition of the word "worship" ("cult" or "service") resembles the definition of "religion." The first and main conception presented is "adoration or paying tribute to a deity in any of its forms and in any religion."[45] The term "worship" (*culto* in Portuguese) has its origin in the Latin word *cultus*, which, originally, carried the meaning of "cultivated" and

---

[42] ANDERSEN, David M. Political Silence at Church: The Empty Threat of Removing Tax-Exempt Status for Insubstantial Attempts to Influence Legislation. 2006 B.Y.U.L. Rev. 115.

[43] MIRANDA, F. C. P. *Comentários à Constituição de 1967 com a Emenda No. 1 de 1969.*

[44] SILVA, J. A. (1976) *Curso de Direito Constitucional Positivo* 25ª Edição. São Paulo: Malheiros Editores Ltda., 2005. 921 pp. 248–53.

[45] FERREIRA, A. B. H. *Novo Dicionário Eletrônico Aurélio versão 6.0.1.* 4ª Edição. [S.l.]: 2009.

afterwards transformed to signify, figuratively, "worshipped" or "honored."[46] One could conclude, therefore, that the word "worship," when not referring to the concept of religion itself, is, at the very least, intimately connected to it, for it is identified as one of its essential elements: the set of practices related to an entity considered absolutely valued. Accordingly, José Afonso treats freedom of worship as a means of protection to the many acts and practices identified as exterior expressions of religion, without regard as to whether they take place at home or in public locations. The constitutionalist author affirms that the 1988 Brazilian Constitution brought an innovation by taking away the determination that this freedom should not disagree with "public order or the good customs" (*ordem pública ou os bons costumes*), which were vague and, because of this, only brought the possibility of subjecting the different religions to arbitrary actions of the State government.

Finally, religious freedom includes the freedom of religious organization, that is, the freedom of establishing and organizing religious institutions and allowing them to relate themselves with the State. José Afonso claims that, presently, in Brazil, there is a regime of separation between the State and religious institutions. This is what a careful reading of Article 19, Part I, of the Brazilian Constitution, for example, allows us to visualize. The text prohibits any favor relating a specific religion, as well as the thwarting of religious activities caused by public administration. The Article makes only one reservation regarding opportunities in which the collaboration between State and religious institutions may favor public interest. According to the author, such a collaboration must, however, be established by an Act or Law of the collaborating federal entity, it must not happen on the religious field, and it must be general in order to comprise all possible religious denominations. Furthermore, it should be stated that there are other constitutional norms, like the right to religious assistance on unities of collective confinement (as protected by Article 5, Part VII), the ministration of facultative religious teachings at public schools of basic education (as protected by Article 210, Section 1), and the civil effects of religious marriage (as protected by Article 226, Sections 1 and 2).[47]

Manoel Gonçalves Ferreira Filho considers religious freedom a facet of the freedom of belief and mentions, specifically, the freedom of worship. He argues that the freedom of worship should be protected according to the law. He also considers that the absence of the requirement of conformity to the public order and good customs does not mean that religions are authorized to disrespect them, since the maintenance of such institutions depends on the maintenance of the legal system.[48]

---

[46] HARPER, D. Cult. In: *Online EtymologyDictionary*. In http://www.etymonline.com/index.php?allowed_in_frame=0&search=cult&searchmode=none, accessed Aug. 27, 2014.

[47] SILVA, J. A. (1976) *Curso de Direito Constitucional Positivo* 25ª Edição. São Paulo: Malheiros Editores Ltda., 2005. 921 pp. 248–53.

[48] FERREIRA FILHO, M. G. *Curso de Direito Constitucional*. 25ª Edição. São Paulo: Editora Saraiva, 2011. 424 pp. 325–26.

2.6 Brazilian Tax Immunity and Exemptions for Religious Organizations

By instituting tax collecting prohibitions, Article 150, Part VI(b), of the Brazilian Constitution has the intention of protecting the practice of any religion and stopping the State from hampering or preventing the expression of any belief by means of its coercive power.

The Brazilian Supreme Court, when asked to rule on tax immunity, declared its protective scope. It went so far as to put property, income, and services "related to the essential goals of the entities" under the protection of Article 150, as seen in its decision on Extraordinary Appeal No. 325.822-2/SP. By doing that, the Court guaranteed the application of immunity to all property whose ultimate goal is the fulfillment of religious activities. That means that even the income from real estate rent, for example, could be included, as long as it is used in religious activities.[49] Such an understanding is even clearer with the analysis of decisions like the one given in Extraordinary Appeal (*Agravo Regimental no Recurso Extraordinário*) No. 694.453/DF, which recognized the application of immunity to the residence of a religious minister because the property was being used for the fulfillment of religious goals of the institution.[50] Thus, the only taxes (*impostos*) that may, occasionally, be considered as paid by religious institutions are the ones paid by the transfer of costs to the price of goods and services, such as the ICMS (Tax on the Circulation of Goods and Services). That was the case in the Appeal in Writ of Mandamus (*Recurso em Mandado de Segurança*) No. 22.582/CE, when the Superior Court of Justice (*Superior Tribunal de Justiça*)[51] confirmed the view that religious organizations' tax immunity did not apply to related third parties, like electric companies.[52]

This constitutional protective norm must guide the tax collection activity of all entities of the Brazilian Federation. One example of how the norm is applied is in the guidelines set forth in legislation in the São Paulo Municipality. São Paulo's Act No. 6,989/66, which establishes the taxation system in the city of São Paulo, explicitly declares the inapplicability of taxes over buildings, urban territory, and services to which constitutional immunities apply, including the protection of Article 150, Part VI(b) of the Constitution. The only requirement given by the act is that real

[49] Extraordinary Appeal (Recurso Extraordinário No. 325.822-2/SP, STF, Plenário, Rel. Ilmar Galvão, 27 de novembro de 2012). In http://www.stf.jus.br/portal/principal/principal.asp, accessed July 26, 2014.

[50] Extraordinary Appeal (Agravo Regimental no Recurso Extraordinário No. 694.453, STF, 2ª Turma, Rel. Ricardo Lewandowski, 25 de junho de 2013). In http://www.stf.jus.br/portal/principal/principal.asp, accessed Aug. 2, 2014.

[51] In Brazil, there are two superior courts: the Supreme Federal Court (*Supremo Tribunal Federal*), which rules on constitutional matters, and the Superior Court of Justice (*Superior Tribunal da Justiça*), which rules federal law matters.

[52] Appeal in Writ of Mandamus (Recurso em Mandado de Segurança No. 22.582/CE, STJ, Primeira Seção, Rel. Herman Benjamin, 10 de fevereiro de 2010.). In http://www.stj.jus.br/portal_stj/publicacao/engine.wsp, accessed Aug. 2, 2014.

estate properties that enjoy such immunity should be regularly registered in the correct department.

Another act at the municipal level of São Paulo is Act No. 13,250/01, complementing the orders of Act No. 6,989/66, which makes the recognition of immunity for temples of any worship subject to verification by public authorities that the property is being used for religious activity. Such verification is regulated by Normative Instruction of the Treasurer of the Municipality of São Paulo (*Instrução Normativa da Secretaria da Fazenda do Município de São Paulo*) No. 03/08. It outlines the procedures for immunity recognition, details to whom a requisition should be presented, specifies the applicable taxes, and provides tax registration numbers and property registration numbers for buildings belonging to the organization. The law establishes that the requisition must be presented to the Division of Immunities, Exemptions, Tax Incentives, and Special Regimes (*Divisão de Imunidades, Isenções, Incentivos Fiscais e Regimes Especiais – DIESP*), which must analyze the request.

Moreover, in the Municipality of São Paulo, there is Act No. 13,879/04, which amends Act No. 13,250/01, restricting immunity to the areas of actual practice of worship and its accessory areas and excluding areas designated for commercial purposes. The law also creates the administrative infraction consisting of the intentional action of omitting or falsifying information directed to attaining undue recognition of immunity. It thus appears that tax immunity for temples of any worship is broadly regulated, at least in the city of São Paulo.

In the field of state law, although not so broadly regulated, the theme of immunity given to religious organizations is also reflected in legislation. In the specific case of the State of São Paulo, there is Decree (*Decreto*) No. 46,655/02, which approved the regulation regarding the Tax on Transmissions *Causa Mortis* and Donations of Any Goods or Rights (*Imposto sobre Transmissão "Causa mortis" e sobre Doação de quaisquer bens ou direitos*). It expresses the inapplicability of these taxes over properties belonging to temples of any worship. Ordinance (*Portaria*) No. 15/03, from the Coordination of State Tax Administration (*Coordenadoria de Administração Tributária do Estado*) establishes the procedures for the formal recognition of immunity, demanding the presentation of a requisition to a Regional Tax Delegate (*Delegado Regional Tributário*), following the model attached to the ordinance.

There is also Decree No. 45,490/00, which approves the regulation of ICMS, in which the inapplicability of this tax over the exiting and subsequent return of equipment and materials promoted by religious organizations (that is, exclusively used in the fulfillment of their essential activities) is explicitly mentioned, in its Article 7. Act No. 6,374/89 complements the commandment by stating, in its Article 7, Sections 1 and 14, that religious organizations are subject to tax collection when they engage in activities unrelated to their essential activities.

Act No. 6,606/89 of the State of São Paulo, which regulates the IPVA (taxes applied to the property of automobiles), also recognizes explicitly the immunity applied to automobiles belonging to religious organizations, in its Article 8, Part V (as modified by Act No. 9,459/96). This law, however, was revoked by Act No. 13,296/08, which only implicitly declares the existence of immunity by regulating its consequences. In order to regulate the formal recognition of immunity applied to automobiles, Ordinance (*Portaria*) No. 56/96 was amended. It now require the presentation of a requisition to the Regional Tax Departments (*Delegacias Regionais Tributárias*) of the Capital or the state (or in *Postos Fiscais*, in the inner state) in which there must be present the organization's bylaws (*estatuto*) and the minutes from the meetings in which the organization's representatives were elected, as well as a declaration about the actual use of the vehicle for the organization's essential goals.

In national and federal laws, there are not many references about the regulation of tax immunity for temples of any worship. In the National Tax Code, there is reference in Article 9 regarding the impossibility of tax collection over religious organizations. Decree No. 3,000/99, which regulates income taxes in Brazil, is very clear about the inapplicability of taxes for religious organizations, since it also mentions the Constitution in Article 168. Religious entities are only required to deliver a "Declaration of Economic-Fiscal Information" (*Declaração de Informações Econômico-Fiscais*) and are subject to penalties for delays, according to Brazilian IRS Normative Instruction (*Instrução Normativa da Receita Federal do Brasil*) No. 1,028/10. Act No. 8,137/90 should also be noted here, as it criminalizes the use of subterfuges to trick the public administration in order to unduly avoid or reduce tax collection.

In view of norms such as the above-mentioned ones, one notices the broad protection given to religious entities by means of tax immunity at all levels of the Brazilian Federation. In a general way, federal entities usually recognize this immunity, only conditioning its application on verification from declarations given by representatives of the institutions and documents proving the religious activity practiced by the institution. One also notices the attempt of governmental bodies, even if discretely, to prevent the use of fraud as a way of attaining undue application of tax immunity. Such is the case when legislation establishes administrative fines for this kind of behavior, as well as criminal penalties attributed to those who engage in such activities.

In Brazil, tax-exempt institutions are immune from income tax, but the following entities are forced to make an annual report to the Brazilian Internal Revenue Service: (1) temples of any denomination (*culto*) (Brazilian Constitution of 1988, Article 150, Part VI(b)); (2) political parties and nonprofit unions of workers (Brazilian Constitution of 1988, Article 150, Part VI(c)); and (3) nonprofit educational and social welfare institutions (Brazilian Constitution of 1988, Article 150, Part VI(c)).

Education and social assistance institutions are considered immune if they provide the services for which they have been established and are open to the general population in a complementary manner to the activities of the State (Law 9,532/1997, Article 12). A nonprofit organization is defined as an institution of education or social assistance that does not have surplus revenue, or if it does, the surplus is entirely applied to the maintenance and development of its social objectives (Act 9,532/1997, Article 12, Paragraph 3, as amended by Act No. 9718/1998, Article 10, and Complementary Act 104/2001).

According to Brazilian law, there are no requirements for churches and temples to get tax-exempt status. However, for the enjoyment of immunity, political parties, nonprofit unions of workers, nonprofit educational institutions, and social welfare institutions have to meet the following requirements: (1) not compensate in any way its officers for services provided; (2) fully implement resources to maintain and develop their institutional objectives; (3) maintain complete bookkeeping of income and expenses to ensure accurate accounting; (4) keep in good order, for a period of 5 years from the date of issue, documents proving the origin of revenue and the effectiveness of expenses, as well as records of any other acts or transactions that may change the financial situation; (5) submit an annual report in accordance with the provisions of the act of the Internal Revenue Service; (6) ensure the allocation of assets to another institution that meets the conditions for enjoyment of immunity in the case of division or dissolution of the corporation or company; and (7) not distribute any part of their assets or income.

For the Brazilian IRS, tax-exempt institutions are nonprofit philanthropic, recreational, cultural, scientific, and civic associations that provide the services for which such restrictions have been imposed and make the services available to the group of people intended (Act No. 9,532/1997, Article 15). They are still considered nonprofit entities if they fail to not present a surplus in their accounts as long as they designate the surplus in full to the maintenance and development of their social objectives (Law No. 9,532/1997, Article 15, Paragraph 3, as amended by Law No. 9718/1998, Article 10).

There can be no coexistence between income from core business, which therefore immune, and yields that are inconsistent with the essential purpose of the entity. Likewise, the coexistence of non-exempt income and exempt income is not possible, since the enjoyment of exemption in half is not possible. All income is exempted if it meets the requirements of Act No. 9,532/1997, or all of it is subject to taxation if the requirements are breached.

There are tax consequences for companies that fail to meet the requirements in the legislation for the enjoyment of immunity and exemption, without prejudice to other penalties provided by law. The Brazilian Internal Revenue Service might suspend the enjoyment of the exemption for the calendar years in which the institution has committed an act constituting an offense present in tax laws, especially if it falsely omits the receipt of donations in assets or cash, or in any way commits tax fraud (Act No. 9,532/1997, Article 15, Paragraph 3).

It is considered a violation of tax laws if the exempt institution, on behalf of its members or leaders, or even in favor of members, shareholders, managers, or directors of an associated company, considers the payment of nondeductible expenses in determining the calculation basis for the income tax and social contribution (Law No. 9.532/1997, Article 13, Sole Paragraph).

Tax exemption does not require prior recognition by the Brazilian Internal Revenue Service (RIR/1999, Article 181).[53]

---

[53] See the Brazilian Internal Revenue Service site (Receita Federal do Brasil), in http://www.receita.fazenda.gov.br/PessoaJuridica/DIPJ/2005/PergResp2005/pr24a31.htm, accessed Sept. 9, 2014.

Aside from tax immunity given to religious organizations, it is possible for such entities to benefit from exemption because they meet certain requirements established by federal law in order to grant them public utility titles (*títulos de utilidade pública*). Even though legislation seeks to make it clear that the mere emission of this title does not imply, necessarily, the attainment of any benefits, it is relatively common for some benefits to be granted based on the recognition of public utility.

On a federal level, Act No. 91/35 establishes the requirements for the issuance of the federal public utility title for "civil societies, associations and foundations" which are: (1) acquisition of legal personality; (2) current and actual functioning and unselfish service to the collectivity; and (3) the absence of any remuneration for any members of its direction organs.

Decree (*Decreto*) No. 50,517/61 regulates this act by requiring the presentation of evidence of: (1) the constitution of the organization in the country; (2) the existence of legal personality; (3) regular functioning according to the organization's bylaws for the 3 years prior to the requisition; (4) absence of any remuneration for board directors or any kind of profit, bonus, or advantage distribution to its members or maintainers; (5) actual educational, scientific research, cultural, artistic, or philanthropist activity, as long as these meet needs in a predominantly universal and indiscriminate way; (6) absence of any criminal record and proven morality of the institution's directors; and (7) commitment to publish annually the income and expenses, if the organization is subsidized by the Union.

One of the benefits that comes from the declaration of public utility is the income tax exemption for donations made by legal entities in favor of entities that possess the federal public utility title. Such exemption, permitted by Act No. 9,249/95, does not benefit public utility institutions directly, but it does so indirectly by giving corporations and other legal entities incentives to donate to these institutions (Article 13, Section 2, Part III). The only additional condition added by this act is that benefitted institutions must provide free services to the employees, to the dependents (relatives) of the donor institutions, or within the community where it functions.

The state legal order of São Paulo also has legislation regarding the issuance of public utility titles. Act No. 2,574/80, similar to the federal regulation, establishes seven requirements to be met by the institution that wants to be contemplated by the title: (1) legal personality; (2) actual and continuous organization operation, within its goals, in the last 3 years; (3) absence of any remuneration for board directors and any profit, bonus, or advantage distribution to any of its members or maintainers; (4) proof of actual operation, during the prior 3 years, of activities related to "education or scientific research, culture, including artistic, philanthropic or, charitable or religious" purposes; (5) if necessary, the registration of institutions in some State entities; (6) proven moral character of its directors; and (7) publication of income and expenses for the prior year.

Among the many advantages given by the state title of public utility, there is a 50 % discount on water and sewage bills. The only limitation provided in the act is the limit of 100 cubic meters of water supply and another 100 for sewer collection, according to Act No. 10,112/98. In addition, philanthropic institutions may be assisted by subsidies from the State of São Paulo, according to Decree No. 22,695/84, if the project or application of resources is approved by the State Counsel for Aid and Grants (*Conselho Estadual de Auxílio e Subvenções*) by means of a contract that determines the rules for application of resources, the prohibition of alienation of acquired goods, and the use of accounts at the Bank of the State of São Paulo (*Caixa Econômica do Estado de São Paulo*) to make transactions with the money.

Finally, at the municipal level in São Paulo there is also the possibility of the issuance of a public utility title. Act No. 4,819/55 authorizes the government to grant the title to entities that have been constituted for more than a year, continuously serving the public, with proven morality and whose board members are not, by any means, remunerated. Similarly, Act No. 12,520 sets forth the procedures to update the documents needed in order to keep the public utility declaration, requiring them to be presented every 3 years. Otherwise, the title should be repealed.

Thus, at every administrative level of the Brazilian Federation, the possibility of issuance of public utility titles exists. The issuance is not automatic, however, and requires adherence to the established procedures. If religious organizations meet the requirements established by law, or constitute other entities that do so, they could benefit, directly and indirectly, from aid policies promoted by Brazilian legislatures.

Bibliography

ANDERSEN, David M. Political Silence at Church: The Empty Threat of Removing Tax-Exempt Status for Insubstantial Attempts to Influence Legislation. 2006 B.Y.U.L. Rev. 115.

ARZT, Donna E., CHON, Margaret. Walking While Muslim, 68 Law & Contemporary Problems 215 (2004–2005).

BRAZILIAN Internal Revenue Service site (Receita Federal do Brasil), in http://www.receita.fazenda.gov.br/PessoaJuridica/DIPJ/2005/PergResp2005/pr24a31.htm, accessed Sept. 9, 2014.

DEAN, Jacob E. Do You Have That New Church App For A Clearer And Broader Definition of Church Under The Internal Revenue Code. 46 Creighton L. Rev. 173.

DEVELOPMENTS in the Law – Religion and the State. 100 Harvard Law Review 1606 (1986–1987).

DONAHUE, William A. (in ANDERSEN, David M. Political Silence at Church: The Empty Threat of Removing Tax-Exempt Status for Insubstantial Attempts to Influence Legislation. 2006 B.Y.U.L. Rev. 115).

DURKHEIM, E. (1912) The Elementary Forms of the Religious Life. London: George Allen & Unwin Ltd., 1915.

ESBECK, Carl H. Table of United States Supreme Court Decisions Relating to Religious Liberty 1789–1994, Religious Liberty. 10 J. L. & Religion 573 (1993–1994).

EVERTON v. Board of Education, 330 U.S. 1 (1947).

EXTRAORDINARY Appeal (Recurso Extraordinário No. 325.822-2/SP, STF, Plenário, Rel. Ilmar Galvão, 27 de novembro de 2012.). In http://www.stf.jus.br/portal/principal/principal.asp, accessed July 26, 2014.

EXTRAORDINARY Appeal, Brazilian Supreme Federal Court (Recurso Extraordinário No. 562.351-RS, STF, 1ª Turma, Rel. Ricardo Lewandowski. 04 de setembro de 2012.) In http://www.stf.jus.br/portal/principal/principal.asp, accessed Aug. 27, 2013.

EXTRAORDINARY Appeal (Agravo Regimental no Recurso Extraordinário No. 694.453, STF, 2ª Turma, Rel. Ricardo Lewandowski, 25 de junho de 2013.) In http://www.stf.jus.br/portal/principal/principal.asp, accessed Aug. 2, 2014.

FERREIRA, A. B. H. *Novo Dicionário Eletrônico Aurélio versão 6.0.1*. 4ª Ed.[S.l.]: 2009.
FERREIRA FILHO, Manoel Gonçalves. Curso de Direito Constitucional. 25ª Edição. São Paulo: Editora Saraiva, 2011.
GALLOWAY v. Town of Greece, 732 F. Supp. 2d 195 (W.D.N.Y. 2010).
GOODWIN, Glenn. Would Caesar Tax God? The Constitutionality of the Governmental Taxation of Churches. 35 Drake L. Rev. 383 (1986).
GREECE v. Galloway: Why We Should Care About Legislative Prayer. Center for American Progress publication. Oct. 1, 2013.
HARPER, D. Religion. In: *Online EtymologyDictionary*. In http://www.etymonline.com/index.php?allowed_in_frame=0&search=religion&searchmode=none, accessed Aug. 21, 2014.
______, Cult. In: *Online EtymologyDictionary*. In http://www.etymonline.com/index.php?allowed_in_frame=0&search=cult&searchmode=none, accessed Aug. 27, 2013.
HORWITZ, Paul. Scientology in Court: A Comparative Analysis and Some Thoughts on Selected Issues in Law and Religion. 47 DePaul Law Review 1 (Fall 1997).
LANERI, Christa E. The Texas Religious Freedom Restoration Act: Does It Really Work?, 16 Texas Wesleyan Law Review 457 (2010).
MIRANDA, Francisco Cavalcanti Pontes de. *Comentários à Constituição de 1967 com a Emenda No. 1 de 1969.*
POWERS, Kevin M. The Sword and the Shield: RLUIPA and the New Battle Ground of Religious Freedom. 22 Buffalo Public Interest Law Journal 145 (2003–2004).
REPORT on the Tenth Anniversary of the Religious Land Use and Institutionalized Persons Act from de U.S. Department of Justice, Sept. 22, 2010 (in http://www.justice.gov/crt/rluipa_report_092210.pdf, accessed May 1, 2014).
SILVA, José. Afonso da. (1976) *Curso de Direito Constitucional Positivo* 25ª Edição. São Paulo: Malheiros Editores Ltda., 2005. pp. 248–53.
Tax Guide For Churches and Religious Organizations. Internal Revenue Service, http://www.irs.gov/pub/irs-pdf/p1828.pdf, p. 3, accessed Dec. 5, 2014.
TRIBE, Laurence Henry. *Church and State in the Constitution*, in Government Intervention in Religious Affairs 31, 32–33 (D. Kelley ed. 1982).
USMAN, Jeffrey Omar. Defining Religion: The Struggle to Define Religion Under the First Amendment and the Contributions and Insights of Other Disciplines of Study Including Theology, Psychology, Sociology, the Arts, and Anthropology. 83 North Dakota Law Review 123 (2007).
UTTER, Jack. American Indians: Answers to Today's Questions. University of Oklahoma Press, 2001, ISBN 0-8061-3309-0.
WELCH, Heather M. The Religious Land Use and Institutionalized Persons Act and Mega-Churches: Demonstrating the Limits of Religious Land Use Exemptions in Federal Legislation. 39 University of Baltimore Law Rev. 255 (2010).
WISCONSIN v. Yoder, 406 U.S. 205 (1972).
WRIT of Mandamus (Recurso em Mandado de Segurança No. 22.582/CE, STJ, Primeira Seção, Rel. Herman Benjamin, 10 de fevereiro de 2010). In http://www.stj.jus.br/portal_stj/publicacao/engine.wsp, accessed Aug. 2, 2014.

Chapter 3
Government Regulation of Religious Organizations

3.1 Legal Nature of Religious Organizations

In many countries, Roman Catholic morality has influenced legislation, which has typically remained denominationally neutral in formal terms. Religious bodies are submitted to generally applicable regulation to some extent, but they have been subjected to particular regulation to their own organizational needs.[1]

Article 44 of the Brazilian Civil Code establishes that "religious organizations" are legal entities of private law. Moreover, section 1 of the same article asserts that such organizations are free to organize and structure themselves, prohibiting the government from denying the registration of their constitutive acts.

Act No. 10,825/03 provided the wording for Article 44. This Act added religious organizations and political parties to the list of autonomous and private legal entities. This Act also amended Article 2,031, sole paragraph, of the Civil Code by establishing that a term that previously applied to all legal entities, requiring them to conform to the new Code's regime, did not apply to religious organizations.

According to Sílvio Venosa, the reason given by the Legislature for that innovation was that Article 53, which defines associations, would not encompass religious institutions completely with all of their peculiarities. Venosa suggests that the motivation for the change (adding religious organizations as an autonomous type of legal person) may be more related to the corporate interests of these entities. For him, the exclusion of religious organizations from some norms, such as the one contained in

[1]According to Eoin Daly, "the historically close relationship between the State and the Roman Catholic Church has had a more informal basis, with the rarely-invoked Article 44 of Bunreacht na bEireann ('the Constitution') remaining the almost exclusive legal basis for the State-religion relationship." In Regulation Religious Function: The Strange Case of Mass Cards, 9 Hibernian L. J. 55, 55 (2010).

F.M. De Sanctis, *Churches, Temples, and Financial Crimes*,
DOI 10.1007/978-3-319-15681-1_3

Article 59 of the Code,[2] is contrary to present legal trends and favors the possibility of these religious organizations to become hermetic.[3]

The 2004 Journal of Civil Law (*Jornada de Direito Civil*), in its Enunciation No. 142 of the Federal Justice Counsel (*Conselho da Justiça Federal*), confirms the associative nature of unions, political parties, and "religious associations." The Civil Code would, therefore, be completely applicable to them.

Nevertheless, other authors, such as Jones Figueirêdo Alves and Mário Luiz Delgado, claim that those institutions constitute different species of legal entities of private law that would not be subject to the commandments contemplated in Articles 53–61, since these articles (especially Article 59, sole paragraph) could lead to a violation of Article 19, Section I, of the Brazilian Constitution.[4]

Even considering that religious organizations are autonomous types of legal entities, they still seem to be subject to the possibility predicted in Article 50, which allows the practice of piercing the corporate veil. Thus, if there is sufficient evidence of diversion of social purpose or property confusion involving goods both from the organization and its associates, then the judge is allowed to pierce the corporate veil in order to broaden the effects of some obligations to the property of some of its members.

That is what one finds when reading decisions such as the one given for Interlocutory Appeal (*Agravo de Instrumento*) No. 0136470-58.2011.8.0000, which recognized the possibility of piercing the corporate veil of religious organizations, as long as either the comingling of assets (religious and personal) or the diversion of purpose is proven (Article 50).[5]

3.2 Charters (Licenses) Needed for Religious Institutions to Function

Aside from the tax relations (or the absence thereof) with the State, religious institutions also maintain important relationships with public administration regarding the regulation of the use of urban spaces where rituals take place. In general, municipal governments demand from religious entities a charter for the temples, which can be obtained depending on the number of people attending their services.

Cities are supposed to not intentionally create zoning ordinances that prevent new churches or temples from being built or that discriminate against certain religions.

[2] Rules about General Assembly of Associations.

[3] VENOSA, S. S. *Direito Civil: Parte geral* (1984). 4ª Edição. São Paulo: Editora Atlas S. A., 2004. 662 pp. 272–73.

[4] ALVES, J. F.; DELGADO, M. L. *Código*, cit., p. 46; DINIZ, M. H. *Código Civil Anotado*. 15ª Edição. São Paulo: Editora Saraiva, 2010. 1432 p. 95.

[5] Interlocutory Appeal (Agravo de Instrumento No. 0136470-58.2011.8.0000, TJ-SP, 19ª Câmara de Direito Privado, Rel. Sebastião Alves Junqueira, 18 de outubro de 2011). In http://www.tjsp.jus.br, accessed Aug. 27, 2013.

A good practice is for zoning laws and regulations to give better guidance in order to reduce discrimination and enable more straightforward resolutions about zoning disputes.[6]

There are continual heated debates over whether churches and houses of worship are shown bias in the zoning process. One side of the argument focuses on the fact that cities intentionally create zoning ordinances to prevent new churches from being built and to discriminate against certain religions.

It is important to understand how zoning ordinances and land use regulations are relevant to churches and religious institutions. If a place of worship is essential to organized religions, it is also a place to perpetuate the sense of unity among members. "Without places of worship, organized religions would become obsolete. With that understood, it must be noted that the opponents argue that churches have an advantage over other institutions because they are shown deference with regards to zoning rights. Cities oppose church zoning requests for a variety of reasons, such as creation of more traffic hazards and noise in a residential area or reduction of tax benefits in a commercial area."[7]

3.2.1 Zoning Regulations in the United States

With the intention of protecting the free exercise of religion by requiring the government to have a "compelling interest" before it could burden or restrict the free exercise of religion, the U.S. Congress passed the Religious Freedom Restoration Act of 1993 (Pub. L. No. 103–141, 107 Stat. 1488, November 16, 1993).[8] It is codified at 42 U.S.C. §§ 2000bb–2000bb-4.[9] Also known as RFRA, this U.S. federal law aims

---

[6] In LANERI, Christa E. The Texas Religious Freedom Restorations Act: Does It Really Work?. 16 Texas Wesleyan Law Review 457 (2010).

[7] *Id.*

[8] The Religious Freedom Restoration Act of 1993 originated as a bill introduced by Howard McKeon of California and Dean Gallo of New Jersey on March 11, 1993. A unanimous U.S. House of Representatives and a near unanimous U.S. Senate (three dissenting votes) passed the bill and President Bill Clinton signed it into law.

[9] **42 USC Chapter 21B: § 2000bb**. Congressional findings and declaration of purposes: (a) Findings. The Congress finds that—(1) the framers of the Constitution, recognizing free exercise of religion as an unalienable right, secured its protection in the First Amendment to the Constitution; (2) laws "neutral" toward religion may burden religious exercise as surely as laws intended to interfere with religious exercise; (3) governments should not substantially burden religious exercise without compelling justification; (4) in Employment Division v. Smith, 494 U.S. 872 (1990) the Supreme Court virtually eliminated the requirement that the government justify burdens on religious exercise imposed by laws neutral toward religion; and (5) the compelling interest test as set forth in prior Federal court rulings is a workable test for striking sensible balances between religious liberty and competing prior governmental interests. (b) Purposes: The purposes of this chapter are—(1) to restore the compelling interest test as set forth in Sherbert v. Verner, 374 U.S. 398 (1963) and Wisconsin v. Yoder, 406 U.S. 205 (1972) and to guarantee its application in all cases where free exercise of religion is substantially burdened; and (2) to provide a claim or defense to persons whose religious exercise is substantially burdened by government.

to prohibit laws that substantially burden a person's free exercise of their religion. It was held unconstitutional as applied to the states in the *City of Boerne v. Flores* decision in 1997, which ruled that the RFRA is not a proper exercise of Congress's enforcement power.[10] But it continues to be applied to the federal government. For example, in 2006, in *Gonzales v. O Centro Espirita Beneficente Uniao do Vegetal*, the U.S. Supreme Court ruled that a church was properly granted an injunction under the RFRA against criminal prosecution for its sacramental use of a hallucinatory substance. In response to *City of Boerne v. Flores*, some individual states passed their own Religious Freedom Restoration Acts that apply to state governments and local municipalities.[11]

---

§ **2000bb-1. a)** In general: Government shall not substantially burden a person's exercise of religion even if the burden results from a rule of general applicability, except as provided in subsection (b) of this section. **(b)** Exception. Government may substantially burden a person's exercise of religion only if it demonstrates that application of the burden to the person—**(1)** is in furtherance of a compelling governmental interest; and **(2)** is the least restrictive means of furthering that compelling governmental interest. **(c)** Judicial relief: A person whose religious exercise has been burdened in violation of this section may assert that violation as a claim or defense in a judicial proceeding and obtain appropriate relief against a government. Standing to assert a claim or defense under this section shall be governed by the general rules of standing under article III of the Constitution.

§ **2000bb-2**. As used in this chapter—**(1)** the term "government" includes a branch, department, agency, instrumentality, and official (or other person acting under color of law) of the United States, or of a covered entity; **(2)** the term "covered entity" means the District of Columbia, the Commonwealth of Puerto Rico, and each territory and possession of the United States; **(3)** the term "demonstrates" means meets the burdens of going forward with the evidence and of persuasion; and **(4)** the term "exercise of religion" means religious exercise, as defined in section 2000 cc–5 of this title.

§ **2000bb-3. (a)** In general: This chapter applies to all Federal law, and the implementation of that law, whether statutory or otherwise, and whether adopted before or after November 16, 1993. **(b)** Rule of construction. Federal statutory law adopted after November 16, 1993, is subject to this chapter unless such law explicitly excludes such application by reference to this chapter. **(c)** Religious belief unaffected. Nothing in this chapter shall be construed to authorize any government to burden any religious belief.

§ **2000bb-4**. Nothing in this chapter shall be construed to affect, interpret, or in any way address that portion of the First Amendment prohibiting laws respecting the establishment of religion (referred to in this section as the "Establishment Clause"). Granting government funding, benefits, or exemptions, to the extent permissible under the Establishment Clause, shall not constitute a violation of this chapter. As used in this section, the term "granting", used with respect to government funding, benefits, or exemptions, does not include the denial of government funding, benefits, or exemptions.

[10]The U.S. Supreme Court held that the RFRA went beyond Congress' power therefore declared the RFRA unconstitutional as applied to the states. See *City of Boerne v. Flores*, 521 U.S. 507, 536 (1997).

[11]In UTTER, Jack. American Indians: Answers to Today's Questions. University of Oklahoma Press, 2001, ISBN 0-8061-3309-0, p. 159.

On the other hand, the Religious Land Use and Institutionalized Persons Act (RLUIPA), codified as 42 U.S.C. § 2000 cc et seq.,[12] is a U.S. federal law that prohibits the imposition of burdens on the ability of prisoners to worship as they please and gives churches and other religious institutions a way to avoid burdensome zoning law restrictions on their property use. It was enacted by the U.S.

---

[12] **42. U.S.C. §2000 cc: a)** Substantial burdens. **(1)** General rule. No government shall impose or implement a land use regulation in a manner that imposes a substantial burden on the religious exercise of a person, including a religious assembly or institution, unless the government demonstrates that imposition of the burden on that person, assembly, or institution—**(A)** is in furtherance of a compelling governmental interest; and **(B)** is the least restrictive means of furthering that compelling governmental interest. **(2)** Scope of application. This subsection applies in any case in which—**(A)** the substantial burden is imposed in a program or activity that receives Federal financial assistance, even if the burden results from a rule of general applicability; **(B)** the substantial burden affects, or removal of that substantial burden would affect, commerce with foreign nations, among the several States, or with Indian tribes, even if the burden results from a rule of general applicability; or **(C)** the substantial burden is imposed in the implementation of a land use regulation or system of land use regulations, under which a government makes, or has in place formal or informal procedures or practices that permit the government to make, individualized assessments of the proposed uses for the property involved. **(b)** Discrimination and exclusion **(1)** Equal terms. No government shall impose or implement a land use regulation in a manner that treats a religious assembly or institution on less than equal terms with a nonreligious assembly or institution. **(2)** Nondiscrimination. No government shall impose or implement a land use regulation that discriminates against any assembly or institution on the basis of religion or religious denomination. **(3)** Exclusions and limits. No government shall impose or implement a land use regulation that—**(A)** totally excludes religious assemblies from a jurisdiction; or **(B)** unreasonably limits religious assemblies, institutions, or structures within a jurisdiction.

§ 2000 cc–1. Protection of religious exercise of institutionalized persons. (a) General rule. No government shall impose a substantial burden on the religious exercise of a person residing in or confined to an institution, as defined in section 1997 of this title, even if the burden results from a rule of general applicability, unless the government demonstrates that imposition of the burden on that person—(1) is in furtherance of a compelling governmental interest; and (2) is the least restrictive means of furthering that compelling governmental interest. (b) Scope of application. This section applies in any case in which—(1) the substantial burden is imposed in a program or activity that receives Federal financial assistance; or (2) the substantial burden affects, or removal of that substantial burden would affect, commerce with foreign nations, among the several States, or with Indian tribes.

§ 2000 cc–2. Judicial relief (a) Cause of action. A person may assert a violation of this chapter as a claim or defense in a judicial proceeding and obtain appropriate relief against a government. Standing to assert a claim or defense under this section shall be governed by the general rules of standing under article III of the Constitution. (b) Burden of persuasion. If a plaintiff produces prima facie evidence to support a claim alleging a violation of the Free Exercise Clause or a violation of section 2000 cc of this title, the government shall bear the burden of persuasion on any element of the claim, except that the plaintiff shall bear the burden of persuasion on whether the law (including a regulation) or government practice that is challenged by the claim substantially burdens the plaintiff's exercise of religion. (c) Full faith and credit. Adjudication of a claim of a violation of section 2000 cc of this title in a non-Federal forum shall not be entitled to full faith and credit in a Federal court unless the claimant had a full and fair adjudication of that claim in the non-Federal forum. (d) Omitted (e) Prisoners. Nothing in this chapter shall be construed to amend or repeal the Prison Litigation Reform Act of 1995 (including provisions of law amended by that Act). (f) Authority of United States to enforce this chapter. The United States may bring an action for injunctive or declaratory relief to enforce compliance with this chapter. Nothing in this subsection

Congress in 2000 to correct the problems created by the RFRA of 1993. The RLUIPA was passed in both the House of Representatives and the Senate by unanimous consent in voice votes, meaning that no objection was raised to its passage, so no vote was taken.

---

shall be construed to deny, impair, or otherwise affect any right or authority of the Attorney General, the United States, or any agency, officer, or employee of the United States, acting under any law other than this subsection, to institute or intervene in any proceeding. (g) Limitation. If the only jurisdictional basis for applying a provision of this chapter is a claim that a substantial burden by a government on religious exercise affects, or that removal of that substantial burden would affect, commerce with foreign nations, among the several States, or with Indian tribes, the provision shall not apply if the government demonstrates that all substantial burdens on, or the removal of all substantial burdens from, similar religious exercise throughout the Nation would not lead in the aggregate to a substantial effect on commerce with foreign nations, among the several States, or with Indian tribes.

§ **2000 cc–3.** Rules of construction. (a) Religious belief unaffected. Nothing in this chapter shall be construed to authorize any government to burden any religious belief. (b) Religious exercise not regulated. Nothing in this chapter shall create any basis for restricting or burdening religious exercise or for claims against a religious organization including any religiously affiliated school or university, not acting under color of law. (c) Claims to funding unaffected. Nothing in this chapter shall create or preclude a right of any religious organization to receive funding or other assistance from a government, or of any person to receive government funding for a religious activity, but this chapter may require a government to incur expenses in its own operations to avoid imposing a substantial burden on religious exercise. (d) Other authority to impose conditions on funding unaffected. Nothing in this chapter shall—(1) authorize a government to regulate or affect, directly or indirectly, the activities or policies of a person other than a government as a condition of receiving funding or other assistance; or (2) restrict any authority that may exist under other law to so regulate or affect, except as provided in this chapter. (e) Governmental discretion in alleviating burdens on religious exercise. A government may avoid the preemptive force of any provision of this chapter by changing the policy or practice that results in a substantial burden on religious exercise, by retaining the policy or practice and exempting the substantially burdened religious exercise, by providing exemptions from the policy or practice for applications that substantially burden religious exercise, or by any other means that eliminates the substantial burden. (f) Effect on other law. With respect to a claim brought under this chapter, proof that a substantial burden on a person's religious exercise affects, or removal of that burden would affect, commerce with foreign nations, among the several States, or with Indian tribes, shall not establish any inference or presumption that Congress intends that any religious exercise is, or is not, subject to any law other than this chapter. (g) Broad construction. This chapter shall be construed in favor of a broad protection of religious exercise, to the maximum extent permitted by the terms of this chapter and the Constitution. (h) No preemption or repeal. Nothing in this chapter shall be construed to preempt State law, or repeal Federal law, that is equally as protective of religious exercise as, or more protective of religious exercise than, this chapter. (i) Severability. If any provision of this chapter or of an amendment made by this chapter, or any application of such provision to any person or circumstance, is held to be unconstitutional, the remainder of this chapter, the amendments made by this chapter, and the application of the provision to any other person or circumstance shall not be affected.

§ **2000 cc–4.** Establishment Clause unaffected. Nothing in this chapter shall be construed to affect, interpret, or in any way address that portion of the first amendment to the Constitution prohibiting laws respecting an establishment of religion (referred to in this section as the "Establishment Clause"). Granting government funding, benefits, or exemptions, to the extent permissible under the Establishment Clause, shall not constitute a violation of this chapter. In this section, the term "granting", used with respect to government funding, benefits, or exemptions, does not include the denial of government funding, benefits, or exemptions.

RLUIPA's land-use sections provide important protections for the religious freedom of persons, places of worship, religious schools, and other religious assemblies and institutions. They codify the constitutional protections for religious freedom and against religious discrimination provided under the Free Exercise Clause, the Free Speech Clause, and the Equal Protection Clause, and provide mechanisms for enforcement of these rights. The land use section contains five separate provisions, which, together, provide comprehensive protection for individuals and religious institutions from zoning and landmarking laws that discriminate based on religion or unjustifiably infringe on religious freedom. The law's institutionalized persons provision prohibits regulations that impose a "substantial burden" on the religious exercise of persons residing or confined in an "institution," unless the government can show that the regulation serves a "compelling government interest" and is the least restrictive way for the government to further that interest. RLUIPA allows aggrieved persons to bring lawsuits under both its land use provisions and its institutionalized persons provision. In addition, RLUIPA authorizes the Attorney General to bring suits to enforce it.

In September 2010, the U.S. Department of Justice issued a Report on the Tenth Anniversary of RLUIPA, as well as a Policy Statement on RLUIPA, which includes detailed questions and answers about the law. "Religious assemblies, especially, new, small, or unfamiliar ones, may be illegally discriminated against on the face of zoning codes and also in the highly individualized and discretionary processes of land use regulation. Zoning codes and landmarking laws may illegally exclude religious assemblies in places where they permit theaters, meeting halls, and other places where large groups of people assemble for secular purposes. Or the zoning codes or landmarking laws may permit religious assemblies only with individualized

---

§ 2000 cc–5. Definitions in this chapter: (1) Claimant. The term "claimant" means a person raising a claim or defense under this chapter. (2) Demonstrates. The term "demonstrates" means meets the burdens of going forward with the evidence and of persuasion. (3) Free Exercise Clause. The term "Free Exercise Clause" means that portion of the first amendment to the Constitution that proscribes laws prohibiting the free exercise of religion (4) Government The term "government"—(A) means—(i) a State, county, municipality, or other governmental entity created under the authority of a State; (ii) any branch, department, agency, instrumentality, or official of an entity listed in clause (i); and (iii) any other person acting under color of State law; and (B) for the purposes of sections 2000 cc–2 (b) and 2000 cc–3 of this title, includes the United States, a branch, department, agency, instrumentality, or official of the United States, and any other person acting under color of Federal law. (5) Land use regulation. The term "land use regulation" means a zoning or landmarking law, or the application of such a law, that limits or restricts a claimant's use or development of land (including a structure affixed to land), if the claimant has an ownership, leasehold, easement, servitude, or other property interest in the regulated land or a contract or option to acquire such an interest. (6) Program or activity. The term "program or activity" means all of the operations of any entity as described in paragraph (1) or (2) of section 2000d–4a of this title. (7) Religious exercise. (A) In general. The term "religious exercise" includes any exercise of religion, whether or not compelled by, or central to, a system of religious belief. (B) Rule. The use, building, or conversion of real property for the purpose of religious exercise shall be considered to be religious exercise of the person or entity that uses or intends to use the property for that purpose.

permission from the zoning board or landmarking commission, and zoning boards or landmarking commission may use that authority in illegally discriminatory ways."[13]

"To address these concerns, RLUIPA prohibits zoning and landmarking laws that substantially burden the religious exercise of churches or other religious assemblies or institutions absent the least restrictive means of furthering a compelling governmental interest. This prohibition applies in any situation where: (i) the state or local government entity imposing the substantial burden receives federal funding; (ii) the substantial burden affects, or removal of the substantial burden would affect, interstate commerce; or (iii) the substantial burden arises from the state or local government's formal or informal procedures for making individualized assessments of a property's uses. In addition, RLUIPA prohibits zoning and landmarking laws that:

(1) treat churches or other religious assemblies or institutions on less than equal terms with nonreligious institutions;
(2) discriminate against any assemblies or institutions on the basis of religion or religious denomination;
(3) totally exclude religious assemblies from a jurisdiction; or
(4) unreasonably limit religious assemblies, institutions, or structures within a jurisdiction."[14]

"The Department of Justice can investigate alleged RLUIPA violations and bring a lawsuit to enforce the statute. The Department can obtain injunctive, but not monetary, relief. Individuals, houses of worship, and other religious institutions can also bring a lawsuit in federal or state court to enforce RLUIPA."[15] Examples of cases or investigations in which the Department of Justice has been involved include[16]:

01. ***United States v. City of Walnut, California***: In September 2010, the Department of Justice filed suit against the City of Walnut, California, over its denial of a conditional use permit to the Chung Tai Zen Center to allow it to build a Buddhist house of worship. The suit alleges that the city had approved similar permits for other places of worship, and until it denied the Zen Center's application, the city had not denied any application for a conditional use permit to build, expand, or operate a house of worship since at least 1980;

02. ***United States v. Suffern, New York***: In June 2010, the Department obtained a consent decree, permitting the continued operation of a "Shabbos house" next to a hospital in a New York village. The facility provides food and lodging to

---

[13] See The United States Department of Justice site, http://www.justice.gov/crt/about/hce/rluipaexplain.php, accessed Apr. 2, 2014.

[14] *Id.*

[15] *Id.*

[16] This list of cases and investigations appears in the Report on the Tenth Anniversary of the Religious Land Use and Institutionalized Persons Act from de U.S. Department of Justice, September 22, 2010 (in http://www.justice.gov/crt/rluipa_report_092210.pdf, accessed May 1, 2014).

Sabbath-observant Jews to enable them to visit sick relatives at the hospital on the Sabbath;

03. ***United States v. Metropolitan Government of Davidson County and Nashville, Tennessee***: After a Christian group named Teen Challenge purchased land to build a residential substance abuse center, the defendants amended the zoning code in order to keep the facility from locating there. The Civil Rights Division of the Department of Justice investigated and filed suit, and reached a settlement in 2009 under RLUIPA and the Fair Housing Act, permitting Teen Challenge to move forward with its plans to build its residential treatment center;

04. ***United States v. City of Hollywood, Florida***: The Department of Justice filed suit in April 2005 against the City of Hollywood, Florida, after it denied a permit to an Orthodox Jewish synagogue located in a residential neighborhood, a permit that the suit alleged was routinely granted to other houses of worship. The suit alleged that the denial and subsequent enforcement actions taken by the city against the synagogue were a result of discrimination toward Orthodox Jews. On the eve of the trial, the Department reached a consent decree with the city and the synagogue that permitted the synagogue to continue to operate at the location and to expand in the neighborhood in the future, and required training for city officials. A separate agreement signed at the same time required the city to pay $2 million in damages and attorneys' fees to the synagogue;

05. ***United States v. Village of Airmont, New York***: The United States alleged in this suit that a New York village enacted a ban on boarding schools specifically to keep Hasidic Jews, who educate their young men in boarding schools called yeshivas, from settling in the village;

06. ***United States v. City of Waukegan, Illinois***: The United States brought suit against the City of Waukegan, Illinois, in 2008, over its exclusion of places of worship in districts that permitted clubs, lodges, meetings halls, and theaters, and its imposition of notices of violation to several small churches operating in these districts. The United States reached a consent decree with the city on February 25, 2008, requiring it to treat places of worship equally with other assemblies;

07. ***United States v. Maui County, Hawaii***: The Civil Rights Division sued the county of Maui in 2003 after the county denied a permit for Hale O Kaula, a small, nondenominational Christian church that has held services on Maui since 1960, to build a church on 5.85 acres of land in an agricultural district. The church encourages practitioners to grow food in accordance with Biblical principles and to live in harmony with the land, and being in an agricultural district was integral to its worship needs. The county permitted various secular assemblies in the district, including rodeo facilities, petting zoos, and sports fields. The county subsequently settled with the church, permitting it to build and paying it damages and attorney's fees;

08. ***Gainesville, Florida***: The Civil Rights Division opened an investigation of the City of Gainesville, Florida, after the city denied a permit to Fire of God Ministries to operate a church in a building formerly used as a Moose Lodge. As a result of the investigation, the city agreed to allow the church to operate on the site, and changed its zoning code to treat religious uses the same as other assembly uses. The Civil Rights Division closed its investigation in April 2008;

09. ***Berkeley, Illinois***: A mosque had operated in a former school building on a 4.5 acre parcel in the Village of Berkeley, Illinois, for more than 20 years. The mosque sought to build a 13,000 square foot addition to accommodate its congregation, which had grown to the point that worshipers spilled into the hallways during services, and to make exterior changes to give the building a more mosque-like appearance, including adding a minaret. The expansion project faced community opposition and repeated permit denials. The Civil Rights Division opened an investigation under RLUIPA in 2007. In March 2008, as a result of the investigation, the Village agreed to allow the mosque's project to move forward;

10. ***Albanian Associated Fund v. Township of Wayne, New Jersey***: A New Jersey Township allegedly delayed a mosque's building application for more than three years, then tried to stop the building project by seizing the property under eminent domain. The mosque filed suit under RLUIPA and various state and federal claims. The Civil Rights Division filed a friend-of-the-court brief against the Township's motion for summary judgment. The United States' brief contended that the mosque produced sufficient evidence to show that the Township deliberately thwarted the mosque's application for a conditional use permit for discriminatory reasons through its exercise of its power of eminent domain. The court agreed with the Division that the use of eminent domain power to bypass zoning regulations could violate RLUIPA. The parties ultimately settled the case, and the Division closed its investigation in 2010;

11. ***Village of Morton Grove, Illinois***: A Muslim school in Morton Grove, Illinois, encountered community opposition to its plans to build a mosque on its property, much of which appeared to be driven by animus against Muslims. The Civil Rights Division opened a RLUIPA investigation, and, after mediation by the Department of Justice's Community Relations Service, the village reached an agreement that permitted the school to build the mosque subject to certain conditions;

12. ***Brighton Township, Pennsylvania***: Brighton Township denied a permit for an Assemblies of God church to build on a 3.25-acre lot because the zoning code had a five-acre minimum for churches. However, the zoning code specifically stated that there was no minimum acreage requirement for adult movie theaters, cabarets, assembly halls, and fraternal organizations. The Civil Rights Division opened an investigation, and the Township amended its zoning code;

13. ***Midrash Sephardi v. Town of Surfside***: Two Orthodox Jewish Congregations were barred from meeting in a space they had rented above a bank in the Florida city's commercial district. The city's zoning code permitted private clubs, lodge halls, dance studios, music studios, and language schools in the district, but excluded houses of worship. The Department filed an amicus brief in the U.S. Court of Appeals for the Eleventh Circuit, and a brief as intervener defending the constitutionality of RLUIPA. The court ruled that the exclusion of houses of worship from the commercial district violated RLUIPA, and that RLUIPA did not exceed Congress's constitutional authority to enforce the Fourteenth Amendment;

14. ***Guru Nanak Sikh Society v. County of Sutter, California***: A Sikh congregation in a California county that only permits houses of worship in residential and agricultural districts purchased land in a residential district, was denied a permit, and then purchased land in an agricultural district, only to be denied a permit there as well. The United States, participating as amicus, argued that the congregation's rights under RLUIPA had been violated, and the U.S. Court of Appeals for the Ninth Circuit agreed;

15. ***West Mifflin, Pennsylvania***: The Civil Rights Division opened an investigation of West Mifflin after an African American Christian congregation was denied a use permit for a church building it purchased from a predominantly white congregation. After the investigation began, officials reversed their decision and granted the use permit;

16. ***Douglas County, Georgia***: The Division opened an investigation of Douglas County after Victory Family Life Church was denied the ability to build a new sanctuary on land it had occupied for 20 years because its 2.8 acres were below the 3-acre minimum newly required for churches, despite comparable assemblies being permitted on small plots. The County amended its code to treat churches equally, and the Division closed its investigation;

17. ***Garden Grove, California***: The United States opened an investigation of the City of Garden Grove, California, in 2007 over its denial of approval for a Buddhist group to convert a commercial building formerly used as a medical center into a temple in the city's office-professional zone. The United States closed its investigation in 2010 after the city agreed to allow the group to locate its temple on the site.

3.2.2 Zoning Regulations in Brazil

Because the relationship between churches and zoning regulations involves municipal governments, there can be great differences among multiple urban regimes. In the municipality of São Paulo, as one example, the current law regarding the regulation of urban spaces is Act No. 10,205/86, which prohibits the occupation of real estate property for institutional purposes (such as the ones fulfilled by religious organizations) without prior authorization from the municipal government. This law also designates the General Secretary of the Subdistricts (*Secretaria Geral das Subprefeituras*) as the competent organ to grant said authorization. Additionally, it allows the municipal administration to carry out inspections in order to assure that the legislation is being followed. Finally, the law provides for a fine for any violation of the law.

Act No. 10,205/86 is currently regulated by Decree No. 49,969/08, which reiterates the requirement to obtain a charter from the municipal government in order to occupy real estate property for non-residential purposes. It also specifies three kinds of licenses: the Operating License (*Auto de Licença de Funcionamento*), the Operating Permit (*Alvará de Funcionamento*), and the Authorization Permit for Public and Temporary Events (*Alvará de Autorização para eventos públicos e temporários*).

The Operating Permit applies to facilities with an occupation of 250 or more persons for an undetermined time. Religious temples are explicitly included in the list of examples of activities covered by this permit. One could also conclude that the third kind of license, the Authorization Permit for Public and Temporary Events, applies to events of religious nature, as long as the events are public, temporary, and involve more than 250 people. Finally, the first type of license, the Operating License, is residually applied to all other cases. Thus, the three licenses could be applied to religious rituals, depending on their frequency and the number of persons attending the event.

The Operating Permit, the most adequate for religious temples, has a concession process that must be started by a requisition of the applicant. The license must be affixed next to the facility's main entrance and contain information as to the maximum number of persons that can safely be accommodated in the building. Obtaining this license requires presentation of documentation that proves that the building is up to code, meets safety requirements, has proper fixtures to avoid noise disturbances, and is accessible to handicapped persons.

3.3 Church Property Disputes

It is not rare to face a perplexing legal issue regarding the ownership of church property. In the wake of the ordination of an openly gay bishop in 2003, local congregations have broken away from the Protestant Episcopal Church in the United States, leading to contentious property disputes over both the real and personal property of the churches. According to Meghaan Cecilia McElroy, "this continual religious saga has led many legal scholars and ordinary citizens alike to wonder who should be entitled to the property after the split."[17]

For instance, the case of *Presbyterian Church v. Mary Elizabeth Blue Hull Memorial Presbyterian Church* established the procedure by which civil courts are to limit their inquiries into intra-church disputes. A Georgia congregation had elected to separate from its mother church on the ground that the latter's statements regarding the ordination of women and opposition to the Vietnam War had significantly departed from established doctrine. The dispute involved the control of local church property. The Georgia Supreme Court ruled in favor of the local congregation, finding that the mother church had departed from its original doctrinal teachings.

[17] MCELROY, Meghaan Cecilia. Possessions is Nine Tenths of The Law: But Who Really Owns a Church's Property in the Wake of a Religious Split Within a Hierarchical Church? 50 William and Mary Law Review 311, 311 (October 2008).

The Georgia courts used the implied trust doctrine. But the U.S. Supreme Court reversed, holding that the first amendment prohibits civil court inquiry into church doctrine. The Court instructed civil courts adjudicating intra-church property disputes to apply "neutral principles of law developed for use in all property disputes."[18]

Theodore Lewis Squillante deems that "where ecclesiastical issues can be separated from secular controversies, civil courts must provide a forum for the resolution of those controversies."[19] The U.S. Supreme Court affirmed this obligation in *Jones v. Wolf*, preserving the right of church members to have access to an objective judiciary.[20]

The evolution of the U.S. Supreme Court's jurisprudence has produced two divergent methods for resolving church property disputes: the deference approach and the neutral principles doctrine. The Court first articulated the deference approach as the proper means for handling intra-church property disputes. A century later, the Court accepted a different manner for resolving property disputes in the wake of a church divorce. The deference approach requires courts to accept the resolution reached by judicial bodies of the hierarchical church on intra-church disputes. The neutral principles doctrine, on the other hand, focuses on courts resolving church property disputes by interpreting church documents relating to the contested property without deciding any questions of religious doctrine. For Meghaan Cecilia McElroy, both approaches articulated by the Supreme Court "reveal an uneasiness by the judicial system to intervene in disputes involving issues of religious doctrine."[21]

"In the case of *Watson v. Jones*, the members of the Walnut Street Presbyterian Church of Louisville, Kentucky, divided into two distinct bodies, each claiming exclusive use of the property owned by the local church. The dispute began shortly after the Civil War ended, when the General Assembly of the Presbyterian Church issued resolutions expressly supporting the emancipation of slaves within the states formerly belonging to the Confederacy. . . . The Walnut Street Church, under the jurisdiction of the Presbytery of Louisville, divided into two factions, one supporting the General Assembly and its denunciation of slavery, and the other supporting the Presbytery and its resistance of the usurpation of authority by the Assembly."[22]

The U.S. Supreme Court has articulated three categories of church property disputes. "The first category includes express trust disputes in which the contested

---

[18] *Presbyterian Church v. Mary Elizabeth Blue Hull Mem'l Presbyterian Church*, 393 U.S. 440 (1969).

[19] SQUILLANTE, Theodore Lewis, Constitutional Law – Freedom of Religion – Church and State – Property – Ecclesiastical Law – A State May Constitutionally Adopt a "Neutral Principles of Law" Approach for Adjudicating Church Property Disputes – *Jones v. Wolf*, 99 S. Ct. 3020 (1979). 48 U. Cin. L. Rev. 1108, 1111 (1979).

[20] *Jones v. Wolf*, 443 U.S. 595 (1979).

[21] MCELROY, Meghaan Cecilia. Possessions is Nine Tenths of The Law: But Who Really Owns a Church's Property in the Wake of a Religious Split Within a Hierarchical Church? 50 William and Mary Law Review 311, 313 (October 2008).

[22] *Id.*

property has been expressly devoted by deed or will to the teaching of a specific religious doctrine." In this case, "the court must determine whether the property has been diverted away from the trust and whether there are persons qualified within the meaning of the original dedication who are willing to teach the doctrines prescribed in the trust. If such persons exist, then they have complete authority to prevent the property from being used in contravention of the trust." The second category is about "congregational church disputes in which the church property is held by an independent organization with no obligation to any higher authority. The third category consists of hierarchical church disputes in which the congregation holding the property is a 'subordinate member of some general church organization in which there are superior ecclesiastical tribunals with a general and ultimate power of control.'"[23]

Mega-churches and mega-temples can accumulate vast amounts of wealth. If they cannot pay creditors, the massive nonpayment could cause serious financial strain for both the creditors and the surrounding community. If there is fraud or abuse of the eleemosynary status, the corporate veil of the mega-church should be pierced.

3.4 The Place of Churches and Temples Within Bankruptcy Law

3.4.1 Churches and Temples Within Brazilian Bankruptcy Regulation

The Brazilian Bankruptcy Act (Act No. 11,101 of February 9, 2005) establishes a policy of providing equal treatment to creditors while affording the debtor some flexibility in formulating a plan. Article 1 of this Act, however, makes it clear that this norm does not apply to religious organizations by stating as follows:

> This Law regulates the judicial reorganization, the bankruptcy extra judicial reorganization and the bankruptcy of entrepreneur and corporation, hereinafter referred to simply as the debtor.

The Brazilian Civil Code (Act No. 10,406, of January 10, 2002) considers religious organizations as legal entities of private law (Article 44, Part IV). Its first Section states as follows:

> The creation, organization, and internal structure and functioning of religious organizations are free, and the government is forbidden from denying them the recognition and registration of the constituent acts necessary for their operation. (Added by Act No. 10,825, of December 22, 2003).

Thus, because religious organizations are legal entities of private law and not corporations or entrepreneurs, they cannot avail themselves to bankruptcy laws.

---

[23] *Id.* (quoting *Watson v. Jones*, 80 U.S. 679 (1871)).

3.4.2 Churches and Temples Within U.S. Bankruptcy Regulation

In the United States, the treatment is the same. Creditors cannot force churches into involuntary bankruptcy because churches are classified as "eleemosynary" institutions. At the same time, creditors are guaranteed equal treatment under the law, while debtors are able to work out their financial situations under protection of the automatic stay.[24] "This protection is an exception to the general principles of the Bankruptcy Code which has a well-established policy of providing 'equal treatment of creditors while affording the debtor some flexibility in formulating a plan.' ... Courts have at various times relied on the state legal status of an institution, the nature of the organization's activities, whether the organization's activities were entirely ancillary to its eleemosynary goal, and whether the eleemosynary organization competed with commercial enterprises. None of these evaluations have been considered determinative."[25]

Mega-churches and mega-temples raise serious questions about the scope of this special protection. Some of them can be qualified as a non- or quasi-religious entities because they own gyms, movie theaters, and amusement parks in addition to their worship and liturgy activities. But, as stated before, the U.S. Supreme Court has not addressed the issue of how to distinguish them from their smaller counterparts with respect to bankruptcy proceedings.

Andrew Stone Mayo recounts an interesting bankruptcy story of one mega-church. "Crystal Cathedral, a California mega-church founded in the 1950s that boasts over ten thousand members, announced in April 2010 that it owed creditors over $55 million. The church estimated that as many as 185 creditors could be waiting for payment. The church stated that it was not looking into bankruptcy, but that it could not afford to pay the creditors at the time. The church refused to enter bankruptcy for six months. It ignored the complaints of creditors, including those with long-standing ties to the church who had been trying to collect money for months with no results. Creditors who did not wish to file a lawsuit could only wait and hope that the church would be able to wade through its messy financial situation or eventually file for bankruptcy. However, should the fact that the church owned a campus with soccer fields, a retreat center, and camping grounds, change the fact that creditors would have no recourse other than individual lawsuits if the church refused to pay?"

The Bankruptcy Code dictates that "an involuntary case may commenced only under chapter 7 or 11 of this title, and only against a person except a farmer, family

---

[24] The Code, however, also protects certain corporations from involuntary bankruptcy. These are corporations that are not "moneyed, business, or commercial" in nature, including "churches, schools, and charitable organizations and foundations." MAYO, Andrew Stone. For God and Money: The Place of the Megachurch Within the Bankruptcy Code. 27 Emory Bankr. Dev. J. 609, 611 (2011).

[25] See MAYO, Andrew Stone. For God and Money: The Place of the Megachurch Within the Bankruptcy Code. 27 Emory Bankr. Dev. J. 609, 650 (2011).

farmer, or a corporation that is not a moneyed, business, or commercial corporation, that may be a debtor under the chapter under which such case is commenced."[26] Thus, the Code maintains the prohibition on involuntary bankruptcy suits against eleemosynary institutions, such as churches, schools, and charitable organizations and foundations.

Bibliography

ALVES, J. F.; DELGADO, M. L. *Código*, cit., p. 46.

ANDERSEN, David M. Political Silence at Church: The Empty Threat of Removing Tax-Exempt Status for Insubstantial Attempts to Influence Legislation. 2006 B.Y.U.L. Rev. 115.

BRAZILIAN Internal Revenue Service site (Receita Federal do Brasil), in http://www.receita.fazenda.gov.br/PessoaJuridica/DIPJ/2005/PergResp2005/pr24a31.htm, accessed March 9, 2014.

DALY, Eoin. Regulation Religious Function: The Strange Case of Mass Cards, 9 Hibernian L. J. 55 (2010).

DINIZ, M. H. *Código Civil Anotado*. 15ª Edição. São Paulo: Editora Saraiva, 2010. 1432 p. 95.

FLAGIELLO v. Pennsylvania, 14 Pa. 486, 208 A.2d 193 (1965).

FRENCH, Thomas M. and ABELS, Jon. Recent Decisions. Indiana Legal Forum. Harris v. Y.W.C.A. of Terre Haute Ind.: Abolition of Charitable Immunity in Indiana. 2 Ind. Legal F. 378 (1968–1969).

INTERLOCUTORY Appeal (Agravo de Instrumento No. 0136470–58.2011.8.0000, TJ-SP, 19ª Câmara de Direito Privado, Rel. Sebastião Alves Junqueira, 18 de outubro de 2011.) In http://www.tjsp.jus.br/, accessed Aug. 28, 2013.

LANERI, Christa E. The Texas Religious Freedom Restoration Act: Does It Really Work? 16 Texas Wesleyan Law Review 457 (2010).

MAYO, Andrew Stone. For God and Money: The Place of the Megachurch Within the Bankruptcy Code. 27 Emory Bankr. Dev. J. 609 (2011).

MCELROY, Meghaan Cecilia. Possessions is Nine Tenths of The Law: But Who Really Owns a Church's Property in the Wake of a Religious Split Within a Hierarchical Church?. 50 William and Mary Law Review 311 (October 2008).

MULLIKIN v. Jewish Hospital Ass'n of Louisville, 348 S.W.2d 930 (Ky 1961).

REPORT on the Tenth Anniversary of the Religious Land Use and Institutionalized Persons Act from de U.S. Department of Justice, September 22, 2010 (in http://www.justice.gov/crt/rluipa_report_092210.pdf, accessed May 1, 2014).

SPRINGER v. Federated Church of Reno, 71 Nev. 177, 283 P.2d 1071 (1955).

SQUILLANTE, Theodore Lewis, Constitutional Law – Freedom of Religion – Church and State – Property – Ecclesiastical Law – A State May Constitutionally Adopt a "Neutral Principles of Law" Approach for Adjudicating Church Property Disputes – Jones v. Wolf, 99 S. Ct. 3020 (1979). 48 U. Cin. L. Rev. 1108 (1979).

UNITED States Department of Justice site, http://www.justice.gov/crt/about/hce/rluipaexplain.php, accessed Apr. 2, 2014.

VENOSA, S. S. *Direito Civil: Parte geral* (1984). 4ª Edição. São Paulo: Editora Atlas S. A., 2004. 662 pp. 272–73.

WELCH, Heather M. The Religious Land Use and Institutionalized Persons Act and Mega-Churches: Demonstrating the Limits of Religious Land Use Exemptions in Federal Legislation. 39 University of Baltimore Law Rev. 255 (2010).

[26] 11 U.S.C. § 303 (2006).

Chapter 4
Criminal Investigations and Cases Involving Financial Crimes Practiced by and Through Religious Institutions

New religious movements are often regarded with suspicion. Some question whether the faith as a whole is fraudulent, or whether particular instances of conduct are fraudulent.[1]

It is a well-known fact that some religious institutions act in controversial ways when it comes to collecting financial resources through donations from church members. This is especially true of protestant churches of neo-charismatic orientation, which are commonly referred in Brazil as "evangelicals." The press and governmental bodies have investigated and released reports of evidence of criminal activity related to financial collections. Some leaders of these organizations have been charged with crimes, such as money laundering, participation in organized crime, and larceny by fraud, among others.

The U.S. Supreme Court ruled, in *United States v. Ballard*,[2] on the prosecution and conviction of the founders of the "I Am" movement for mail fraud, based on their soliciting funds accompanied by representations that they had the power to heal illnesses and injuries. The Court did not explicitly sanction fraud convictions based solely on a lack of sincerity. Justice Jackson explained that some degree of skepticism is a normal feature of religious belief, so it would be dangerous to make sincerity a triable question. For him, the Constitution requires us to tolerate a certain amount of fraud rather than weaken the guarantees of the First Amendment. However, he left open the possibility that a fraud conviction could be sought on grounds unrelated to religion, such as a misrepresentation about what would be done with solicited donations.

Religious values do not endorse corruption and fraud. This is true of several religious bodies, including Islamic laws. Islam looks to moral development within

[1] In HORWITZ, Paul. Scientology in Court: A Comparative Analysis and Some Thoughts on Selected Issues in Law and Religion. 47 DePaul Law Review 1, 28 (Fall 1997).

[2] United States v. Ballard, 322 U.S. 78, 92–95 (1944).

F.M. De Sanctis, *Churches, Temples, and Financial Crimes*,
DOI 10.1007/978-3-319-15681-1_4

the individual to strengthen resolve and foster self-restraint.[3] Corruption is a "deep-rooted phenomenon that exists in innumerable forms, knows no cultural boundaries, operates in the private as well as the public sector, occurs in rich countries and poor, and defies comprehensive definition."[4] This logically extends to internal religious authority.

4.1 Crimes Practiced Within Religious Organizations

4.1.1 "Among Brothers" Operation ("Entre irmãos")

Related irregularities and crimes allegedly took place in a religious institution called Igreja Cristã Maranata (ICM) based in the State of Espírito Santo, Brazil. The denomination's leaders supposedly took advantage of the tax exemption granted to churches of any worship and began to use the goods of the church for their own benefit, investing in private assets such as real estate, vehicles, and businesses. There were suspicions that the acquisition of computer equipment and software, such as computers and video conferencing equipment, was illegally done in the United States and in Paraguay. On November 26, 2012, "Among Brothers" Operation was initiated with the aim of investigating fraud committed in the institution. Documents and illegally imported equipment were seized. The operation consisted of carrying out 12 search and seizure warrants issued by both the federal and the state courts of Espírito Santo. The investigations revealed evidence of the involvement of members of the Church's executive board, who, by illicit payments and unbacked invoices issued by suppliers participating in the scheme, promoted irregular cash outflow of resources and the state tax. There was suspicion of a number of other irregularities, ranging from the use of policemen to guard and protect ICM members and temples (the abuse of police functions), overpriced services hiring, parliamentary amendments aimed at deviating funds for a foundation linked to the ICM, and the remittance of dollars in suitcases carried by church followers.[5]

---

[3] According to Ved P. Nanda, in many Islamic or Muslim countries, the people feel obligated to conduct their lives in conformity with the precepts of the Qu'an and Sunna. These countries profess to be governed by authoritative statements of the traditional law of Islam, Shari'a law (in NANDA, Ved P. Islam and International Human Rights Law: Selected Aspects, 87 American Society International Law 327, 328 (1993)).

[4] ARAFA, Mohamed A. Corruption and Bribery in Islamic Law: Are Islamic Ideals Being Met in Practice?. 18 Annual Survey of International & Comparative Law 171, 171–2 (2012).

[5] In Gazeta Online, Operação cumpre mandados para apurar desvios de doações da Igreja Maranata, Nov. 26, 2012, http://gazetaonline.globo.com/_conteudo/2012/11/noticias/cidades/1376718-operacao-cumpre-mandados-para-apurar-desvios-de-doacoes-da-igreja-maranata.html, accessed May 1, 2014.

4.1.2 "Backlands' Moonlight" Operation ("Luar do Sertão"*)*

Reverend Sun-Mun Moon, known as Reverend Moon, was a religious leader of Korean origin who founded the Unification Church. He was accused of illegally attempting to circumvent the legal obstacle to the formation of large estates that Brazilian law has in place for foreign individuals. He did this by instituting the Family Federation for World Peace and Unification through which he operated the New Hope Project in Pantanal region of the Brazilian state of Mato Grosso do Sul in 2000. There were fears at the time of "denationalization" of part of the country, because of the large areas of land acquired. Reverend Moon faced an investigation and an inquiry by the State Congressional Committee. He died in September 2012.[6]

4.1.3 "Trash" Operation

Research originating from information received from the Customs Port of Vitória, in the Brazilian state of Espírito Santo, revealed several importations of large quantities of used tires coming from countries in Europe and Asia that were clearly forbidden by a presidential decree (Decree No. 3,919 of September 14, 2001). Not only was this an environmental crime and fraud, there was also suspicion of underpricing tire imports, tax evasion, and money laundering.

As identified in one of the telephone interceptions, one of the targets of the investigation talked to a pastor about transactions with checks. The target got a check from a church in order to "operate" his company, but when the transaction was supposed to be performed, $50,000 was instead deposited in the target's personal account. He justified the transaction saying the check was returned to the church.[7] The church was accused of wrongdoing and several companies were seized as part of this investigation in February 2008.

4.1.4 "Miracle" Operation

This operation occurred in November 2006 and involved an illegal exchange of goods consisting of electronic and computer products that were afterwards replaced by religious musical instruments and publications. The illegal operation was revealed by an import clearance aimed at a small church located inside a favela in the city of Rio de Janeiro.

---

[6] See MidiamaxNews, Reverendo Moon, que tem fazenda e fiéis em MS, está internado em estado 'irreversível', Aug. 31, 2012, http://www.midiamax.com.br/noticias/814178-reverendo+moon+tem+fazenda+fieis+ms+esta+internado+estado+irreversivel.html, accessed Sept. 9, 2014.

[7] Brazilian Internal Revenue Service (Receita Federal do Brasil), Deflagrada operação de combate à fraude de pneus usados, http://www.receita.fazenda.gov.br/AutomaticoSRFsinot/2008/02/20/2008_02_20_10_46_12_561402307.html, accessed Oct. 1, 2014.

4.1.5 *The Universal Church of the Kingdom of God (Igreja Universal do Reino de Deus – IURD)*

In 2007, the Universal Church of the Kingdom of God's leader, bishop Edir Macedo Bezerra, was arrested on charges of larceny, "false-healing," and quackery. The pastor was released after 15 days in jail, but since then, the church has been thoroughly investigated for other criminal activity.[8]

Under the command of Bishop Macedo, money raised in church services was transferred to companies named Cremo and Unimetro which, in turn, remitted the money to two other companies based in tax havens: Cabeinvest and Investholding. The money would then return to Brazil in the form of loans simulated in contracts between the two companies located in tax havens and intermediaries. The repatriated funds would then be used to buy media companies. According to the investigation by state prosecutors, the total income of the church from 2001 to 2008 was nearly $4 billion. Such information was confirmed by the Council for Financial Activities Control (COAF, the Brazilian Intelligence Unit).

A criminal case against Bishop Macedo and nine other members of the church was filed in 2009 at the state court of São Paulo (Case No. 1,121/2009). On August 10, 2009, state judge Glaucio Roberto Brittes De Araújo upheld the charges and issued the indictment against all defendants.[9] The judge's opinion states as follows:

> There are enough elements of materiality and indication of the participation of each and every one of the defendants in the infractions imputed to them for the criminal charges to be received.
>
> Indication of the commission, by the group, of the behaviors described by the criminal charges stand out from the case file, especially from: the Council for Financial Activities Control – COAF (Brazilian Intelligence Unit) report; from the successive atypical contracts (pages 115/285 and 978/995); from the financial operations that are incompatible with the economic and physical conditions of Cremo S.A. (pages 328/329), including interbank transactions (*TED, transferência eletrônica disponível*) with significant amounts received from the Universal Church of the Kingdom of God – IURD; from the information from the State Treasury Office and from the Brazilian Internal Revenue Service; from the statements of its ex-delegates and church followers (pages 422/426, 955/957, 968/970, 1246/1249); from bank statements; from other documents including those sustaining the preliminary injunction.
>
> According to the result of initial investigations, there were many peculiar transfers of resources – that were allegedly collected through illegal means during religious services – to companies that were not really practicing activities consistent with its corporate purpose, but, instead, were passing them on to businesses interesting to the defendants. By effectively

[8] Relembre as denúncias e investigações sobre a Igreja Universal. *Estadão.com.br*, Aug. 11, 2009, http://www.estadao.com.br/noticias/cidades,relembre-as-denuncias-e-investigacoes-sobre-a-igreja-universal,416987,0.htm, accessed Aug. 21, 2014.

[9] In Brazil, grand jury indictments only apply to cases of homicide, abortion, and suicide assistance or participation. All other criminal charges are given to a single judge who decides individually whether the charges have merit and should be accepted by the trial court.

controlling legal persons or participating in simulated transactions, they increased private assets, without any exchanges, thus ultimately thwarting the goal of tax exemptions given to Churches. The dynamics of facts preconized by prosecution is consistent, theoretically, with the subsumption of the acts to the criminal offenses cited.

Thus, in face of a preliminary and perfunctory analysis of the aforementioned investigation data, the charges presented are reputed admissible, considering the presumption of innocence and the due process of law.

It is impracticable for the description of the facts to be more specific, for each defendant, than those presented in the diagrams contained in the prosecution's pleading, whereas the evidence of the adherence of each one of them to the undertakings is crucial for the establishment of the procedural relationship. Those undertakings are glimpsed, by the way, through: contracts signed – especially those supposedly simulated, performance in positions within the companies involved, and personal references made by witnesses.

Considering the principles of the presumption of innocence and the due process of law, any profound evaluation of the inquest's evidence, any conclusion regarding the preceding behaviors, any final judgment about the simulations or any incursion in the subject of description and classification of the actions attributed to each defendant would be unnecessary and premature.

It is of interest the fact that the content of the indictment allows each one of those accused to defend and contemplates concrete cogent evidence, obtained during the inquisitorial phase, especially by virtue of investigations and documents' analysis. Under these conditions, the pleading cannot be considered vague or devoid of a just cause, thus authorizing criminal persecution under the scrutiny of an adversarial process.

Therefore, in light of the aforementioned reasons, I RECEIVE the current indictment. Let all necessary measures be taken in order to preserve the secrecy of the information referred to on page 120 of the appended records.

Let the defendants be summoned to present written responses to the charges within ten days, according to article 396 of the Brazilian Code of Criminal Procedure, altered by Act No. 11.719/2008.

In the summons document, let it be clear that those accused must present their responses through a lawyer and, in case they do not have financial conditions to appoint one, a Public Defender shall be appointed to represent them.

The court clerk charged with the summons shall collect forthwith the manifestation of the defendants regarding potential interest in appointing a Public Defender.

If the summon is done by letter rogatory, let the requested judge be asked to send us a copy of the court clerk's certificate by fax, not forgetting to send it by usual means.

Once expired the established time lapse, if there is no response, let the judicial staff certify the expiry of the deadline and appoint the Public Defender.

If there is response, let the case file return to me.

Let the criminal record be requisitioned, asking, first and foremost – independently from any other order – , certificates from the Assignment Office, the Criminal Enforcement Judge of this jurisdiction and from the criminal procedures potentially notified in the first one, as well as the Criminal Enforcement Judge potentially indicated in the last, if it is the case. The documents shall be attached in their own appended records.

I grant the Public Prosecution's request in page 1274, item 3.

Let the orders be followed.

São Paulo, August 10, 2009.

Glaucio Roberto Brittes De Araújo

STATE JUDGE

The ninth Criminal Court of São Paulo accepted the indictment, acknowledging that there had been diversion of social purpose when resources from donations were employed on corporations that only sought to profit for church leaders. According to the indictment, part of the tax immune money collected by the church was transferred to fake shelf companies. Then, the funds were transferred to foreign companies in tax havens. In order to return the money to Brazil, these foreign companies used financial operations that involved money loans to natural persons linked to Edir Macedo, who allegedly used these funds to acquire companies, real estate property, and other goods.[10]

On October 19, 2010 (published on October 26, 2010), the state appellate court ordered the case to be transferred to Federal Justice. The state appellate court determined that it did not have jurisdiction over the case because the international component of the money laundering scheme properly placed the matter in federal court.[11]

---

[10] Denúncia de promotores aponta "prática de fraude" contra a Universal e fiéis. Globo.com, Aug. 11, 2009, http://g1.globo.com/Noticias/Brasil/0,,MUL1263488-5598,00.html, accessed Aug. 23, 2013.

[11] The opinion states, in part, as follows: "2. From the analysis of the facts imputed to the defendants, a preliminary question arises from the case that must be faced before any procedural or substantial matter. It is indicated in the pleading that the money collected from Universal Church of the Kingdom of God's followers was transferred to publicly traded corporations CREMO and UNIMETRO, which, on their own turn, sent it to other two companies headquartered in tax havens, called INVESTHOLDING LIMITED and CABLEINVEST LIMITED, located, respectively, in Cayman Islands (British territory in the Caribbean, south of Cuba) and Channel Islands (UK islands located near the French coast). According to the accusatory pleading, that capital sent to foreign countries would return to Brazil by means of simulated and intermediaries owned by the criminal group. Then, repatriated money was, allegedly, used to acquire communication companies, such as TV Record. CREMO and UNIMETRO, controlled by some of the defendants and formally directed by others, were, allegedly, according to the indictment, used to disguise and occult the nature, origin, location, disposition, movement, and property of those expressive funds that came from larceny by fraud perpetrated against church followers and the religious entity itself. CABLEINVEST and INVESTHOLDING, according to the prosecution, constitute **offshore companies,** i.e., companies located on privileged investment zones abroad. They are located in territories known as tax havens, where tax exemptions, reduced income taxes, as well as business secrecy attract companies and entrepreneurs searching for greater profitability and privacy. **Offshores** are subject to a differentiated legal regime, thus, extraterritorial, when the residence of owners and shareholders are taken into consideration. They exist, legally, because some countries adopt radical tax exemption policies aimed at attracting investments and foreign capital. Thus, the behaviors attributed to defendants involve, hypothetically, foreign territories, marking the alleged crimes of money laundering with a transnational character. Transnationality is a characteristic of a criminal behavior whose execution and fulfillment occurs on foreign territory, outside national borders. This theme is a subject of the United Nations Convention against Transnational Organized Crime, concluded on

December 15, 2000, in Palermo, Italy, ratified by Legislative Decree No. 231/03 and promulgated by Presidential Decree No. 5.015/04. It is called Palermo's Convention. In view of the insertion process of the Convention's text in national Law, it integrates our national legal order with a federal act status. This is the major position of national legal doctrine, which is aligned to the understanding of the Supreme Federal Court itself. A brief incursion into this international norm is indispensable for full knowledge of the matter. Article 1 of the Palermo Convention states that *The purpose of this Convention is to promote cooperation to prevent and combat transnational organized crime more effectively*. Its Article 3, which regulates its scope, is very explanatory regarding the meaning of transnationality. According to item 2 of Article 3, *an offence is transnational in nature if: a) It is committed in more than one State; b) It is committed in one State but a substantial part of its preparation, planning, direction or control takes place in another State; c) It is committed in one State but involves an organized criminal group that engages in criminal activities in more than one State; or d) It is committed in one State but has substantial effects in another State*. In the present case, the money that was allegedly acquired by illegal means was supposedly sent to two tax havens, integrated into the property of two offshore companies and returned as simulated loans, which would characterize the internationalization of the offence hypothetically committed. With this evident transnationality, a matter arises regarding what court has jurisdiction to process criminal cases of money laundering and its related crimes. About jurisdiction, Act No. 9.613/98, in its Article 2, item III, states that *Federal Justice's jurisdiction includes: a) those crimes practiced against the financial system and financial-economic order, or to the detriment of goods, services and interests of the Union, or its public companies and independent agencies; b) those crimes whose preceding crimes are within Federal Justice's jurisdiction*. Out of these expressly stated hypotheses, the jurisdiction would belong to State Justice. There are two situations (line) that can find their basis in the general rule of Article 109, items IV and VI, of the Constitution, and a third (line) which arises from the connection rule recognized by Superior Court of Justice's Precedent No. 122, which states: *Federal Justice has jurisdiction for processing and judging, in a unified manner, related crimes that normally belong to State jurisdiction, since Article 78, II, a, of the Brazilian Criminal Procedures Code, is inapplicable*. For part of national legal doctrine, Federal Justice always has jurisdiction to process and adjudicate money laundering offences, given the complexity of the legal subject involved, which certainly includes the national financial system. For Souza Nucci, as an example, *when money is laundered, taxes are left uncollected and the national economy might be affected. In sum, in face of this, there is an interest of the Union and there must be an ascertainment within the federal sphere* (*in* Leis Penais e Processuais Penais Comentadas 4ª ed., 2009, Ed. RT, PP. 834/835). In spite of this venerable doctrinal understanding, I believe that jurisdiction must be verified in each case. It will be State Justice's if none of the hypotheses referred to in item III (Article 2 of Act No. 9.613/98) – which, we must emphasize, is not a thorough list – is applicable. Apart from these cases, another determining factor for excluding State Justice's jurisdiction is precisely transnationality, which makes it, in my view, imperative for Federal Justice's jurisdiction. I start from the premise that Federal Justice's jurisdiction is not limited by the three hypotheses of Article 2, item III, of Act No. 9.613/98. In that non-thorough list, there must be the inclusion of transnational money laundering, which is not present in Act No. 9.613/98, but is shaped and regulated by Palermo's Convention, obviously, not as a different crime definition, but as a subject of combat measures that must be created and implemented by signatory countries. The aforementioned Convention did not create an autonomous international money laundering definition – it could not do so. In light of the principle of the necessity of a legal definition for crimes, it is indispensable that legislation – in the strict sense – must be enacted, according to ordinary legislative procedure and as a manifestation of the will of the Parliament, for a criminal offence to be created. The Convention established, in fact, general prevention and combat measures against money laundering and corruption in general. It uses instruments such as confiscation and seizure of goods, special investigation techniques, international cooperation programs, protection of witnesses and victims, and extradition provisions. It also specifies requirements for laundering to acquire transnationality characteristics and, from that, the jurisdiction for processing and adjudicating in Brazil must observe currently

On September 12, 2012, federal judge Marcelo Costenaro Cavali of the second Federal Trial Court, partly upheld the charges against the church leaders. His decision as quoted in another judicial opinion, states, in part, as follows[12]:

enacted norms, interpreting them systematically. Therefore, money laundering partially or totally carried out abroad constitutes, per se, a crime that induces Federal Justice's jurisdiction. In other words, transnationality constitutes another criterion, other than those given by Article 2, III, of Act No. 9.613/98, for the laundering offence to be subject of adjudication and processing by Federal Justice. Even if predicate offences are within State Justice's jurisdiction, transnationality is a determining element for establishing federal jurisdiction. That is what happens in the current case, in which the pleading mentions, as predicate offences, larceny by fraud practiced within religious organizations (Article 1, item VII, of Act No. 9.613/98). Such conclusion arises from Article 109 of the Federal Constitution, which, in its item V, determines that federal judges have jurisdiction for processing and judging crimes predicted in international treaties or conventions, if, once initiated the execution in the Country, the result has or should have happened abroad, or vice-versa. Now, transnational money laundering, as noted, is defined in Palermo's Convention, ratified by Legislative Decree 231/03 and promulgated by Presidential Decree 5.015/04, inserting itself, in that manner, into our national legal order. Without doubt, it is an offence defined – yet not legally defined, or typified – in an international convention, whose execution, initiated in Brazil, touched the territory of another country. Thus, yet another hypothesis defines federal jurisdiction: once the *iter criminis* of the money laundering offence was initiated, if any of the offence's phases (assets collection, occultation or disguise and integration) occurs in Brazilian territory and abroad, then, based on Article 109, V, of the Constitution, the jurisdiction of Federal Justice is set. Therefore, if the pleading attributes to the defendants the participation in capital laundering in which offshore companies, located in the Cayman Islands and Channel Island – safe havens to which the money that came from larcenies by fraud practiced against church followers was sent and then returned to Brazil as simulated loans, so that they could be used to buy companies – were used, then transnationality is constituted. We are, thus, facing a constitutional commandment, an absolute jurisdiction rule, whose strictness does not admit any alteration or prorogation, under penalty of violating the principle of the natural judge (Constitution, Article 5, LIII). In sum, notwithstanding the solution aimed by HC No. 990.09.289589-0 – the closure of the criminal procedure of defendant Veríssimo de Jesus – by better analyzing the matter, I review, in this opportunity, the prior understanding set and, by the aforementioned arguments, I recognize that State Justice has no jurisdiction for processing and adjudicating this criminal procedure, nor does this Court have jurisdiction to judge the current *habeas corpus* petition. The scope of the current judgment is limited to the recognition of the lack of jurisdiction of this Court of Justice. 3. For these reasons, by my vote, *ex officio*, I recognize the State Justice's jurisdiction does not cover processing and judging the proposed criminal procedure against the defendants, as well as judgment on the merits of the current *habeas corpus* petition, by which reason I annul the procedure since the pleading was received – including the pleading itself– and I order the case file and the criminal procedure (Proc. No. 1121/09 – control number) to be sent to Federal Justice, which has jurisdiction over the case." (*Habeas Corpus* n.° 990.10.247420-8, 16th Criminal Panel, Judge Almeida Toledo, in São Paulo State Appellate Court site, http://esaj.tjsp.jus.br/cjsg/getArquivo.do?cdAcordao=4776713&cdForo=0, accessed Oct. 12, 2014). *See also* Justiça comum não pode julgar caso da Universal, in Consultor Jurídico, http://www.conjur.com.br/2010-out-20/justica-comum-nao-competencia-julgar-universal-tj-sp, Oct. 20, 2010, accessed Oct. 12, 2014; FERREIRA, F. Justiça de SP anula processo contra bispos da Universal. Folha.com: São Paulo, Oct. 2010, http://www1.folha.uol.com.br/poder/817422-justica-de-sp-anula-processo-contra-bispos-da-universal.shtml, accessed Aug. 23, 2013. The decision will be analyzed by the Brazilian Supreme Court (Recurso Extraordinário com Agravo, ARE n.° 737566, Justice Teori Zavascki, http://www.stf.jus.br/portal/processo/verProcessoAndamento.asp?incidente=4375014, accessed Oct. 13, 2014.

[12] Information obtained from *Habeas Corpus* n.° 0038794-85.2011.4.03.0000/SP, 5th Panel, Federal Appellate Judge Luiz Stefanini, which upheld the trial court decision (in Tribunal Regional Federal da 3ª Região site, published Sept. 11, 2012, http://web.trf3.jus.br/acordaos/Acordao/BuscarDocumentoGedpro/2279490, accessed Oct. 14, 2014).

"[...] Finally, the prosecution describes those mechanisms by which the money collected from IURD's followers was supposedly transferred in a clandestine and repeated way, according to statements given by Waldir Abraão.

One of these mechanisms for transferring unreported currency from Brazil allegedly included the participation of partners and operators, initially from IC Câmbio e Turismo Ltda., and, between 1993 and 2005, from Diskline Câmbio e Turismo Ltda. – based in São Paulo, with a branch office in Rio de Janeiro.

Luiz Augusto Cunha Ribeiro and Cristina Marini Rodrigues da Cunha Brito, defendants in a criminal procedure ascertaining illegal transfers to foreign countries (pages 17/19 of the Police Investigation No. 2550–78.2010.403.6181, and pages 13/16 of the Police Investigation No. 2550–78.2010.403.6181, respectively), were partners at Diskline and described in detail the operations with IURD, which were summarized by Public Prosecution:

'Between 1991 – IC Câmbio e Turismo Ltda.'s creation year – and 1993, when they became partners at Diskline Câmbio e Turismo Ltda., along with Sílvio Roberto Anspach, aka 'Fifo', a notorious money changer from this capital, the operations for sending values to foreign countries happened exclusively in Rio de Janeiro. Since then, IURD started to operate with Diskline in Rio de Janeiro and São Paulo.

The aforementioned money changers' statements demonstrate the enormous amount of bills brought to currency exchange houses using vehicles and armed security guards from IURD. Marcelo says that the bills came in bags and many of them were 'crumpled, torn, glued with Durex, sweaty and scribbled', which made it difficult for the money to be counted by the machines at the currency exchange house. Higher value bills – fifty and one hundred reals – came from the so-called 'businessmen masses', with greater contributing capability. The values received were counted and checked, always in presence of a IURD pastor. Cristina stated that, because of the security needed to handle such a great amount of money in cash, she and IURD rented adjacent vaults in financial institutions and transferred the cash between vaults in such institutions. On other occasions, the cash transfer was made by putting the money in the trunks of some vehicles in the IURD temples' parking lots. Luiz Augusto, who left Diskline around 1997, stated that, because of these operations for transferring money, he had close contact with IURD members, mainly Mauro Macedo – Edir Macedo's cousin – and Paulo Roberto Gomes da Conceição. Luiz Augusto also got together with Edir Macedo in New York. By that time, Edir asked him to study other ways to carry out the structured operation to send values to foreign countries, so that these operations 'sounded legitimate'. On that occasion, Edir also mentioned to Luiz the possibility of IURD creating a bank in foreign countries[...]"

"[...] from the aforementioned reports, the accusation concludes that, directed by EDIR MACEDO, mastermind of IURD's criminal policy, and JOÃO BATISTA, national president of the Church, ALBA MARIA and PAULO ROBERTO determined and oriented the illegal money transfers to the following foreign bank accounts, which received, according to documents adduced as evidence, millions of reals from IURD's believers between 1999 and 2005:

(i) Chase Manhattan Bank – NY: a) account No. 3100 6678 0465, owned by Genesis Holding Group; b) account No. 140 094 221, of Lehman Brother Inc. subaccount No. 74326634-1-2-115; c) other three accounts owned by the Universal Church of the Kingdom of God (IURD);

(ii) Republic Nacional Bank – NY: account No. 310 407 915 owned by I.F.P.C. Inc.;

(iii) HSBC – NY: account No. 610 114 948, owned by T.I.F.P.C. Inc;

(iv) Northern Trust International Banking Corp – NY: account No. 238 522 of Merryl Lynch, as a beneficiary: a) subaccount 163-07Q32, of Harman Holdings; b) subaccount 163–07158, by Steele Resources or Steele Internacional Ltda.;

(v) JP Morgan – NY: account owned by Universal Church of the Kingdom of God (IURD).

Based on these facts, the accusation imputes to EDIR MACEDO, as an organizer of criminal activities, according to article 62 of the Brazilian Penal Code, to JOÃO BATISTA, president of the IURD in Brazil and partner of Cremo, to ALBA MARIA, representative of offshore companies in Brazil, operator of Cremo, signed by her, along with PAULO ROBERTO, director of Banco de Crédito Metropolitano, succeeded by Credinvest Facility, the following criminal offenses […]

[…] As to the crime of transferring unreported currency to foreign countries (Act No. 7.492/1986, article 22, single paragraph), I understand the indictment must be received.

The accusatory pleading's allegations that the values were sent clandestinely to foreign companies had already been proven, in an incipient way, by the notarized statement of Waldir Abrão. However, more recently, with the statements given by money changers responsible for the transactions, the *modus operandi* was really made clear.

Such money changers supposedly were operators of IC Câmbio e Turismo Ltda. companies and, between 1993 and 2005, of Diskline Câmbio e Turismo Ltda. Luiz Augusto Cunha Ribeiro, Cristina Marini Rodrigues Cunha Brito and Marcelo Bismarcker, defendants in a proceeding ascertaining the occurrence of the remittance of unreported money to foreign countries, were partners at Diskline Câmbio e Turismo Ltda. and described in detail the operations supposedly made in favor of IURD (pages 13/16, 17/19 and 20/22).

An important amount of money that would be clandestinely – merely by accounting operation – sent, as it happens in underground banking systems, came, according to Marcelo Bismarcker, in bags, with many crumpled, glued, torn and scribbled bills. The money was supposedly delivered by IURD security guards, armed with shotguns, pistols and revolvers (page 20).

Luiz Augusto Cunha Ribeiro affirmed that the close contact between members of IURD was mainly with defendant PAULO ROBERTO, as well as Mauro Macedo. EDIR MACEDO also allegedly got together with him in New York, where he supposedly asked him to search for operations for money remittance that 'sounded legitimate' (pages 17/19).

Cristina Marini Rodrigues Cunha Brito affirmed that ALBA MARIA was responsible for giving orientations about the clandestine remittance of funds, also stating that IURD was Diskline's main client (page 15).

Many documents were gathered that are able provide sustainable evidence to such statements, demonstrating, thus, the clandestine remittances (pages 23/77 and 91).

As national president of IURD, JOÃO BATISTA, along with EDIR MACEDO, was supposedly the one responsible for controlling the events, orienting the way the funds should be sent abroad by illicit means. PAULO ROBERTO and ALBA MARIA, on their own turn, were, allegedly, the operational branch for these transactions, the members of IURD responsible for ordering money changers to send money abroad by clandestine ways.

The requisition for bank secrecy for the accounts that supposedly received money in this way was granted. The bank account statements and/or documents linked to accounts No. 365-1-024410, No. 365-1-018248, No. 365-1-007852 – kept at MORGAN CHASE – No. 365-5-00081565, No. 365-5-0010265 – kept at THE CHASE MANHATTAN BANK -, No. 610114956 and No. 610114948 – kept at HSBC BANK USA – all obtained by the international cooperation request completed by the USA, are contained in the CD appended to page 98.

Appended to the case file, there is also the notarized statement of Waldir Abrão, describing this supposedly illegal mechanism (pages 153/175).

The underground banking operations correspond, in my view, to article 22, *caput*. The operation occurs with a structure for withdrawing currency at distance: an amount of a determined currency is deposited in the account of the seller in Brazil, which delivers a corresponding amount of money abroad [...]"

"[...] Only during the examining phase of the procedure will it be possible to compare all documents gathered with the pleading and the statements given by money changers, as well as other evidence, to ascertain if there was, in fact, remittance of unreported money in a clandestine way to foreign countries from Brazilian territory.

Thus, the pleading must be received, in order for the facts to be verified with due deepness, in light of the adversarial system and full defense rights.

In regard of the attribution of conspiracy (Brazilian Penal Code, article 288), the definition of the crime demands the association of more than three persons in a gang, aiming to commit crimes.

At first, the facts narrated fulfill the minimum requirements for the pleading to be received. In fact, it can be extracted from the pleading that the defendants EDIR MACEDO, ALBA MARIA, JOÃO BATISTA and PAULO ROBERTO allegedly associated, in a stable, longstanding, premeditated way and with unity of desires for committing the crimes of larceny, misrepresentation and unreported remittance of funds to other countries.

Departing from the offenses of larceny and misrepresentation, as previously demonstrated, the money-laundering and unreported remittance of funds to other countries still remain.

One concludes, from the imputation, that the defendants acted in a concerted manner to enable the delivery of national currency in Brazil in exchange for the equivalent in foreign currency abroad by means of a clandestine mechanism– i.e., disregarding the Central Bank of Brazil control – known as underground banking. Also in a concerted way, these assets were sent abroad without any communication regarding their existence to authorities in Brazil.

The pleading shows – even though in a generic manner, which is admitted in crimes practiced within legal persons – the participation of each and every one of the accused in contacting money changers, attributing to EDIR MACEDO the role of leader of this kind of action.

Supposedly, the defendants also acted in an associated manner in constituting and administrating shelf companies – Cremo Empreendimentos S.A. and Unimetro Empreendimentos S.A. – with the aim of concealing its true owner, which, in theory, can characterize the misrepresentation offense.

JOÃO BATISTA and PAULO ROBERTO allegedly were directors of Cremo Empreendimentos S. A. and ALDA MARIA director of Unimetro Empreendimentos S. A. EDIR MACEDO, on his own turn, as leader of the group composed by entities connected to the IURD, was supposedly the greatest beneficiary and mastermind of these deceits.

All those accused were key figures in structuring the actions of IURD, which consisted in using shelf companies, simulated legal businesses and clandestine remittances of assets to other countries, always intending to hide, from its followers and competent authorities, the true owners of the high financial movement verified.

At the moment the pleading was received, the coherent narrative of the supposedly illegal facts is enough, at least, to give the defendants the opportunity to express themselves about the imputations, without denying reanalysis after written responses to the accusations are presented.

Lastly, regarding the crime of money laundering, the pleading attributes its commission to the accused, identifying larceny and criminal organization as precedent crimes (page 135).

According to the typical structure of money laundering offenses adopted by Brazilian criminal legislation, these infractions can only be characterized if a predicate crime – included in the list located in Article 1 of Act No. 9.613/1998 – can be identified.

That is to say that capital laundering is a crime dependent on a preceding crime. If the illegal character of the supposed larceny offenses is removed, as demonstrated earlier, as a logical result, the imputation of money laundering cannot be sustained.

However, the Federal Public Prosecutor also attributed to the defendants the crimes of sending unreported currency to foreign countries, a crime against the national financial system, which is also a predicate crime for money laundering, as stated by Article 1, item VI, of Act No. 9.613/1998.

In order to hide those assets that resulted from sending unreported funds to other countries, the defendants allegedly included straw-men as partners in their companies, even though these were not real owners.

Some legal businesses were also simulated – real estate sales in Niterói/RJ, aircraft sales of a Cessna, money lending – between Cremo Empreendimento S. A. and Record S. A. or IURD, which were able to demonstrate that these intermediaries were not the real owners of those companies.

At first, at least in this perfunctory analysis typical for receiving the pleading, if these facts are confirmed, then it is possible that some funds resulted from unreported currency remittance to other countries that were covertly retransferred to Brazil, as described by the prosecution.

There are documents appended to the case file related to such businesses and alleged shelf companies (pages 140/152 and pages 115/285 from records No. 0001910-41.2011.403.6181), by which the Federal Public Prosecutor intends to demonstrate that these offenses really happened.

The link between the facts, in my view, is complexly ascertained, in such a way that it is not admissible to overcome the *in dubio pro societatis* principle that guides the judgment about receiving or not receiving the pleading [...]"

"[...]In view of these arguments, I RECEIVE PARTIALLY THE PLEADING presented by Federal Public Prosecutor against EDIR MACEDO BEZERRA (hereinafter called 'EDIR MACEDO'), . . . ALBA MARIA SILVA DA COSTA (hereinafter called 'ALBA MARIA'), . . . JOÃO BATISTA RAMOS DA SILVA, and PAULO ROBERTO GOMES DA CONCEIÇÃO (hereinafter called 'PAULO ROBERTO') . . . regarding the imputation of the crimes of conspiracy (Brazilian Penal Code, article 288, *caput*), unreported currency sending to other countries (Act No. 7.492/1986, Article 22, single paragraph, first and second figures) and money laundering (Act No. 9.613/1998, Article 1, VI). I REJECT THE COMPLAINT, however, with regard to the allocation of commission of offenses of embezzlement (Penal Code, Article 171, *caput*), based on Article 395, Item I, Criminal Procedure Code, given its manifest ineptitude, and perjury (Penal Code, Article 299, *caput*), based on Article 395, item II, Criminal Procedure Code, given the occurrence of the statute of limitations claim. They include the accused to submit reply to the complaint within ten (10) days in which they could claim all that interests their defense and may give rise to their acquittal, provide documents and evidence, and specify the evidence sought, call witnesses, calling them and demonstrating the relevance of their hearing as well as their relation to the facts described in the complaint. I emphasize at the outset that, in the case of merely providing confidence witnesses, the witnesses must submit written declarations, which will be given the same value. At that time, if the defendant becomes aware that the statutory period has expired without manifestation, or if he is not in a financial position to hire a lawyer, something which should be reported to the bailiff upon their communication, the Court will appoint an advocate to act in his defense, who should be aware, though, that he should follow this criminal action in all its terms and acts until the final judgment, in accordance with Article 367 of the Criminal Procedure Code: the process will continue without the presence of the defendant, who personally summoned or cited for any act, fails to appear without good reason, or in the case of change of residence, not to communicate the new address to the court. The defendant must also be aware that further subpoenas related to the case will be made in the presence of his lawyers and published in the official press. Due to adversarial principle which must govern the Brazilian criminal proceedings for constitutional order, particularly in light of the recent reform of the Criminal Procedure Code, the initiative and subsequent evidential burden should be primarily in the hands of the parties and only complementarily in the hands of that judicial body. Federal prosecutors are responsible to bring to the court criminal record/or other records about the defendants (article 8, II, III, V, VII and VIII of Complementary Law No. 75/93), because such papers relate to their institutional prerogatives (Article 129, VIII, of the Constitution and Article 236, III, Supplementary Law No. 75/93). Such information must be provided and attached to the file in accordance with Article 231 of Criminal Procedure Code. In this sense, moreover, it has been oriented by jurisprudence (*Habeas Corpus* 200503000451893, Second Panel of the Federal Appellate Judge of the Third Region, Judge Rapporteur Cotrim Guimarães, published on Sept. 22, 2006; *COR* 2009.04.00.041563-0, Eighth Panel of the Federal Appellate Court of the Fourth Region, Judge Rapporteur Paulo Afonso Vaz Brum, published on Dec. 9, 2009; ...). The office must expedite requests for international cooperation for citation and summons of the defendant EDIR MACEDO in the United States. The course of the limitations period is suspended until the fulfillment citing of defendant EDIR MACEDO, under Article 368 of the Criminal Procedure Code. In addition, in view of the existence of documents in the record that are protected by confidentiality, and in order to safeguard the interests of any persons involved, I determine the confidentiality of the documents under Article 792, 1st paragraph, Criminal Procedure Code, and Article 155 of the Civil Procedure Code, by analogy with Article 3 of the Criminal Procedure Code, Article 7, 1, item 2, of the Statute of the Brazilian Bar Association (Law no. 8,906, April 7, 1994). Only authorities who officiate the case and the defendants should have access pursuant to Binding Precedent n. 14, Feb. 2, 2009, from the Supreme Court, and Resolution n.° 58, May 25, 2009, of the Council of the Federal Judiciary (restricted advertising). However, except for these documents that are limited to tax and banking data, I highlight that the decisions and proceeding are public, according to Article 93, Section IX, of the Federal Constitution.

São Paulo, September 11, 2011.

Marcelo Costenaro Cavali

FEDERAL JUDGE

As of August 2014, this case is still being processed by the aforementioned Federal Trial Court.

4.1.6 *The Worldwide Church of God's Power (***Igreja Mundial do Poder de Deus***)*

The Worldwide Church of God's Power (WCGP) is the fastest growing church in Brazil. In 2009, WCGP had 500 temples. In 2013, there were more than 5,000.

WCGP's legal and financial troubles began in 2012 when it was the target of an operation called Safe Harbor (*Porto Seguro*). During the operation, the federal police and the public prosecutor's office seized nine jets allegedly purchased by the WCGP abroad without paying taxes in Brazil. On October 27, 2013, the IRS auctioned one of these jets, a Falcon 900. The church's leader, Valdemiro Santiago, denied that he owned the aircraft, claiming that the jet was just borrowed. The church was subjected to blocked bank accounts.

In 2014, the IstoÉ magazine published a comprehensive analysis of the financial crisis occurring behind the scenes of WCGP. According to the analysis, the financial crisis was caused by "gangs of thief pastors, millionaire debts with TVs, amateur management from the board and misguided investments in building grandiose temples."[13] The church owed R$8 million (around US$3.4 million) to Bandeirantes Group TV (Band) in September 2014, a debt predicted to reach R$13 million (US$5.4 million) by the next month. In its recent fundraising campaign, WCGP asked its followers to donate R$21 million (around US$8.75), intending to use this amount to pay commitments with TV stations. All the while, WCGP's leader, Valdemiro Santiago, was being investigated by prosecutors and the Civil Police of São Paulo. The magazine says that since January 2013, the Special Group on Economic Crimes (Gedec) and the Division of Investigations of Tax Crimes of the Civil Police searched for evidence of suspected money laundering and concealment of assets, rights, and values.

The current crisis was allegedly created by the diversion of about 30 % of the funds raised. "Every month, R$30 million (US$12.5 million) goes down the drain," said a leader of WCPG in Rio de Janeiro (the magazine did not disclose his name). "About two and a half years ago, for example, Valdemiro discovered one of these gangs in ABC region led by the bishop and his assistants and expelled them," he explained. He went further, reporting that the bank account printed on booklets distributed in many of the temples was not from the church, but from this group of malicious pastors.

Dennis Muñoz, lawyer and deputy president of WCGP, denies that the church is experiencing a crisis. "These problems decreased by 70 % in recent times," he explained. Regarding the allegations of "gangs of pastors," he said that church has always quickly taken the necessary steps.

The president of the WCGP, Congressman José Olímpio, talked about the issue of rent arrears: "We are paying a lot of installments, we have many works in progress. Failing to pay a month becomes a problem for the following monthly payment."

---

[13] ARAGON, Jarbas. Revista denuncia crise na Igreja Mundial do Poder de Deus, GolpelPrime site, Oct. 27, 2013, http://noticias.gospelprime.com.br/crise-igreja-mundial-do-poder-de-deus/, accessed June 29, 2014.

In January 2014, Band sued the church requesting the payment of an alleged debt of R$10,156,259.57 (US$4.1 million) for non-payment of fees for the transfer of space in the channel lineup. In the lawsuit, Band obtained a favorable decision, foisting one of the biggest setbacks in the history of the evangelical empire. Judge Carlos Eduardo Borges Fantacini, state judge in São Paulo of the 26 Trial Court, ordered the seizure of church vehicles and the restriction of licensing and transfer thereof.

The church supposedly agreed with Band in late 2012 to purchase Channel 21, which occupied 22 programming. But the contract was discontinued for alleged nonpayment of installments and failure to comply with certain clauses. The WCGP sued Band Group seeking an indemnity of R$200 million (US$83,333 million), claiming unilateral breach of contract on the grounds that a clause ensured the opportunity to honor the plots 45 days after the due date. The Band Group, of which Band and Channel 21 are subsidiaries, counter-claimed against the Universal Church of the Kingdom of God, asking for R$100 million (US$41,666 million) related to delayed installments, reimbursement of expenses, fines, and interest.

*4.1.7 The Rebirth in Christ Church (***Igreja Renascer em Cristo***)*

Similar charges have fallen over the Rebirth in Christ Church, founded by Estevam Hernades Filho and his wife Sônia Haddad Morais Hernandes, the so-called church apostles. In 2006, they were accused of larceny by fraud, money laundering, and misrepresentation, and authorities ordered the arrest of both. Through a *habeas corpus* petition, the Superior Court of Justice revoked the arrest order in December of that same year.[14] In January of 2007, Estevam and Sônia were arrested by the FBI in Miami, accused of entering the United States with an amount of roughly US$56,500, much higher than what they declared to customs authorities.[15] On December 31, 2009, they pled guilty to smuggling, conspiracy, and perjury, and a U.S. court sentenced them to 10 months in jail.[16]

On July 12, 2012, Brazilian Supreme Court granted *habeas corpus* in favor of both and other members in order to halt a criminal procedure in which both were

[14] STJ cassa mandado de prisão contra bispos da Igreja Renascer. *G1.globo.com*, São Paulo, Dec. 2006, http://g1.globo.com/Noticias/SaoPaulo/0,,AA1393688-5605,00.html, accessed Aug. 26, 2014.

[15] Polícia dos EUA prende bispos da Renascer em Miami. *G1.globo.com*, São Paulo, Jan. 2007, http://g1.globo.com/Noticias/Brasil/0,,AA1413589-5598,00.html, accessed Aug. 26, 2014.

[16] TOZZI, A. Casal Renascer é condenado nos EUA. *Estadão.com.br*, Dec. 2009, http://www.estadao.com.br/noticias/impresso,casal-renascer-e-condenado-nos-eua,36748,0.htm, accessed Aug. 26, 2014.

defendants charged with money laundering.[17] The Court held that "criminal organization" (*organização criminosa*) could not be a predicate crime to constitute the crime of money laundering under Act No. 9,613/98.

Justice Marco Aurélio, responsible for the *habeas corpus* No. 96.007/SP, claimed in his vote and speeches during the debates that there was need to halt the criminal procedure because the crime of "criminal organization," established by the United Nations Convention against Transnational Organized Crime, had not been internalized by Brazilian Law. That is because the treaty does not assign any penalty for the crime and it was merely received by Brazilian government through a presidential decree. Thus, it violates Article 5, Part XXXIX, of the Constitution, because it was not promulgated as law and it has no provision for penalties. Therefore, if the crime of "criminal organization" does not exist in Brazilian law, it cannot constitute a predicate for money launder. The alleged crime of larceny by fraud could not be used as the necessary predicate crime either, as it did not appear in the list of the money laundering law.

During debates regarding questions raised by Justice Dias Toffoli, Justice Ayres Britto questioned Marco Aurélio's premises, claiming the Plenary of the Supreme Federal Court had already determined the term "criminal organization" means the same as conspiracy, which would enable it to serve as a predicate crime for money laundering. To these claims, Marco Aurélio responded that if "criminal organization" corresponded to "conspiracy," then it would open a precedent for any offense to be included as a predicate crime for money laundering as long as there is collusion among multiple agents.[18]

In addition to the Hernandes couple, the federal prosecution also charged a bishop of the church, José Antônio Bruno, who had used resources from an agreement

---

[17] COSTA, F. Supremo arquiva ação penal contra líderes da Igreja Renascer. *G1.globo.com*, Brasília, June 2012, http://g1.globo.com/sao-paulo/noticia/2012/06/supremo-arquiva-acao-penal-contra-lideres-da-igreja-renascer.html, accessed Aug. 26, 2014.

[18] Among those few cases of open access to the public, there is the aforementioned *Habeas Corpus* No. 96.007/SP, in which charges of money laundering, from Act No. 9.613/98, were dropped. In that case, the criminal proceeding was halted because of deficiencies in the indictment: it did not present any evidence of a predicate crime from the thorough list in Article 1 of the Act (an essential condition to the configuration of money laundering). Considering charges made by the aforementioned Operation Carwash, one could consider that the facts presented in the operation were clearly cases of money laundering. It is important to remember that, currently, the description given by Article 1 was reformulated, by Act No. 12,683/2012, in a way that, now, the mere criminal origin of the money is enough to constitute the crime of money laundering, without regard to the list. Considering the charges from the indictment on Operation Carwash, one could consider that the facts presented in the operation are clear cases of money laundering, since the entity in question was used to hide the illegal origin of certain values. Possibly, if the judgment of HC No. 96.007/SP were done under the shield of the new wording given to the law, the STF would have allowed the procedure to continue based on the possibility that the money had come from larceny by fraud, which was claimed by the prosecution. Habeas Corpus No. 96.007-SP, STF, 1ª Turma, Rel. Marco Aurélio, June 12, 2012, http://www.stf.jus.br/portal/principal/principal.asp, accessed Aug. 26, 2014.

between the federal government and Renascer Foundation (*Fundação Renascer*) for purposes not provided by the agreement.[19]

Another case, involving the leaders of the aforementioned church, a fraud report to the Brazilian authorities, and capital flight, although still under appeal, generated important legal arguments. The facts were based on a sequence of various events and crimes with consequences in both Brazil and the United States, where the defendants, owners of the church, were convicted and already served their sentences in the United States:

THE ABSENCE OF BIS IN IDEM AND NATIONAL SOVEREIGNTY

On those facts, the defendants could have been caught *in flagrante delicto* in Brazil, even before stepping onto American soil, where they allegedly made false statements to local authorities, among other crimes (pages 03/04 of Attachment, Volume I), for which they were convicted and sentenced in a United States court.

Brazilian prosecution still has an interest in prosecuting the case based on different facts performed at various points in time: by embarking in Brazil, in violation of Brazilian law, in particular by perpetrating, in theory, the crime of tax evasion (on Jan, 7, 2007), and entering the United States of America with false statements to the U.S. customs (on Jan. 08, 2007).

Now, a contrary view, as the defense contends, in practice, would surely mean to skip a step, to skip the laws to which Brazilians are required to comply, i.e., to disregard them. The punishment by U.S. authorities demonstrated application of the right infringed upon entering the United States, while, in Brazil, the violation occurs, in theory, by leaving the country.

There is no subjective right to criminal detraction (Article 42 of the Penal Code), i.e., the computation of time served abroad in compliance with any imposition of penalty in Brazil, given the factual and temporal diversity that occurred.

Thus, any interpretation to the contrary would result in a violation of Brazilian sovereignty which should be observed by all. The depositary of a share of power is not its owner, but a servant. Those who exercise it do not do it for their own or their group interests. Water and oil do not mix. The authorities are subject to the popular will, the people, the true lawmaker, and judge. The people make and unmake, create and destroy, that is the essence. Now whoever acts on its behalf must always be aware, considering the real and genuine popular will. He or she becomes responsible for what he or she builds or performs, subjecting himself or herself to the law, to its expression.

Would it be legitimate to determine if it is justifiable to give up sovereignty, i.e., disregard that particular violation of the will of our people (the Brazilian criminal law) as supplied by U.S. people's will (foreign law)?

Would it be appropriate, then, to subject any condemned only to foreign authorities for acts first committed here, that by they themselves, already imply a criminal offense to a Brazilian norm?

---

[19] MPF pede condenação de fundação e bispo da Renascer: Para o órgão, houve desvio e má aplicação de R$2 milhões de dois convênios com o Fundo Nacional para Desenvolvimento da Educação (FNDE), *Estadão.com.br*, São Paulo, Aug. 16, 2012, http://www.estadao.com.br/noticias/geral,mpf-pede-condenacao-de-fundacao-e-bispo-da-renascer,595757,0.htm, accessed Aug. 28, 2014.

The penalty to be applied in Brazil represents the popular will, the expression of our people claiming for the existence of solid and legitimate institutions, and it cannot be dismissed. It requires respect.

There is only one possible interpretation to be adopted, which will reflect in the spirit of other defendants and, especially of the people to which the authorities are subject: the preservation of law by which Brazilians manifest.

No "*bis in idem*" should, in casu, be recognized.

MERIT

The evidence contained in the case file was conclusive to point out that the conduct perpetrated by defendants ESTEVAM HERNANDES Moraes Filho and Sonia Haddad HERNANDES is perfectly outlined by the criminal offense in Article 22, sole paragraph, first figure, of Law No. 7,492, of June 16, 1986, which provides: "(...) whoever, in any capacity, promotes, without legal authorization, the exit of currency to other countries (...)."

The criminal definition outlined by said provision defines a material crime that portrays the behavior of promoting, without legal authorization, the exit of currency of the country, being certain that its consummation happens with the effective output of currency to other countries, which happens when the boundaries of national territory are trespassed.

In this vein, I transcribe the wise lessons of Rodolfo Tigre Maia, for whom the sole paragraph of Article 22 of the *lex specialis*: *"provides for two absolutely autonomous modalities of illegality. The first involves the illegal transfer of currency to other countries. The objective criminal definition, in this case, incriminates the action of promoting, that is to say, to fulfill, perform or execute, in any way (in any capacity) the withdrawal of capital (gold, checks drawn against overseas markets, credits, etc.), without authorization, to other countries (...) the crime is material, having as a consuming result the effective 'exit of capital or currency from the country', which occurs when the boundaries of national territory are trespassed, and its executive process, in general, admits fractionation which, therefore, makes it possible for the crime to be only attempted yet not consummated."* (emphasis added).

Unlike the *caput* of Article 22 of Law 7,492/1986, its sole paragraph must be classified as a blank criminal norm because, for illegality to happen, there is need of a law that will clarify whether or not there is legal authorization for money and capital to be sent abroad.

It should be noted that this authorization does not necessarily imply the necessity of a rule enacted by the Legislature, just the existence of an integrative administrative act, in a way that it will be important to verify the existence of an authorization for the operation of the remittance of currency or capital, so that the expression authorization should be interpreted as a release granted by the competent public authorities.

Considering this approach, national legislation requires that values over $10,000.00 (ten thousand dollars) are to be sent abroad exclusively by bank transfers.

Article 65 of Law No. 9,069, dated June 29, 1995, reads as follows:

Art 65. The flow into the country and out of the country, of national and foreign currencies shall be processed exclusively by bank transfer, leaving it to the banking establishment to accurately identify the client or beneficiary.

§ 1 An exception to the provisions in this Article is the possession, in cash, of values:

I – when in local currency, equal to R$ 10,000.00 (ten thousand reals);

II – when in foreign currency, equivalent to R$ 10,000.00 (ten thousand reals);

III – when its entrance to or exit from the country is disclosed, in the manner prescribed by regulation.

§ 2 The National Monetary Council, in accordance with directives of the President, shall regulate the provisions of this Article, regulating even the limits and conditions for entry into the country and exit from the country of national currency.

§ 3 Failure to comply with this Article, notwithstanding criminal penalties provided for in specific legislation, and after due process, will result in loss of the excess of the limits referred to in § 1 of this Article, in favor of the National Treasury.

In its own turn, Article 89 of Provisional Measure 2,158/2001 states that:

Art 89. It is a Federal Revenue Department competence to apply the penalty in § 3 of art. 65 of Law No. 9,069, dated June 29, 1995.

§ 1 The administrative process for calculating and applying the fee will be instituted with the drafting of an assessment notice, accompanied by a term of apprehension, and, if applicable, the term of custody.

§ 2 Once subpoenaed, personally or by edict, if an objection is not filed within twenty days there will be judgment by default.

§ 3 If an objection is presented, preparatory authorities will have fifteen days to refer the case to trial.

§ 4 The period mentioned in § 3 may be extended when there is a need for further investigation or expert reports.

In the instant case, the accused embarked on TAM Flight JJ 8090 in São Paulo International Airport in Guarulhos, on January 7, 2007, as shown from the inset documentation on pages 11/19 (individualized list of boarding passengers in that flight and reservations on behalf of the defendants), carrying packed money in unusual ways, including inside a Bible cover, and did not submit the Statement of Possession of Values to the Internal Revenue Service of Brazil which can be done via internet.

The official letter ALF/GRU/Case/No. 29/2007 (fl. 49) forwarded by the Federal Revenue Department of Brazil, done by the Inspector of Customs of São Paulo/Guarulhos International Airport, noting the absence of Statement of Possession of Values and, when boarding the dock, still in native soil, is fully able to reveal the intention of the accused in evading their legal obligations herein:

*In due diligence performed on the IRS system, **no Statement of Possession of Values was found in the name of the aforementioned persons**, as well as other tax information related to this shipment of São Paulo/Guarulhos International Airport on January 07, 2007, flight JJ8090, TAM, Miami/USA (...) (emphasis added).*

The amounts held by the defendants that were seized at Miami Airport – United States of America, equivalent to US$ 56,467 (fifty-six thousand four hundred sixty-seven U.S. dollars), effectively support the criminal materiality of the offense, for they denote that the defendants were carrying foreign currency since their boarding in the São Paulo International Airport (Guarulhos), which can be proven by evidence and indicia contained on this procedure, which reveals the certainty necessary to support a condemnation decree.

In this sense, given their vehemence and clarity, the elements of conviction produced legal certainty in this respect, and were, per se, sufficient to shape the conclusions of this Court, thus removing the assertion of the defense toward the lack of evidence that the defendants were carrying money when departing from Brazil.

Not possible that the defendants had received the values found with them only inside the aircraft, as the defense would have us believe, especially in view that such amounts were found in places that require preliminary preparation demonstrating that, from the moment they left this country's territory, defendants already had possession of alien currency.

The documentation that was shared between the existing criminal procedures in the United States of America and in São Paulo State Justice also serves as evidence for this procedure, since it was duly consented by U.S. authorities (pages 329 and 331) given that, in a similar way, it also corroborates the fact that the accused stepped into Miami – USA already in possession of the sum of US $56,467 (fifty-six thousand four hundred and sixty-seven U.S. dollars), which makes it clear that they were carrying foreign currency from Guarulhos International Airport – Guarulhos/São Paulo.

The information sent by the Department of Homeland Security – Office of the Attaché at the Embassy of the United States of America, notably in the document entitled DETAILS OF RESEARCH, whose copy had also been extracted from the documents of the case file moved before the State Court also asserts that:

Passengers inserted data on the same CBP Form 6059B and were referred for a more thorough luggage check. Even though the passenger Estevam HERNANDES has declared not to be carrying cash, he verbally amended the family statement by informing they were carrying a value greater than US$ 10,000, and his wife, Sonia, also stated that she was in possession of US$ 10,000.

In response to the official letter No. 202/07 – NUCART/DPF/AIN/SP, forwarded by Federal Police at the São Paulo International Airport (Guarulhos), the Attaché at the U.S. Embassy in Brasilia also had clarified the following:

The information requested relates to our internal investigation based on the detentions in Miami, Florida. The aforementioned individuals were arrested on January 8, 2007, while trying to smuggle into the United States.

The law in the United States is similar to that of Brazil, relatively to persons entering and leaving the U.S., which by law, have to declare amounts over $10,000 (ten thousand dollars). Since the couple did not declare cash in excess of $10,000, they violated our law. During an inspection of our personnel in Miami found concealed a total of $56,000.

There is no reason for cogitating the existence of a mistake of law, for the defendants deliberately sought to hide the cash they were carrying, packing US$ 9,088 inside the cover of a Bible and in Sonia Haddad Moraes Fernandes's luggage; US$ 10,000 in defendant ESTEVAM HERNANDES FILHO's coat; US$ 10,000 in their son's (Gabriel) backpack and US$ 9,700 packaged inside a CD case, which, by itself, let it be restated, is indicative factor that the goal of the defendants was to hide from Brazilian authorities the possession of foreign currency totaling US$ 56,467 (fifty six thousand and four hundred sixty-seven U.S. dollars).

Both Estevam Hernandes Filho and Sônia Haddad Moraes Fernandes acknowledged that they were carrying a sum greater than the one legally permitted, and, thus chose to employ "effective" mechanisms to circumvent competent authorities, in a way that it is safe to affirm, with a good margin of security, that the defendants were aware of the illegal nature of their conduct, which constituted the imprinted offense in Article 22, sole paragraph, of Law no. 7,492, of June 16, 1986.

On the other hand, with the defendants engaged in intense international religious activity, of which they are major leaders, it would not be believable that – accustomed to international travel and the need to send and receive funds to and from abroad, as they were – they were unaware of the declaration requirement for tax authorities about international remittances in such high values, or even the need to send them via exchange contracts.

In this sense, there is no doubt about criminal authorship and materiality, since the defendants were arrested in *flagrante delicto* in the United States in the possession of U.S. dollars, a fact not denied by them.

The defensive argument pointing to the absence of evidence capable of proving a necessary collusion between the defendants does not deserve reception. The individualization of the conduct remains patent on the case file, as seen elsewhere, since SONIA HADADD MORAES HERNANDES and ESTEVAM HERNADES FILHO boarded together at São Paulo International Airport (Guarulhos) to Miami, United States of America, both having perpetrated the crime of illegally sending funds abroad.

There was specific imputation by the Federal Public Prosecutor of the collusion, contrary to what claims the defense, especially considering that the crime outlined in Article 22 of Law No. 7,492, of June 16, 1986, can be perpetrated by one or more persons, making it a single agent offense.

It became clear by the documentation present in case files, including photos, that SONIA HADDAD MORAES HERNANDES and ESTEVAM HERNANDES FILHO left Brazil carrying US$ 9,088 inside the cover of a Bible and in their luggage, US$ 10,000 in a coat belonging to one of the defendants, US$ 10,000 in the backpack of their son Gabriel, and US$ 9,700 packaged inside a CD case, elements that confirm the criminal practice individually (pages 03/11).

The witness Cecilia Yoshie Watanabe said that, in the past, she only took care of the SÔNIA's schedule, having reported that the accused allegedly anticipated the trip from Monday to Sunday making what he called a "surprise" for the family. The witness was unable to clarify what the commitment was (fl. 365) that would have made ESTEVAM not initially accompany his family, nor whether the defendants met before heading to the airport. Also she had not seen the defendants' luggage. Cecilia allegedly only requested an earlier date in a travel agency, not knowing if they were traveling in early, mid or end of January 2007. Therefore, she did not weaken the documentation that based the accusation which categorically specifies the luggage of each one of the defendants.

Thus, it cannot be envisioned that the defendants were unaware of the illegal nature of their actions, since they duped authorities by allocating cash in a peculiar way and in smaller amounts (in cash), revealing they were aware of national legislation regarding the correct way to transfer alien currency abroad, which shows that they acted indifferently to this knowledge and promoted the outflow of foreign currency that was not spontaneously subject to supervision by Brazilian authorities.

Incidentally, the Federal Regional Court of the 3rd Region considered that the provision of the sole paragraph had been characterized, as an attempted behavior of someone who would not willingly submit foreign currency to verification and supervision of competent authority, which was followed by the discovery of cash due to the search imposed on them, so that, in this case, with much greater emphasis on the subsumption of facts to the criminal behavior outlined in article 22, sole paragraph, part of the *lex specialis* that, is characterized, for it was fully consummated.

It is worth noting, moreover, that the offense in question is carried out independently of the damage and the lawful origin of values, for which reason these subjects shall not be dealt with.

Again, there is no recommendation for the recognition of a mistake of any kind, be it a mistake of law or a mistake of fact, since there is no talking about an excusable, either inevitable or avoidable mistake. Given the qualification of the accused and the circumstances in which the crime occurred, it was perfectly possible that the defendants were conscious and aware of the unlawfulness of the facts practiced by both. Undeniably, there was a will to practice the criminal offense, to practice a punishable behavior to accomplish both goals that were just taken care in crime direction and not taking heed against criminal practice.

I do not recognize, however, as adequate, the charges related to Article 299 of the Criminal Code (fraud report) since there was no omission in the statement that should appear in the particular document (Declaration of Possession of Values), due to its total absence. Even if that imputation had been considered appropriate, one cannot fail to recognize the absorption of misrepresentation by the crime of sending unreported funds to foreign countries, not only by its specificity, but by the fact that the latter constitutes a more serious crime, or, finally, before the *antefactum* not punishable.

A certainty, then, shapes itself in the mind of the Magistrate that analyzed the evidence, always taking into account the goals modernly accepted for criminal sanctions: positive general and specific deterrence.

Based on the foregoing and everything else that the file contained, I UPHOLD the present criminal procedure for:

a) Acquitting ESTEVAM HERNANDES FILHO [...] and SÔNIA MORAES HERNANDES HADDAD [...] of the imputation addressed to them, of the offense outlined in Article 299 of the Criminal Code, based on Article 386, paragraph I, of the Code of Criminal Procedure.

b) Convicting the defendants ESTEVAM HERNANDES FILHO [...] and SÔNIA MORAES HERNANDES HADDAD [...] to the penalties of the offense specified in Article 22, sole paragraph, part of Law No. 7,492, of June 16, 1986, combined with Article 18, I, of the Criminal Code.

Consequently, I turn to establish the penalties.

Considering the elements contained in Article 59 of the Criminal Code, it appears that not all circumstances are favorable to them. Incidentally, with regard to social behavior, even though the witnesses presented by defense revealed a concern and a social behavior aiming at those who need the most (pages 343/347, 348/353, 362/367 and 368/377), the following facts should be registered:

1) Culpability – It could not be considered as normal for the specific case. Being leaders of an order of a religious character, they were expected to conduct themselves in ways compatible with that which they preach: the fulfillment of the common good, never acting by their own illegal interests. They profess the observance of what they consider to be a divine commandment, a dogmatic and moral system that undeniably requires from its most important adherents, the leaders of a particular religious branch, the exemplarity of their behavior. To claim to be acting in the service of the Creator, through devotion of faith and piety, is incompatible with those who act based on their illegitimate private interests. Culpability, which does not have only a meaning of disapproval or censure in basing the judgment of conviction, presents itself with greater forcefulness to the extent that the criminal act was clothed in excessive intentionality (intense intent), which was made clear by the use of unusual methods;

2) Perpetrators' personalities – They demonstrated with their criminal actions, a unique self-centeredness that detaches easily from the social parameters for satisfaction of direct economic benefits. They surprised everyone with unusual criminal behavior. They did not base their actions in the underlying values of ethics or correction, even though they profess the gospel. These attitudes revealed distorted personality traits, ignoring Brazilian authorities and Brazilian law. They reversed, thus, the maxim: the instrument (goods, money) becomes the entity and the entity becomes an instrument. They are governed by this instrument, not by Him or by the good precepts of faith they claim to profess and believe. There

is a clear contradiction between what they do and what they say they believe. They reveal, therefore, a misfit personality;

3) Motives – The motivation would be irrelevant if the defendants were not who they are. As religious leaders, they desecrated sacred things and the divine commandments, the humble and dignified life. They could not favor the continuity of unjust enrichment, set in motion next to the entanglement of dogmas of the Christian faith;

4) Circumstances and consequences of the crime – Their *modus operandi* generated harmful consequences to those who have always believed in the defendants' good faith as protagonists of a religious sect. They started to create feelings of perplexity and obscurity with the harmful set of attitudes that favored the "having" and not the "being": hiding foreign currency in the Bible, in a CD case, in a coat and in the backpack of their son. How many have questioned, from the facts, whether or not they had trod a path of blind unthinking reverence? Have not the defendants started to create religiously maimed people who have lost the courage to think for themselves, breaking their full human development? The illegal activities of the defendants indeed led to the discrediting of many people, to the dismay and more and more doubts and obscurities, in a way that many lose the belief in the ability of humans to achieve positive actions. In others, due to the responsibilities assumed by the accused for what they speak and do, they refrain from any reflection. They refuse the truth, such is their faith. For example, witnesses Cecilia Yoshie Watanabe, Leandro Roberto Barros Miglioli, Newton Heli Delgado, and Jorge Rueda Cailo Kamezawa, aside from certifying and affirming the social services provided by the convicted defendants and the Rebirth in Christ Church (for abandoned children, drug addicts, prisoners, and the elderly), reaffirmed their feelings of admiration of the defendants, literally asserting that they knew nothing that could discredit them. The last (Jorge) even said that before joining the Church, he made remittances from Japan (where he lived) to Brazil through the official channels and, even so, still refuses to see any blemish in their lives, considering that it was nothing but a 'misunderstanding'.

Thus, I fix for each of the defendants, the base penalty of three (03) years and six (06) months plus the payment of 141 (one hundred forty-one) fee-days. The fine penalty is fixed in order to save linear correspondence with the *quantum* of the applied penalty.

In the second phase of penalty dosimetry, there are aggravating circumstances, in particular the breach of duties inherent to the ministry, or religious activity, in accordance with Article 61, Section II, "g" (third figure) of the Criminal Code in order to increase the penalty by 1/6 (one sixth).

There are no mitigating circumstances to be considered.

In the last phase of penalty dosimetry, no causes for the increase or decrease of penalty are left to be weighed.

Therefore, the total penalty fixed for each of the defendant will reach a total of four (04) years of imprisonment, plus the payment of 164 (one hundred and sixty-four) daily fine.

Given that defendants frequently travel to the United States of America on vacation (as affirmed by the mustered defense witness Cecilia Yoshie Watanabe – pages 362/367), in addition to possessing, in cash, a large sum of foreign money, which reveals important economic capacity, I FIX fee-days in five (05) minimum wages prevailing at the time of the facts. The values shall be corrected on the payment date.

Based on Article 44, § 2, of the Criminal Code, as amended by Article 1 of Law No. 9,714, of November 25, 1998, I SUBSTITUTE the custodial sentence imposed on those convicted for two penalties restricting rights, to be served by both:

1. Provision of services to philanthropic entities, to be determined by the Court of Criminal Executions, by the time of the sentence, considering what is needed for preventing and repressing the imputed offense (Article 46, § 4, of the Criminal Code, with the writing given by Article 1 of Act No. 9,714, of November, 1998);

2. Temporary suspension of rights, during the time of the penalty, in the form of prohibition from attending certain places (Article 47, item IV of the Criminal Code), namely gambling houses; lotteries; casinos; property auctions, except for charitable ones, in which case they must have legal authorization; farms; luxury stores; bookmakers; other countries except for those with religious temples and with the existence of due judicial authorization.

If the penalties restricting rights are revoked, the accused should start serving their sentences in semi-open regime in the wake of what was recorded in the dosimetry of the penalty (Art. 33, § 3 of the Criminal Code).

I allow defendants to appeal in freedom.

Once this decision becomes unappealable, the names of the accused shall be released in the Docket Book of the Guilty.

I fix for each one, in face of the scope of incalculable moral damage to people, believers or not (indirect victims), the reparation for the criminal offense in R$ 150,000.00 (one hundred fifty thousand reals), which must be paid to charitable entities during implementation of the penalties and upon prior proof of legal origin, based on Art. 387, Section IV, of the Code of Criminal Procedure.

Even though tax immunity has been a well-established and constitutionally guaranteed way for achieving religious freedom, there are those who understand there is a need for discussing borderline issues, such as the contrast between the wealth of temples and the lack of resources of its followers, the financing by people who profess no religion, discriminatory conduct of many cults, and a lack of control over what are their earnings, facilitating unlawful practices.

For example, Eduardo Sabbag states:

In a temple proliferation scenario, given the 'extreme ease with which a sect is established', and the occurrence of numerous abuses, we are encouraged to reflect critically on the extent of the phenomenon and its consequences.

From the beginning, we have said that it is unfortunate that such expansion entails, in some cases, a fraudulent scenario in which some 'pseudo churches' operate under the cloak of faith. By diffusing a hypocritical religiosity, they even mask illegal activities under the guise 'representatives of the good'.

Indeed, it is commonplace in the Press the disclosure of resounding cases in which certain religious entities conduct illegal businesses, taking advantage of the pious image the activity naturally impinges. The question arises then: could the constitutional legislator, when intending to guarantee freedom of religion, have imagined such misrepresentation of his intention?

Regardless of whether or not the question of the pertinence of tax immunity is addressed, one cannot fail to recognize it.

The Constitution of the Federal Republic of Brazil, dated October 5, 1988, in its Article 5, Sections VI, VII, and VIII, well testified on religious freedom, even including it as an entrenchment clause, according to the following terms:

VI – freedom of conscience and of belief is inviolable, the free exercise of religious cults being ensured and, under the terms of the law, the protection of places of worship and their rites being guaranteed;

VII – under the terms of the law, the rendering of religious assistance in civil and military establishments of collective confinement is ensured;

VIII – no one shall be deprived of any rights by reason of religious belief or philosophical or political conviction, unless he invokes it to exempt himself from a legal obligation required of all and refuses to perform an alternative obligation established by law;

The national Magna Carta, thus, establishes the secularism of the Brazilian State (Article 19):

Article 19. *The Union, the states, the Federal District and the municipalities are forbidden to:*

I – establish religious sects or churches, subsidize them, hinder their activities, or maintain relationships of dependence or alliance with them or their representatives, without prejudice to collaboration in the public interest in the manner set forth by law;

The constitutional legislator also evinced this concern by ensuring religious freedom in its Article 105, Section VI, so much that the constituents ensured the immunity of religious temples or rather, the non-levy of taxes on temples of any worship, with the following:

Article 150. *Without prejudice to any other guarantees ensured to the taxpayers, the Union, the states, the Federal District and the municipalities are forbidden to:*

(…)

VI – institute taxes on:

(…)

b) temples of any denomination.

The Civil Code in this context establishes the autonomy of each religious institution, not demanding any requirements for their formation, greatly facilitating the possibility of their use for illicit purposes:

Art 44. Legal entities of private law are:

I – associations;

II – companies;

III – foundations;

IV – religious organizations (Included by Law No. 10,825, of December 22, 2003);

V – political parties (Included by Law No. 10,825, of December 22, 2003).

§ 1. The creation, organization, internal structure and functioning of religious organizations are free, being forbidden to the government denying them recognition or registration of the constituent and acts necessary for their operation. (Included by Law No. 10.825, of December 22, 2003) (…)

In face of such considerations and the remittance to foreign countries of large sums of foreign currency in cash, not spontaneously subject to the supervision of Brazilian authorities, done by leaders who profess religiosity, and, also, considering the *modus operandi* by which the offenses have been perpetrated, especially with the transfer of money being made inside the cover of a Bible, it becomes necessary to assert about the existence of profitable activity that will eventually collide with the institution of tax immunity.

In this respect, the office of the Court shall require the Internal Revenue Service of Brazil to closely inspect the Rebirth of Christ Church and the defendants now convicted, by sending in the official letter, in addition to this decision, the wording of the statement given by Leandro Roberto Barros Miglioli (pages 368/377). He stated he received as a bishop of Rebirth Church, the amount of R$ 12,000.00 (twelve thousand reals), which corresponds to 10 % (ten percent) of the value collected within his church, stating not to know what was the final destination of the 90 % (ninety percent) left. He affirmed, also, he receives from R$ 12,000.00 (twelve thousand reals) to R$ 15,000.00 (fifteen thousand reals) from a pet shop located at Shopping Tamboré, aside from money (between R$ 1,500.00 and R$ 1,700.00) due to a dog hotel in Villa Rica Park residential, in Santana do Parnaíba/SP, within his own residence of 250 sqm acquired years after joining that religious entity and not with values received from the pet shop. The witness revealed that he got rid of drug addiction thanks to the Rebirth of Christ Church.

The confidentiality of these records is restricted to documentation (page 323).

This restriction does not extend to this decision or to other documents that do not have a sensitive nature, being worthy of note that the content of the accusatorial petition reveal the commission of financial crime and documentation forgery, highlighting the prevalence, in casu, of the public interest, in a way that the situation should be governed by the general rule that the court decisions must be public, in line with Article 93, item IX of the Federal Constitution, Article 792 of the Code of Criminal Procedure, Article 155 of the Code of Civil Procedure, combined with Article 3 of the criminal procedural statute and in accordance with Article 6, the final part of Resolution no. 58 of May 25, 2009, of the Federal Justice Council.

Furthermore, I note that the secrecy of proceedings arose in the fourteenth century to protect those accused persons linked to the king who could, therefore, suffer retribution. The aim was also to stimulate appeals by those offended when they are fit for criminal prosecution.

The Federal Constitution also establishes the precept of publicity of the acts of the public administration of any of the Powers, providing, in Article 37, caput, the following: *The governmental entities and entities owned by the Government in any of the powers of the Union, the states, the Federal District and the Municipalities shall obey the principles of lawfulness, impersonality, morality, publicity, and efficiency, and also the following (...).*

In the decision on the issue of Binding Precedent No. 14 by the Supreme Federal Court, which ensured full and unrestricted access to the evidence already documented in investigative procedure, the eminent Justice Celso de Mello stated: *we must not lose sight of the fact that the Constitution does not favor secrecy, nor allows it to transform into government 'praxis', under penalty of serious harm to the democratic principle, for there is no possible space, in political models which establish democracy, for mystery.*

Moreover, the Justice stated: *I have as unquestionable, for that reason, that the requirement of publicity of the acts that form within the state apparatus reflects on consequences that result from an essential principle, that the new legal-constitutional order in our country did not remain indifferent, for which reason the establishment of a secrecy regime in criminal proceedings is coated by a cloak of exceptionality.*

In this procedure, I understand that secrecy does not have the scope to reap access to court decisions that also have the concern of protecting third parties, such that one should recognize the democratic maturity of Brazilian citizens in distinguishing security measures, prior to any criminal procedure, its beginning with the indictment, a conviction and ultimately a decision with *res judicata*.

Moreover, there is no place for secret criminal proceedings in a State under the rule of law. So much so that the sessions of the Supreme Federal Court are televised by Justice TV with the case of the indictment in Inquest No. 2,254-4/MG (*Mensalão* Case) being an example of the eminently public character of Brazilian criminal procedures.

Costs *ex lege*.

Register it and apply it.

December 1, 2009

Fausto Martin De Sanctis

FEDERAL JUDGE

4.1.8 "Vatileaks": The Institute for the Works of Religion (Vatican Bank)

So far, the most well-known crisis involving the Catholic Church was the sexual abuse of minors by some members of the U.S. Catholic clergy. The crisis led to two fundamental issues regarding how individuals with a disposition to prey sexually upon minors gained admission to the priesthood and how they managed to remain in that position even after allegations and evidence of such abuse. Although it is not possible to pinpoint any cause of the problem, it could be said that dioceses did not properly screen candidates for the priesthood properly, and seminaries did not adequately train candidates for the priesthood.[20]

[20] On the other hand, the presence of homosexually oriented priests or the discipline of celibacy would have not caused the crises. Many outstanding priests of a homosexual orientation lived chaste and were not involved in such crisis. According to the National Review Board for the Protection of Children and Young People, composed of lay Catholics and chartered by the United States Conference of Catholic Bishops, in 2002, causes of this failure include the following: Bishops and other church leaders did not understand the broad nature of the problem but treated allegations as sporadic and isolated; some bishops and other church leaders often put what they erroneously believed to be the institutional concerns of the local church above the concerns of the universal church. The fear of scandal caused them to practice secrecy and concealment; the threat of litigation caused some bishops to disregard their pastoral role and adopt an adversarial stance not worthy of the church; some bishops and other church leaders failed to comprehend fully the extent and magnitude of the harm suffered by victims of sexual abuse by priests; they did not do enough in the way of "fraternal correction" to ensure that their brethren dealt with the problem in an effective manner; they placed the interests of the accused priests above those of the victims; canon law and canonical procedures made it too difficult to remove a predator priest from ministry. The National Review Board for the Protection of Children and Young People, A Report on the Crisis in the Catholic Church in the United States, http://www.bishop-accountability.org/usccb/causesandcontext/2004-02-27-CC-Report.pdf, Feb. 27, 2004, accessed Dec. 6, 2014, pp. 7–9.

The June 2002 United States Conference of Catholic Bishops considered a collective response to the crisis and wrote the Charter for the Protection of Children and Young People to establish national standards for dealing with abuse cases involving minors. The Essential Norms include, among other things, a mandate that any priest who has engaged in a single act of sexual abuse of a minor be removed permanently from the ministry.[21]

Perhaps less well-known, but still significant on an international level, are the financial scandals that the Catholic Church has been involved in. The Institute for Works of Religion (IOR, or the "Vatican Bank") is a privately held financial institution located inside Vatican City. Founded in 1942, the IOR's role is to safeguard and administer property intended for religious or charity work. The bank accepts deposits only from top Church officials and entities, according to Italian legal scholar Settimio Caridi. It is run by a president but overseen by five cardinals who report directly to the Vatican and the Vatican's secretary of state. Because so little is known about the bank's daily operations and transactions, it has often been called "the most secret bank in the world." Hence, the IOR is a sort of central body of the Holy See (as the Church's government is called) whose profits are at the Pope's disposal. Its purpose is to provide for the protection and administration of moveable and immovable assets transferred or entrusted to the institute and destined for religious works or charity. Financial transparency and successful cooperation with Europe's anti-money-laundering agency Moneyval should continue to remain a priority for the institution.

The Vatican bank is not a true bank. It does not issue checkbooks. It does not make loans. It is more of a fund deposit and transfer institution than a bank. The IOR generates income by placing deposits in short-term government securities and in interest-bearing accounts at other banks.

On September 21, 2010, Italian police declared that it was investigating Gotti Tedeschi and another manager from the IOR under charges of money laundering. On that occasion, 23 million Euros were blocked after a Banco d'Italia division alerted authorities about two suspicious transactions from an Italian bank to JP Morgan Chase and the Banca del Fucino bank. The original account, as well as the two destination accounts, was controlled by the IOR, which allegedly defied Italian law by not declaring the origin of the money.[22]

The Vatican Bank was involved in various scandals, among them, "loss of millions of dollars, bank failures, arms sales to nations in conflict, creating front companies in tax havens, financing cout d'Etat, mafia money laundering and mysterious 'suicides'." It is an entity, but without a clear link to the ecclesiastical affairs or other

[21] "When even a single act of sexual abuse by a priest or deacon is admitted or is established after an appropriate process in accord with canon law, the offending priest or deacon will be removed permanently from ecclesiastical ministry, not excluding dismissal from the clerical state, if the case so warrants." The National Review Board for the Protection of Children and Young People, A Report on the Crisis in the Catholic Church in the United States, http://www.bishop-accountability.org/usccb/causesandcontext/2004-02-27-CC-Report.pdf, Feb. 27, 2004, accessed Dec. 6, 2014.

[22] Vatican Bank "investigated over money-laundering." Sept. 21, 2010, http://www.bbc.co.uk/news/world-europe-11380628, accessed Aug. 26, 2014.

bodies of the Holy See and the pope is its unique controller. The Vatican Bank, unlike other international financial institutions, "is not supervised by any internal or external agency, nor there are written records of their transactions."[23]

As an answer to those suspicions, the former pope, Benedict XVI, established on December 30, 2010, a Financial Information Authority to supervise all monetary and commercial activities from all institutions related to the Vatican. The entity had the function of ensuring that such operations met the requirements of international norms against money laundering and terrorism financing.[24] Apparently, as an answer to the Vatican initiative, Rome's prosecutor liberated the previously blocked values.[25] In June 2013, Pope Francis ordered the creation of a Special Investigative Pontifical Commission to evaluate the IOR.[26] The commission convenes at least bi-annually and oversees the compliance of the IOR with its statutory norms.[27]

Shortly after the creation of this commission, a new scandal hit the Holy See, when Monsignor Nunzio Scarano was arrested under charges of aiding an attempt of smuggling 20 million Euros from Switzerland to Italy. According to the investigation, the cleric was accused of money laundering for hiding a sum of 560,000 Euros, attributing to them, as source, the donations of worshippers.[28]

In 2012, Italian prosecutors detained the head of the Vatican Bank, Ettore Gotti Tedeschi, after searching his home and former office for suspected criminal behavior. The Vatican Bank appeared to be "embroiled in yet another financial scandal. After a number of very embarrassing episodes in recent years, the Pope [Benedict XVI] pledged to comply with international standards on illicit finance and clean up the bank's image. The European Union has an important role to play in helping the Vatican mitigate risks and come into full compliance; the Financial Action Task Force (FATF), set up by the G-7 to combat money laundering and terrorist financing as a responsibility as well."[29]

---

[23] FRATTINI, Eric. A SANTA ALIANÇA. Cinco séculos de espionagem no Vaticano. São Paulo, Brazil: Boitempo Editorial, 2009, p. 351–52.

[24] Papa aprova novas medidas contra lavagem de dinheiro: Francisco reforça regulação de órgãos de controle financeiro, ministérios e instituições. Folhape.com.br, Aug. 8, 2013, http://www.folhape.com.br/cms/opencms/folhape/pt/geral/mundo/arqs/2013/08/0037.html, accessed Aug. 26, 2013.

[25] Italy releases over $33 million in Vatican bank assets. Catholicnewsagency.com, June 1, 2011, http://www.catholicnewsagency.com/news/more-than-33-million-released-from-vatican-bank/, accessed Aug. 27, 2013.

[26] Papa nomeia comissão de inquérito para o Banco do Vaticano: Integrantes responderão diretamente a Francisco. Globo.com, June 26, 2013, http://oglobo.globo.com/mundo/papa-nomeia-comissao-de-inquerito-para-banco-do-vaticano-8818007, accessed Aug. 26, 2014.

[27] Cardinal commission for Vatican bank could undergo changes, CNA Daily News, published on Jan. 10, 2014, http://www.patheos.com/blogs/catholicnews/2014/01/cardinal-commission-for-vatican-bank-could-undergo-changes/, accessed Jan. 15, 2014.

[28] Prelado e mais 2 homens são presos em investigação sobre o Banco do Vaticano. Oglobo.globo.com, June 28, 2013, http://oglobo.globo.com/mundo/prelado-mais-2-homens-sao-presos-em-investigacao-sobre-banco-do-vaticano-8840405, accessed Aug. 28, 2014.

[29] JORISH, Avi, The Vatican Bank: The Most Secret Bank In the World June 26, 2012, http://www.forbes.com/sites/realspin/2012/06/26/the-vatican-bank-the-most-secret-bank-in-the-world/, accessed Jan. 15, 2014.

According to a Forbes article, it appeared that "the Vatican's promise to comply was nothing less than controversial in the Holy See's inner circle. A book published in 2012 by Italian journalist Gianluigi Nuzzi details intrigue, corruption, power struggles, bribes, money laundering, and a lack of desire to follow the dictates of the [Financial Action Task Force (from the Organization for Economic Cooperation and Development)] — and its European sister organization, MONEYVAL— to fight illicit finance."[30] The scandal became known as "Vatileaks" and involved the release of over 4,000 internal Vatican documents. It was an embarrassment to the Vatican and "cast a cloud over its effort to demonstrate financial transparency and shed its reputation as a tax haven."[31]

"FATF and the MONEYVAL are uniquely placed to pressure the IOR to reform. Both organizations have scores of trained staff members who can assist the Vatican to implement a robust anti-money-laundering regime that would satisfy both the EU and the international community. It would also be beneficial if the Italian government were to step in, given its close ties with the Vatican. Traditionally, the Ministry of Economy and Finance has designed the policy aspects of Italian money-laundering and terrorism-finance efforts, while the financial intelligence compliance functions fall under the Ufficio Italiano dei Cambi (UIC), in collaboration with the Guardia di Finanza (GdF). Italy has received high marks from the international community for its part in ensuring the safety and soundness of the international financial sector. Italian government agencies would thus seem to be the ideal candidates to lead the Vatican back to the straight and narrow road."[32]

In July 2013, there are reports that the charges against Tedeschi—who had been ousted from his functions[33]—were dropped.[34]

On July 11, 2013, Pope Francis signed a Decree changing the criminal law of the Vatican to criminalize sexual abuse, financial misconduct, and the leakage of sensitive information.[35] That same month, the Vatican froze the account of a senior cleric, Monsignor Nunzio Scarano, who was suspected of involvement in money-laundering. He and two others were arrested by Italian police on suspicion of trying to illegally move 20 million Euros. Soon thereafter, Pope Francis issued a decree designed to combat money laundering and prevent terrorism financing.[36]

---

[30] *Id.*

[31] *Id.*

[32] *Id.*

[33] SCHERER, S. Vatican bank president Gotti Tedeschi ousted – statement. Reuters, May 21 2012, http://www.reuters.com/article/2012/05/24/vatican-bank-idUSL5E8GOGVL20120524, accessed Aug. 26, 2014.

[34] Gotti Tedeschi verso archivazione: Rischio richiesta giudizio per Cipriani e Tulli. Ansa.it., July 2013, http://www.ansa.it/web/notizie/rubriche/cronaca/2013/07/02/Ior-Gotti-Tedeschi-verso-archiviazione_8963101.html, accessed Aug. 30, 2014.

[35] Papa endurece leis contra pedofilia e atos de corrupção. Francisco assina decreto que prevê reforma do código penal do Vaticano, que era visto como desatualizado. *Folha de São Paulo,* mundo A17, July 12, 2014.

[36] Pope Francis tightens Vatican bank controls. BBC News Europe, Aug. 8, 2013, http://www.bbc.co.uk/news/world-europe-23621235, accessed Jan. 15, 2014.

The Guardian revealed "a surprising secret commercial property empire owned by the Vatican." The church used cash originally handed over by Mussolini in return for papal recognition of the Italian fascist regime in 1929 to build up an international portfolio over the years using a disguised offshore company structure. The value of "Mussolini's nest-egg" now exceeds £500 m. In 2006, at the height of the recent property bubble, the Vatican spent £15 m of those funds to buy 30 St James's Square in London. It owns other properties in the UK—at 168 New Bond Street and in the city of Coventry, as well as blocks of apartment buildings in Paris and Switzerland. The Vatican has gone surprising lengths to preserve secrecy about the Mussolini millions. The Guardian reports as follows:

> The St James's Square office block was bought by a company called British Grolux Investments Ltd, which also holds the other UK properties. Published registers at Companies House do not disclose the company's true ownership, nor make any mention of the Vatican.
>
> Instead, they list two nominee shareholders, both prominent Catholic bankers: John Varley, recently chief executive of Barclays Bank, and Robin Herbert, formerly of the Leopold Joseph merchant bank. Letters were sent from the Guardian to each of them asking whom they act for. They went unanswered. British company law allows the true beneficial ownership of companies to be concealed behind nominees in this way.
>
> The company secretary, John Jenkins, a Reading accountant, was equally uninformative. He told the Guardian journalists the firm was owned by a trust but refused to identify it on grounds of confidentiality.
>
> (…)
>
> Research in old archives, however, revealed more of the truth. Companies House files disclose that British Grolux Investments inherited its entire property portfolio after a reorganisation in 1999 from two predecessor companies called British Grolux Ltd and Cheylesmore Estates. The shares of those firms were in turn held by a company based at the address of the JP Morgan bank in New York. Ultimate control is recorded as being exercised by a Swiss company, Profima SA.
>
> British wartime records from the National Archives in Kew complete the picture. They confirm Profima SA as the Vatican's own holding company, accused at the time of "engaging in activities contrary to Allied interests". Files from officials at Britain's Ministry of Economic Warfare at the end of the war criticized the pope's financier, Bernardino Nogara, who controlled the investment of more than £50 m cash from the Mussolini windfall.
>
> Nogara's "shady activities" were detailed in intercepted 1945 cable traffic from the Vatican to a contact in Geneva, according to the British, who discussed whether to blacklist Profima as a result. "Nogara, a Roman lawyer, is the Vatican financial agent and Profima SA in Lausanne is the Swiss holding company for certain Vatican interests." They believed Nogara was trying to transfer shares of two Vatican-owned French property firms to the Swiss company, to prevent the French government blacklisting them as enemy assets.
>
> Earlier in the war, in 1943, the British accused Nogara of similar "dirty work", by shifting Italian bank shares into Profima's hands in order to "whitewash" them and present the bank as being controlled by Swiss neutrals. This was described as "manipulation" of Vatican finances to serve "extraneous political ends".
>
> The Mussolini money was dramatically important to the Vatican's finances. John Pollard, a Cambridge historian, says in Money and the Rise of the Modern Papacy: "The papacy was now financially secure. It would never be poor again."

From the outset, Nogara was innovative in investing the cash. In 1931, records show he founded an offshore company in Luxembourg to hold the continental European property assets he was buying. It was called Groupement Financier Luxembourgeois, hence Grolux. Luxembourg was one of the first countries to set up tax-haven company structures in 1929. The UK end, called British Grolux, was incorporated the following year.

When war broke out, with the prospect of a German invasion, the Luxembourg operation and ostensible control of the British Grolux operation were moved to the US and to neutral Switzerland.

The Mussolini investments in Britain are currently controlled, along with its other European holdings and a currency trading arm, by a papal official in Rome, Paolo Mennini, who is in effect the pope's merchant banker. Mennini heads a special unit inside the Vatican called the extraordinary division of APSA – Amministrazione del Patrimonio della Sede Apostolica – which handles the so-called "patrimony of the Holy See".

According to a report last year from the Council of Europe, which surveyed the Vatican's financial controls, the assets of Mennini's special unit now exceed £680 m (£570 m).

While secrecy about the Fascist origins of the papacy's wealth might have been understandable in wartime, what is less clear is why the Vatican subsequently continued to maintain secrecy about its holdings in Britain, even after its financial structure was reorganised in 1999.[37]

The Vatican has not addressed the real issues: that their global property and investments are hidden behind layer after layer of false fronts and holding companies. Money laundering is when funds from criminal acts is "washed" into an account with a seemingly legitimate purpose. This is usually done through an offshore company, meaning there are no government rules or regulations in place to prevent the transactions or prosecute the perpetrators.

Gianluigi Nuzzi reveals that several leaks focused on Vatican finances, charging corruption and cronyism. Documents obtained by him would style the Vatican bank as a rogue offshore bank, which included purportedly encrypted and secret accounts, raise questions about the Vatican's willingness to cooperate with international regulators and expose internal debates over whether a new Vatican financial watchdog agency is actually useful, beside disclose that the IOR money laundered about $280 million on behalf of Mafia.[38]

MONEYVAL released the Mutual Evaluation Report of "The Holy See (including Vatican City State)" on July 4, 2012, based upon compliance with FATF and Directive 2005/60/EC (third EU Directive, Anti-Money Laundering Directive). MONEYVAL also acknowledged that the Vatican had never taken steps to actually

---

[37] LEIGH, David, TAND, Jean François and BENHAMOU, Jessica. How the Vatican built a secret property empire using Mussolini's millions. Papacy used offshore tax havens to create £500 m international portfolio, featuring real estate in UK, France, and Switzerland. The Guardian, Jan. 21, 2013, http://www.theguardian.com/world/2013/jan/21/vatican-secret-property-empire-mussolini, accessed Feb. 18, 2014.

[38] NUZZI, Gianluigi. *Ratzinger was Afraid. The Secret Documents the Money and the Scandals that Overwhelmed the Pope* Casaleggio Associati edition, Mar. 15, 2013, Kindle format (see http://www.amazon.it/Ratzinger-was-afraid-Adagio-ebook/dp/B00BMLDG3O/ref=sr_1_1?ie=UTF8&qid=1363343619&sr=8-1).

uncover or stop money laundering, the real identity of IOR account holders had yet to be discovered, and, per their report, there is "a lack of clarity about the role, responsibility, authority, powers and independence of the Financial Intelligence Authority (FIA[39]) as supervisor."[40]

"In today's interconnected financial world, instituting measures to mitigate abuse of the international financial sector is part of the cost of doing business. Unquestionably, one of the most serious public policy challenges the international community will face in the foreseeable future is how to use every tool in its arsenal to make progress against those who exploit tainted money. While the Vatican answers to a higher calling, the EU, FATF and MONEYVAL should insist that its earthly responsibilities are equally important."[41]

4.1.9 Congregation Aish Kodesh (Woodmere, NY)

In June 2011, board members of a Modern Orthodox shul, Congregation Aish Kodesh, started to investigate its community finances after some of the shul's checks started to bounce. After a meeting, they discovered that more than $500,000 had been wired from the shul's bank account to another account owned by a law firm belonging to the shul's treasurer.

A forensic accountant hired by the shul discovered that the fraud started back in 2008, while the treasurer was serving the first of two three-year terms as a board member. Apparently, the shul had two bank accounts: one for operating expenses at a local bank and another, which was an endowment fund. Officials claimed that the treasurer deposited checks made out to the expense account into the endowment fund, which he was later able to send to another account owned by him. The board's chairman also affirmed that, even though the shul had a two-signature policy for its checks, somehow this limitation was bypassed by the perpetrator.[42]

---

[39] The Financial Intelligence Unit for the HS/VCS, is the FIA – Financial Intelligence Authority (Autorità di Informazione Finanzaria – AIF), which has been operational since April 1, 2011. The unit was established by His Holiness Benedict XVI in his Apostolic letter dated Dec. 30, 2010, in the form of a Motu Proprio on preventing and countering illegal activities in the financial and monetary field. It is a public institution with autonomous administrative authority.

[40] See the site of Council of Europe, Mutual Evaluation Report of "The Holy See (including Vatican City State)," http://www.coe.int/mwg-internal/de5fs23hu73ds/progress?id=v7L6iiaJVo, accessed June 10, 2014, p. 159.

[41] JORISH, Avi, The Vatican Bank: The Most Secret Bank In the World June 26, 2012, http://www.forbes.com/sites/realspin/2012/06/26/the-vatican-bank-the-most-secret-bank-in-the-world/, accessed Jan. 15, 2014.

[42] ORBACH, Michael. Woodmere Shul's Treasurer Charged With $600G Theft. Thejewishweek.com, June 29, 2011, http://www.thejewishweek.com/news/new_york/woodmere_shuls_treasurer_charged_600g_theft, accessed July 29, 2014.

4.1.10 Beth El Synagogue (Southbury, CT)

On December 19, 2013, a former president of the Beth El Synagogue, a Southbury Jewish community, was sentenced to 30 months in prison, followed by 3 years of supervised release (during which 6 months would be in home confinement and 120 of community service would be performed) for embezzling more than $600,000. She was also ordered to pay restitution to the synagogue in the amount of $531,985.25.

According to court documents and statements, the embezzlement began in November 2010 while she was serving as the synagogue's vice-president. In June 2011, she became president of the synagogue and used this position to open a checking account and a money market account in the name of the synagogue. She even used the institution's address for a while, but later requested the bank to change the mailing address on those accounts to her own address.

In order to carry out the offense, the accused deposited bank checks into the accounts she created. Such checks reflected funds gained through investments in other financial institutions. Then the money was drawn from the accounts through more than 60 unauthorized ATM and over-the-counter transactions in amounts that ranged from $500 to $2,000. The perpetrator then used these funds to pay school-related expenses for her children, vehicle expenses, traveling expenses, and even expenses to lease a horse for one of her children[43]

4.1.11 Cordoba Initiative and American Society for Muslim Advancement (New York, NY)

In February 2013, Imam Feisal Abdul Rauf, chairman of the Cordoba Initiative and the American Society for Muslim Advancement, was accused of diverting millions of dollars donated to these organizations and using the money to promote a luxurious lifestyle. Rauf was already a controversial figure for proposing that a mosque and a Muslim cultural center be built near the site of the terrorist attacks of September 11, 2001.

The lawsuit in question claimed that the Muslim leader falsified tax returns of both of the organizations that he founded. He allegedly used $167,000 from private donations and $3,000,000 from the Malaysian government to pay for vacations, real estate, entertainment, a luxury sports car, and other personal advantages.[44]

---

[43] UNITED States Attorney's Office. Former President of Southbury Synagogue Sentenced to 30 Months in Prison for Embezzling More Than $600,000. Justice.gov., Dec. 19, 2013, http://www.justice.gov/usao/ct/Press2013/20131219-2.html, accessed July 29, 2014.

[44] DYE, Jessica. Imam Feisal Abdul Rauf Embezzlement Lawsuit: Former Head of 'Ground Zero Mosque' Accused of Squandering Millions. Huffingtonpost.com, May 2, 2013, http://www.huffingtonpost.com/2013/02/05/imam-feisal-abdul-rauf-embezzlement_n_2625660.html, accessed Sept. 1, 2014.

In June 2013, the lawsuit was dropped after the accusing donors and the imam reached an agreement.[45]

4.1.12 Islamic Center of Washington, D.C.

In November 2006, the Islamic Center of Washington, D.C., led by Imam Abdullah M. Khouj, sued Farzad Darui for embezzlement. Darui was in charge of security duties and, according to the lawsuit, he supposedly altered hundreds of thousands of dollars' worth of checks that Khouj had written for legitimate mosque expenses. The financial resources came from an account funded by the Saudi Arabian government for expenses at the Islamic center. These funds were allegedly used by Darui to pay for his own businesses at Blue Line Travel and Zaal, Inc., an investment and management company.[46]

Darui claimed that Khouj had actually written those checks to meet the needs of two women close to the imam and for security tips given by informants.

In August 2010 federal prosecutors dropped the charges against Darui without specifically stating why they decided to do so.[47]

4.1.13 Thailand's Buddhist Jet-Setting Monk

In July 2013, Wirapol Sukphol, a Buddhist monk from Thailand, became a headline subject in the country after a video went viral YouTube showing the monk in his orange robe, with aviator sunglasses and a Louis Vuitton carry-on, boarding a private jet. The opulence depicted in these images sparked criticism and made many complaints start to surface—like the ones about his fortune of 1 billion baht (approximately US$32,000,000).

Since then, an arrest warrant was issued implicating Wirapol on charges of statutory rape, embezzlement, and online fraud to seek donations. Authorities were still unsure how he was able to amass such a great amount of money. There are also investigations about his involvement in money laundering, drug trafficking, and manslaughter.

[45] ROSS, Barbara; GREGORIAN, Dareh. 'Ground Zero mosque' imam settles lawsuit accusing him of using donor money to fund lavish lifestyle. Nydailynews.com, June 7, 2013, http://www.nydailynews.com/new-york/ground-zero-mosque-imam-settles-lawsuit-accusing-donor-money-fund-lavish-lifestyle-article-1.1365904, accessed Sept. 1, 2014.

[46] SCHWARTZ, Stephen. The Mosque and the Imam. Ahl-Alquran.com, http://www.ahl-alquran.com/English/show_article.php?main_id=4450, accessed Sept. 1, 2014.

[47] HSU, Spencer S. Federal prosecutors drop theft case against Islamic Center business manager. Washingtonpost.com, Aug. 15, 2010, http://www.washingtonpost.com/wp-dyn/content/article/2010/08/14/AR2010081402552.html, accessed Sept. 4, 2014.

While building his reputation as a monk with supernatural powers, Wirapol cultivated many rich followers, which helped him fund great projects like building temples, hospitals, and what was advertised as the world's largest Emerald Buddha. After the scandal, the Thailand Anti-Money Laundering Office found out about 41 bank accounts linked to the monk. Some of them kept about 200 million baht (around US$6,400,000) in circulation.[48]

4.1.14 *Tian Lai Temple (Hunan, China)*

In November 2011, a Buddhist monk named Zhang Kai was sentenced to 6 years in prison for bigamy and embezzlement. The investigation, carried out by Chinese authorities, revealed that Zhang acted as both the abbot of the Tian Lai Temple and the head of the city of Loudi's Buddhist association. At the same time, he was also the abbot of the Gu Tian Wang Temple.

While he kept these positions, he founded a company named Loudi Kaiyuan, which had management cooperation agreements with the Tian Lai Temple and a loan agreement with the Gu Tian Wang Temple. Chinese police claim that the company asked for 4,680,000 yuan (US$750,000) from both temples, but the monk kept 940,000 yuan (US$150,000) for himself to invest in another temple, the Ti Mu Temple. Apparently, Zhang owned 70 % of this last temple's shares.[49]

4.2 Churches and Temples as Front Organizations

Although not related to real religious institutions, another criminal practice that involves the legal status of churches is the use of fake churches and temples.

Even though it is a relatively new practice, there are already reports of investigations in which police claim that legally constituted churches were being used as facades to move illegal money and give it legitimate features.

In Brazil, because of the relatively recent emergence of news about financial crimes practiced within religious organizations and the notorious difficulty of judicial system to speed up criminal procedures, there are only a few judicial decisions regarding the subject.

---

[48] GECKER, Jocelyn. Wirapol Sukphol, Jet-Set Buddhist Monk Shocks Thailand with Religious Scandal. Huffingtonpost.com, July 18, 2013, http://www.huffingtonpost.com/2013/07/18/thailand-riveted-by-jetse_n_3615742.html, accessed Sept. 4, 2014.

[49] HSING-TONG, Lee. Buddhist monk in Hunan convicted of bigamy, embezzlement. Wantchinatimes.com, Nov. 20, 2012, http://www.wantchinatimes.com/news-subclass-cnt.aspx?id=20121120000006&cid=1103, accessed Sept. 4, 2014.

4.2.1 *"Car Wash" Operation ("Lava rápido")*

This investigation originated from a complaint forwarded by the inspection sector of the Brazilian IRS, which revealed serious criminal activities. A religious entity (incorporated with the aim of fulfilling social "activities of religious organizations") handled R$400 million between 2006 and 2009 by intermediaries. There were suspicions that the religious institution bank account had been used as a way to send money illegally abroad by business importers to cover the costs of under-valued importation.

On October 31, 2012, with the participation of the IRS, authorities executed 12 seizure warrants and 6 temporary detentions. In the course of the investigation it was that the church never existed, having only been formed for the passage of money.

Crimes against the national financial system and against the state revenue service, including money laundering, tax evasion, and tax fraud, were all investigated. Businessmen, civil servants, and magistrates were allegedly involved.[50]

4.2.2 *Religious Front Company for a "Doleiro" Network*

In another interesting case, a certain company set up in Brazil under the purpose of "Religious Organization Activities" moved, in its bank account, about R$250 million. There is a suspicion that the real holder of the bank account is an illegal currency exchange broker ("doleiro") who carried out clandestine transfers of money to or from abroad for illicit purposes. The Brazilian IRS started the investigation in April 2011 because it considered that the movement of the company's bank account was incompatible with its financial sources. It was discovered that the "company" (church) did not even exist.

Interviewed people that belonged to the board stated that they did not know that they were members of the church. Another person worked as a proxy of them under the bank and had the power to move values of the bank account belonging to the church. A treasurer of the "company" said that the real owner of it was a "doleiro." An accounting firm was hired by the "company." The accountant revealed that they were responsible only for its setup. Instead, the IRS discovered that they also were responsible for providing the annual report and all the accountability services to disguise the non-existent religious activities. Visiting the church, the IRS agents

[50] Juiz é investigado por acúmulo de R$ 30 milhões em 30 meses Terra, May 11, 2013, http://noticias.terra.com.br/brasil/policia/juiz-e-investigado-por-acumulo-de-r-30-milhoes-em-30-meses,310aaa682739e310VgnVCM20000099cceb0aRCRD.html, accessed Dec. 6, 2014; Operação Lava-Rápido desarticula quadrilha envolvida em crimes financeiros Jornal do Brasil, Oct. 31, 2012, http://www.jb.com.br/pais/noticias/2012/10/31/operacao-lava-rapido-desarticula-quadrilha-envolvida-em-crimes-financeiros/), accessed Dec. 6, 2014.

discovered that in the place for services there was a drugstore and a fitness center, which existed for more than 20 years.

An employee of the fitness center said to them that there was never any religious activity. The IRS discovered that the proxy of the church had several real estate properties and failed to report them. He was responsible for illegal transactions from Brazil to abroad giving his name to hide several remittances. It was revealed that 750 individuals and companies deposited into and or withdrew from the "church" bank account.

In the credit perspective (deposits in the church's bank account), it was revealed that import companies were sending money outside the country to pay creditors (suppliers of goods). The invoices of these sales contained values below the real value of goods.

On the other hand, in the debit perspective (withdraws), many individuals were the beneficiary of the transactions, including residents in many different states of Brazil.

Several Suspicious Activity Reports were filed by banks to COAF, the Brazilian Financial Intelligence Unit, mentioning that the "company" and/or its proxy were responsible for non-based financial transactions, that is, not compatible with its size or its declared current activity. A well-established network was setup in order to a place for "doleiros" (non-authorized money brokers). For the Brazilian IRS agents, remittance companies located in the United States (New Jersey) would help the network to disguise the transactions from Brazilian authorities through illegal wire transfers. They also discovered many construction companies were clients of other companies that belonged to the proxy of the church, a scheme well designed for tax fraud. Finally, clients of the aforementioned proxy operated in the football (soccer) sector, including a confederation and local organized committee of FIFA, and made several deposits into the church bank account. The case is still under investigation.

4.2.3 *First Church of Life (Orange County, CA)*

In 2002, an indictment against four persons in the U.S. District Court in Los Angeles charged with 48 accounts of mail fraud, money laundering, and other federal offenses. According to the prosecution, the defendants, since 1993, were using what prosecutors called "sham churches" (front religious organizations) to solicit funds by telephone and mail. Three organizations of this kind were allegedly used by the defendants to create at least 12 "sham charities" (phony charitable organizations) that were used to collect funds from the public. Donors were told that they could make tax-deductible donations to causes such as the treatment of AIDS and monetary relief for families of officers hurt or killed in the line of duty.[51]

[51] REZA, H. G. 4 indicted in Alleged Fake-Church Scam in O.C. Latimes.com, Oct. 25, 2012, http://articles.latimes.com/2002/oct/25/local/me-charity25, accessed Aug. 28, 2014.

4.3 Tax Fraud and Larceny by Fraud Using Churches and Temples

In 2010, a businessman in Brazil set up two churches as the owner of both of them. One is located in a commercial office of 25 square meters and the other in a place rented to a travel and tourism company. In 2012, he set up a third one in a summer house.

Eventually, a total of 25 real estate properties were purchased by the businessman on behalf of the church. One of them was bought less than a month after the creation of the church and paid with cash.

The Brazilian Financial Intelligence Unit (COAF) received Suspicious Activity Reports revealing that the church's proxy moved annually around $300,000 and reported that the money was the output of followers' donations. Cash withdrawn from the bank account belonged to the church.

After alleging doctrinal divergence, the businessman resigned as president. The new president is a drug addict and appointed the same businessman who founded the church as its proxy (for the religious organization). In 2013, more real estate and luxury vehicles were purchased on behalf of the church. The deal was made through private contracts registered by a specific notary.

The president of the church is responsible for the annual report to the Brazilian IRS of the businessman. The church sold part of the real estate and because of tax immunity no taxes were paid to the IRS.

There is a suspicion that the church was created to disguise the transfer of goods in favor of the real owner, who had been concealed under the religious institution. Besides tax fraud, there is an investigation to discover if the beneficiary of the scheme is also a drug dealer.[52]

Larceny by fraud is one of the most mentioned crimes when talking about crimes practiced through religious institutions. Nevertheless, there is a question as to what measure the character of larceny by fraud could be attributed to the donations given by worshippers. As immoral—and even against some religious principles—as the collection of donations based on promises may be, it probably should not be subject of a criminal prosecution, since the error in which the victim is supposedly induced does not consist of a fake conscience about a situation of facts, or it is often hard to prove, but it is what we are able to do when we face the supernatural. The acceptance of such a judgment by state organs about the divine would open a dangerous precedent to legitimize the State to act as a censor, choosing conceptions about what is and what is not acceptable in the religious field, compromising the secularism of the State.

As Luiz Regis Prado says in his work, the deceit—the essential element of the constitution of larceny by fraud—consists of a "situation of fact detached from

[52] Polícia Federal Descobre Igreja Usada Para Lavagem De Dinheiro Nov. 2, 2012, http://www.amigodecristo.com/2012/11/policia-federal-descobre-igreja-usada-para-lavagem-de-dinheiro.html, accessed Sept. 20, 2014.

reality."[53] The same sense is found in the lessons of Cezar Roberto Bitencourt, defines deceit as a "false representation or evaluation of reality."[54] Insofar as religion concerns the supernatural, that is, the unknowable through sensorial human experience, it does not deal with statements about the reality, but with dogmas that extrapolate the possibility of human verification. Thus, larceny by fraud would be inapplicable to cases when someone uses statements about the divine to obtain advantages—even if these are morally wrong.

The situation, however, changes completely when the deceit consists of a false conscience about a situation of facts. Suppose the existence of a religious entity that promotes the collection of resources promising that they will be entirely applied to charitable work. If, instead of using those resources on said works, the directors of the institution applied them to another finality—such as the increase of their personal patrimony—then the crime of larceny is clearly configured, for the application of those values is a fact, capable of being proven by human experience. That was the case of the First Church of Life, in which individuals founded a fake church that collected funds that were supposedly applied to charitable causes. Those resources, however, were never used for these ends, so the donors were tricked about a fact, that is, the actual use of donated resources.

With those considerations, one could notice that the application of crime defined in Article 171 of the Brazilian Penal Code (fraud), when the crime is practiced within churches, depends on an analysis about the error to which the victim is allegedly induced. Thus, there is need, in order to punish directors of religious organizations by larceny by fraud, of finding elements that demonstrate the intention of tricking its worshippers about the destination of resources given by them.

Aside from larceny by fraud and money laundering, it should be noted that it is possible that a front religious organization may be used to avoid the collection of taxes based on the immunity conferred by the Constitution. These cases, apart from administrative penalties, Act No. 8,137/90 defines crimes against the tax order which include the behaviors of omitting information or giving false declarations to suppress or reduce tax incidence. One could realize, then, that the crime could be well applied to the cases in which the status of religious organizations is used to escape tax collection.

Bibliography

ARAGON, Jarbas. Revista denuncia crise na Igreja Mundial do Poder de Deus GolpelPrime site, Oct. 27, 2013, http://noticias.gospelprime.com.br/crise-igreja-mundial-do-poder-de-deus/, accessed June 29, 2014.

BITENCOURT, C. R. Tratado de Direito Penal – Parte Especial 3. 4ª Edição. São Paulo: Editora Saraiva, 2008.

---

[53] PRADO, L. R. *Curso de Direito Penal Brasil, Volume 2.* 7ª Edição. 2ª Tiragem. São Paulo: Editora Revista dos Tribunais Ltda., 2008. 800 p. 445.

[54] BITENCOURT, C. R. *Tratado de Direito Penal – Parte Especial 3.* 4ª Edição. São Paulo: Editora Saraiva, 2008. 439 p. 233.

CARDINAL commission for Vatican bank could undergo changes CNA Daily News, Jan. 10, 2014, http://www.patheos.com/blogs/catholicnews/2014/01/cardinal-commission-for-vatican-bank-could-undergo-changes/, accessed Jan. 15, 2014.

CARDOSO, Rodrigo. Uma igreja com contas bloqueadas. IstoÉ independente Magazine, Feb. 28, 2014, http://www.istoe.com.br/reportagens/350111_UMA+IGREJA+COM+CONTAS+BLOQUEADAS, accessed June 30, 2014.

COSTA, F. Supremo arquiva ação penal contra líderes da Igreja Renascer. G1.globo.com, Brasília, June 2012, http://g1.globo.com/sao-paulo/noticia/2012/06/supremo-arquiva-acao-penal-contra-lideres-da-igreja-renascer.html, accessed Aug. 26, 2014.

COUNCIL of Europe, Mutual Evaluation Report of "The Holy See (including Vatican City State)" http://www.coe.int/mwg-internal/de5fs23hu73ds/progress?id=v7L6iiaJVo, accessed June 10, 2014.

DEFLAGRADA operação de combate à fraude de pneus usados. Brazilian Internal Revenue Service (Receita Federal do Brasil), in http://www.receita.fazenda.gov.br/AutomaticoSRFsinot/2008/02/20/2008_02_20_10_46_12_561402307.html, accessed Oct. 1, 2014.

DENÚNCIA de promotores aponta "prática de fraude" contra a Universal e fiéis. Globo.com, Aug. 11, 2009, http://g1.globo.com/Noticias/Brasil/0,,MUL1263488-5598,00.html, accessed Aug. 23, 2013.

DYE, Jessica. Imam Feisal Abdul Rauf Embezzlement Lawsuit: Former Head of 'Ground Zero Mosque' Accused of Squandering Millions. Huffingtonpost.com, May 2, 2013, http://www.huffingtonpost.com/2013/02/05/imam-feisal-abdul-rauf-embezzlement_n_2625660.html, accessed Sept. 1, 2014.

EXTRAORDINARY Appeal (Recurso Extraordinário com Agravo, ARE) n.° 737566, Justice Teori Zavascki, in http://www.stf.jus.br/portal/processo/verProcessoAndamento.asp?incidente=4375014, accessed Oct. 13, 2014.

FERREIRA, F. Justiça de SP anula processo contra bispos da Universal. Folha.com: São Paulo, Oct. 2010, http://www1.folha.uol.com.br/poder/817422-justica-de-sp-anula-processo-contra-bispos-da-universal.shtml, accessed Aug. 23, 2013.

FRATTINI, Eric. A SANTA ALIANÇA. Cinco séculos de espionagem no Vaticano. São Paulo, Brazil: Boitempo Editorial, 2009.

GAZETA Online, Operação cumpre mandados para apurar desvios de doações da Igreja Maranata, Nov. 26, 2012, http://gazetaonline.globo.com/_conteudo/2012/11/noticias/cidades/1376718-operacao-cumpre-mandados-para-apurar-desvios-de-doacoes-da-igreja-maranata.html, accessed May 1, 2014.

GECKER, Jocelyn. Wirapol Sukphol, Jet-Set Buddhist Monk Shocks Thailand with Religious Scandal. Huffingtonpost.com, July 18, 2013, http://www.huffingtonpost.com/2013/07/18/thailand-riveted-by-jetse_n_3615742.html, accessed Sept. 4, 2014.

GOTTI Tedeschi verso archivazione: Rischio richiesta giudizio per Cipriani e Tulli. Ansa.it, July 2013, http://www.ansa.it/web/notizie/rubriche/cronaca/2013/07/02/Ior-Gotti-Tedeschi-verso-archiviazione_8963101.html, accessed Aug. 30, 2014.

HABEAS *Corpus* no. 0038794–85.2011.4.03.0000/SP, 5th Panel, Federal Appellate Judge Luiz Stefanini, (in Tribunal Regional Federal da 3ª Região site, Sept. 11, 2012, http://web.trf3.jus.br/acordaos/Acordao/BuscarDocumentoGedpro/2279490, accessed Oct. 14, 2014.

HABEAS *Corpus* no. 96.007-SP, STF, 1ª Turma, Rel. Marco Aurélio, June 12, 2012. In http://www.stf.jus.br/portal/principal/principal.asp, accessed Aug. 26, 2014.

HABEAS *Corpus* no. 990.10.247420-8, 16th Criminal Panel, Judge Almeida Toledo, in São Paulo State Appellate Court site, in http://esaj.tjsp.jus.br/cjsg/getArquivo.do?cdAcordao=4776713&cdForo=0, accessed Oct. 12, 2014.

HORWITZ, Paul. Scientology in Court: A Comparative Analysis and Some Thoughts on Selected Issues in Law and Religion. 47 DePaul Law Review 1 (Fall 1997).

HSING-TONG, Lee. Buddhist monk in Hunan convicted of bigamy, embezzlement. Wantchinatimes.com, Nov. 20, 2012, http://www.wantchinatimes.com/news-subclass-cnt.aspx?id=20121120000006&cid=1103, accessed Sept. 4, 2014.

HSU, Spencer S. Federal prosecutors drop theft case against Islamic Center business manager. Washingtonpost.com, Aug. 15, 2010, http://www.washingtonpost.com/wp-dyn/content/article/2010/08/14/AR2010081402552.html, accessed Sept. 4, 2014.
ITALY releases over $33 million in Vatican bank assets. Catholicnewsagency.com, June 1, 2011, http://www.catholicnewsagency.com/news/more-than-33-million-released-from-vatican-bank/, accessed Aug. 27, 2013.
JORISH, Avi, The Vatican Bank: The Most Secret Bank In the World, June 26, 2012, http://www.forbes.com/sites/realspin/2012/06/26/the-vatican-bank-the-most-secret-bank-in-the-world/, accessed Jan. 15, 2014.
JUIZ é investigado por acúmulo de R$ 30 milhões em 30 meses Terra, May 11, 2013, http://noticias.terra.com.br/brasil/policia/juiz-e-investigado-por-acumulo-de-r-30-milhoes-em-30-meses,310aaa682739e310VgnVCM20000099cceb0aRCRD.html, accessed Dec. 6, 2014.
JUSTIÇA comum não pode julgar caso da Universal Consultor Jurídico, http://www.conjur.com.br/2010-out-20/justica-comum-nao-competencia-julgar-universal-tj-sp, Oct. 20, 2010, accessed Oct. 12, 2014
LEIGH, David, TAND, Jean François and BENHAMOU, Jessica. How the Vatican built a secret property empire using Mussolini's millions. Papacy used offshore tax havens to create £500 m international portfolio, featuring real estate in UK, France and Switzerland. The Guardian, Jan. 21, 2013, http://www.theguardian.com/world/2013/jan/21/vatican-secret-property-empire-mussolini, accessed Feb. 18, 2014.
MIDIAMAXNEWS, Reverendo Moon, que tem fazenda e fiéis em MS, está internado em estado 'irreversível' Aug. 31, 2012, http://www.midiamax.com.br/noticias/814178-reverendo+moon+tem+fazenda+fieis+ms+esta+internado+estado+irreversivel.html, accessed Sept. 9, 2014.
MP não revela origem ilícita do dinheiro da Universal. Consultor Jurídico, http://www.conjur.com.br/2009-ago-11/justica-sp-recebe-denuncia-integrantes-igreja-universal, Aug. 11, 2009, accessed Sept. 19, 2014.
MPF pede condenação de fundação e bispo da Renascer: Para o órgão, houve desvio e má aplicação de R$2 milhões de dois convênios com o Fundo Nacional para Desenvolvimento da Educação (FNDE) Estadão.com.br, São Paulo, Aug. 16, 2012, http://www.estadao.com.br/noticias/geral,mpf-pede-condenacao-de-fundacao-e-bispo-da-renascer,595757,0.htm, accessed Aug. 28, 2014.
NATIONAL Review Board for the Protection of Children and Young People, A Report on the Crisis in the Catholic Church in the United States http://www.bishop-accountability.org/usccb/causesandcontext/2004-02-27-CC-Report.pdf, Feb. 27, 2004, accessed Dec. 6, 2014.
NUZZI, Gianluigi. *Ratzinger was Afraid. The Secret Documents the Money and the Scandals that Overwhelmed the Pope*, Casaleggio Associati edition, Mar. 15, 2013, Kindle format (see http://www.amazon.it/Ratzinger-was-afraid-Adagio-ebook/dp/B00BMLDG3O/ref=sr_1_1?ie=UTF8&qid=1363343619&sr=8-1).
ORBACH, Michael. Woodmere Shul's Treasurer Charged With $600G Theft. Thejewishweek.com, June 29, 2011, http://www.thejewishweek.com/news/new_york/woodmere_shuls_treasurer_charged_600g_theft, accessed July 29, 2014.
PAPA aprova novas medidas contra lavagem de dinheiro: Francisco reforça regulação de órgãos de controle financeiro, ministérios e instituições. Folhape.com.br, Aug. 8, 2013, http://www.folhape.com.br/cms/opencms/folhape/pt/geral/mundo/arqs/2013/08/0037.html, accessed Aug. 26, 2013.
PAPA endurece leis contra pedofilia e atos de corrupção. Francisco assina decreto que prevê reforma do código penal do Vaticano, que era visto como desatualizado. Folha de São Paulo, mundo A17, July 12, 2014.
PAPA nomeia comissão de inquérito para o Banco do Vaticano: Integrantes responderão diretamente a Francisco. Globo.com, June 26, 2013, http://oglobo.globo.com/mundo/papa-nomeia-comissao-de-inquerito-para-banco-do-vaticano-8818007, accessed Aug. 26, 2014.
PF prende 6 por sonegação fiscal e lavagem de dinheiro em SP. G1.globo.com, Oct. 31, 2014, http://g1.globo.com/sao-paulo/noticia/2012/10/pf-prende-6-por-sonegacao-fiscal-e-lavagem-de-dinheiro-em-sp.html, accessed Aug. 28, 2014.

POLÍCIA dos EUA prende bispos da Renascer em Miami. G1.globo.com, São Paulo, Jan. 2007, http://g1.globo.com/Noticias/Brasil/0,,AA1413589-5598,00.html, accessed Aug. 26, 2014.

POLÍCIA Federal Descobre Igreja Usada Para Lavagem De Dinheiro. Nov. 2, 2012, http://www.amigodecristo.com/2012/11/policia-federal-descobre-igreja-usada-para-lavagem-de-dinheiro.html, accessed Sept. 20, 2014.

POPE Francis tightens Vatican bank controls. BBC News Europe, Aug. 8, 2013, http://www.bbc.co.uk/news/world-europe-23621235, accessed on Jan. 15, 2014.

PRADO, L. R. Curso de Direito Penal Brasileiro – Volume 2. 7ª Edição. 2ª Tiragem. São Paulo: Editora Revista dos Tribunais Ltda., 2008.

PRELADO e mais 2 homens são presos em investigação sobre o Banco do Vaticano. Oglobo.globo.com, June 28, 2013, http://oglobo.globo.com/mundo/prelado-mais-2-homens-sao-presos-em-investigacao-sobre-banco-do-vaticano-8840405, accessed Aug. 28, 2014.

RELEMBRE as denúncias e investigações sobre a Igreja Universal. Estadão.com.br, Aug. 11, 2009, http://www.estadao.com.br/noticias/cidades,relembre-as-denuncias-e-investigacoes-sobre-a-igreja-universal,416987,0.htm, accessed Aug. 21, 2014.

REZA, H. G. 4 indicted in Alleged Fake-Church Scam in O.C.. Latimes.com, Oct. 25, 2012, http://articles.latimes.com/2002/oct/25/local/me-charity25, accessed Aug. 28, 2014.

ROSS, Barbara; GREGORIAN, Dareh. 'Ground Zero mosque' imam settles lawsuit accusing him of using donor money to fund lavish lifestyle. Nydailynews.com, June 7, 2013, http://www.nydailynews.com/new-york/ground-zero-mosque-imam-settles-lawsuit-accusing-donor-money-fund-lavish-lifestyle-article-1.1365904, accessed Sept. 1, 2014.

SCHERER, S. Vatican bank president Gotti Tedeschi ousted – statement. Reuters, May 21 2012, http://www.reuters.com/article/2012/05/24/vatican-bank-idUSL5E8GOGVL20120524, accessed Aug. 26, 2014.

SCHWARTZ, Stephen. The Mosque and the Imam. Ahl-Alquran.com, http://www.ahl-alquran.com/English/show_article.php?main_id=4450, accessed Sept. 1, 2014.

STJ cassa mandado de prisão contra bispos da Igreja Renascer. G1.globo.com, São Paulo, Dec. 2006, http://g1.globo.com/Noticias/SaoPaulo/0,,AA1393688-5605,00.html, accessed Aug. 26, 2014.

TOZZI, A. Casal Renascer é condenado nos EUA. Estadão.com.br, Dec. 2009, http://www.estadao.com.br/noticias/impresso,casal-renascer-e-condenado-nos-eua,36748,0.htm, accessed Aug. 26, 2014.

UNITED States Attorney's Office. Former President of Southbury Synagogue Sentenced to 30 Months in Prison for Embezzling More Than $600,000. Justice.gov., Dec. 19, 2013, http://www.justice.gov/usao/ct/Press2013/20131219-2.html, accessed July 29, 2014.

VATICAN Bank "investigated over money-laundering". Sept. 21, 2010, http://www.bbc.co.uk/news/world-europe-11380628, accessed Aug. 26, 2014.

Chapter 5
International Religious Activities and Legal Cooperation for Repatriation of Assets

December 2008 brought headlines that shocked the world: prominent banker Bernie Madoff, instead of providing legitimate investment services, was running a fraudulent operation (a chain or Ponzi scheme). Over the course of several years, Madoff gulled thousands of investors who shelled out over $65 billion. In March 2009, he pled guilty to nine counts, including financial fraud, money laundering, and perjury. In June of that same year, he was sentenced to over 150 years in prison.

Madoff was given more than just a custodial sentence. Prosecutors sought forfeiture of all of his revenue from the scheme, a total of $170 billion. They are trying to recover this amount, alleging that Madoff's assets and those of his wife were acquired with the proceeds of crime and should therefore be confiscated by the government. Their aim is to deprive him of four houses totaling $22 million, a Steinway piano worth $39,000, and silverware worth $65,000.[1]

This case, as well as others involving the commission of crimes that result in large amounts of money acquired by their perpetrators, demonstrates the importance for freezing and seizing assets that come from criminal activities. Depriving financial criminals (fraudsters, embezzlement, money launderers, and white-collar criminals) of their ill-gotten proceeds and the instrumentalities of their trade not only achieves important law enforcement objectives but also provides an effective means of recovering funds for victim restitution.

In fact, the U.S. Department of Justice confiscated some $4,952.7 million in 2013. The purpose of asset seizure and forfeiture is to deter crime by disrupting, damaging, and dismantling criminal organizations.[2]

---

[1]HENRIQUES, Diana B. Madoff Is Sentenced to 150 Years for Ponzi Scheme *New York Times*, June 29, 2009, http://www.nytimes.com/2009/06/30/business/30madoff.html?pagewanted=all&_r=0; MERCED, Michael J. De la, Prosecutors Try to Claim Madoffs's Properties *New York Times*, Mar. 17, 2009, B6.

[2]THE UNITED STATES DEPARTMENT OF JUSTICE, Asset Forfeiture Program, Annual Financial Statements, Fiscal Year 2013, Audit Report No. 14-08, February 2014, http://www.justice.gov/jmd/afp/01programaudit/index.htm, accessed Nov. 2, 2014, p. 6.

F.M. De Sanctis, *Churches, Temples, and Financial Crimes*,
DOI 10.1007/978-3-319-15681-1_5

Because religious institutions are possible victims—and, sometimes, even instruments—of financial crimes, the confiscation of assets related to them becomes an important issue for crime-fighting authorities. There are two features present in churches and religious movements that make them somewhat attractive for ill-intentioned persons. One of them is a phenomenon that has emerged in recent years: the miscellaneous functions of churches and temples called mega-churches. Part church or temple, part civic community, they function like small towns. Their capacity for collecting large amounts of resources is so great that it has raised questions about how much of a church's activities, labor, and funds can be devoted to influencing legislation and to what extent engage in—or encourage their members to engage in—direct lobbying of policy makers, and what are the legal implications of a church taking a particular stance on a public policy, domestically or internationally. So much money is handled within these institutions that they might get the attention of people with bad—and criminal—intentions. The other feature is that churches and temples are institutions in transition and are continuously expanding their worship and services to new cities and countries. Their increasing international character has transformed them into possible victims and tools for money laundering, tax evasion, and many other financial offences. This is why the fight against financial crimes needs an approach that involves religious institutions.

The confiscation of ill-gotten resources by the government strengthens public safety in general by allowing federal investment in state and federal police forces, and in education to prevent serious crimes. All of the money or assets transferred to the government results in special crime-fighting and prevention programs, as well as combined efforts on the part of the states and the federal government and its agencies, culminating in proper enforcement methods to curtail crime. The ideal is to create a safe place for freedom, security, and justice. This is no small feat, for it necessarily requires a joint effort on the part of the police, prosecutors, and courts to obtain property illegally acquired. Forfeiture, confiscation, and repatriation require cooperation. Learning from decisions made in searching for and seizing the proceeds of crime will result in improvement of the work and training of public agents, and the adoption of new measures to fight crime.

When assets are confiscated, the message that gets sent to organized crime is that financially, crime no longer pays, and is not in the best interests of its practitioners. It drives home the message that some types of behavior really are prohibited, and that to insist on engaging in them is to pay the price.

According to professor Jean-Germain Gros, "failed states are those whose power grids have experienced sustained and massive breakdown, or political brownout, wherein state authorities are no longer able to project power either at the centre or at the periphery, and are subsequently, if temporarily, replaced by non-state generators of social power. . . . The connection between the failed state and crime in the post-Cold War world is simply this: the failed state, for reasons that will be exposed immediately, is a magnet for criminal elements both inside and outside its borders. In other words, the failed state is both a perpetrator and a victim of international crime."[3]

[3] GROS, Jean-Germain. Trouble in Paradise: crime and collapsed states in the age of globalization (in *The British Journal of Criminology*, 2003, v. 43, pp. 63–80).

The "failed states" can be transformed into "successful states" if there is an improvement in the international cooperation toward the seizure and forfeiture of ill-gotten assets.

Confiscation differs from pecuniary penalties because of the implicit perception that the violation determines the payment. When assets are forfeited, the amount varies in accordance with the proceeds derived from criminal behavior. The greater the proceeds from crime, the larger the confiscation. Defendants in comfortable financial circumstances ought to be subject to forfeiture of assets not trivial to them. In other words, ill-gotten goods should be taken in proportion to criminal behavior. Pecuniary fines and confiscation are measures independent of one another, yet incorrectly distinguished by many jurists. Because they are calculated differently, they cannot be combined for purposes of establishing the penalty imposed, for this would reduce the penalty.

The system as a whole works best when confiscation is kept as one of the solutions among the several outcomes of sentencing.

The clear message sent by proceeding with such measures is that unlawful behavior is in fact prohibited.

In addition to criminal proceedings, there is also the possibility of administrative and civil confiscation. Financial Action Task Force Recommendation No. 4 makes it clear that no prior criminal conviction is required for the forfeiture of assets.

This is something that occurs frequently in the United States (actions *in rem*, that is, proceeding against the thing itself) whenever the property or its possession is related to criminal activity.[4] As these claims are framed, the ownership or possession of the property is considered illegal, in which case the interested party may intervene to prevent loss to the government. In such cases, it is incumbent upon the government to prove "by a preponderance of the evidence, that the property is subject to forfeiture," and "if the Government's theory of forfeiture is that the property was used to commit or facilitate the commission of a criminal offense," the Government must prove "a substantial connection between the property and the offense."[5]

In the case of fungible goods such as cash, a common source of funding for churches and temples, showing the connection between the asset and the crime is quite complicated. But pursuant to U.S. law, once the Government proves that property found in any place or account is derived from crime, then identical property found in the same place is subject to forfeiture. For example, if the Government proves that $100,000 in an account is revenue from drugs, and the trafficker spends $50,000 of that amount but has another legitimately earned $50,000 in the same account, then the full $100,000 will be subject to forfeiture.[6]

---

[4] Cf. *United States v. Bajakajian*, 524 U.S. 321, 330–31 (1998); *United States v. One-Sixth Share*, 326 F.Wd 36, 40 (1st Cir. 2003).

[5] 18 U.S.C. § 983(c).

[6] 18 U.S.C. § 984(a)(2): *Except as provided in subsection (b), any identical property found in the same place or account as the property involved in the offense that is the basis for the forfeiture shall be subject to forfeiture under this section.* 18 U.S.C. § 984 (b): *No action pursuant to this section to forfeit property not traceable directly to the offense that is the basis for the forfeiture may be commenced more than 1 year from the date of the offense.*

In harmony with this, the UN Conventions against Organized Crime (Art. 12(a)) and against Corruption (Article 46) operate on the idea that confiscation is enforceable even in the event of the death of the accused or expiration of the statute of limitations.

Civil and criminal confiscations are not mutually exclusive. Were the Government to file both actions, each on its own grounds, and lose one, this in no way precludes continuing to seek confiscation in the remaining action.[7]

The symbolism in the forfeiture of personal property is striking. Losing the proceeds of crime is as upsetting, if not more so, than facing imprisonment. Hence, confiscation has become a priority strategy in the fight against organized crime. However, inasmuch as criminal activity has become transnational, and criminal investments have increased incredibly outside of national boundaries, a vast network has emerged to make use of the proceeds of crime, and has taken root in loopholes and legal hurdles in the way of crime-fighting efforts.

Criminals often work off of an interpretation established in case law. This is what justifies shoring up asset forfeiture even though the assets may have been transferred to some third party who nevertheless ought to have perceived that these were the proceeds of unlawful conduct, or had been transferred precisely to avoid confiscation (establishment of a good-faith third party).[8]

No burdens should be placed on police and state's attorneys' efforts to temporarily freeze or solicit the freezing of assets liable to disappear if nothing is done, and all such measures are, to be sure, subject to consideration by the courts. Nor is any such interference warranted when the assets are located abroad.

Governments ought therefore to allow the freezing, seizure, confiscation, and repatriation of assets in order to facilitate the fight against organized crime, itself a global business, in such a way as to force criminals to change their ways. With churches and temples, the theory does not change in the case of crimes committed within or through them.

Financial Action Task Force Recommendation No. 30 establishes the possibility of conducting freezing and seizure operations, even when commission of the antecedent crime may have occurred in another jurisdiction (country). It also recommends the implementation of specialized multidisciplinary groups or task forces. Thus, the importance of international cooperation to vitalize all necessary efforts to assist States in their mission to fight crime is evident.

According to Fletcher Baldwin, Jr., there are three dimensions involved in the ongoing fight against international money laundering: consistent policies between national and international efforts, an efficient legal and institutional apparatus, and close cooperation between the public and private sectors.[9]

---

[7] McCAW, Catherine. Forfeiture as a Form of Punishment: A Case for Integrating Asset Forfeiture into Criminal Sentencing. 38 American Journal of Criminal Law 181, 195 (2011).

[8] Confiscation and Asset Recovery: Better Tools to Fight Crime. *States New Service*, Brussels, March 12, 2012, www.lexis.com, accessed May 26, 2012.

[9] See BALDWIN, Fletcher. Art Theft Perfecting The Art of Money Laundering. (Jan. 2009 for the 7th Annual Hawaii International Conference on Arts & Humanities). An unpublished work, sent to the U.S. Library of Congress on April 20, 2012, by University of Florida College of Law Professor Emeritus Levin, by request of the author, pp. 47–8.

For an effective and cohesive universal policy against money laundering, participation by and commitment of all States to international cooperation is imperative.

It has taken many years to establish international cooperation for the repatriation of objects of cultural heritage. For instance, if in 1816 a cultural work were outside of its country of origin, there was little to be done even if the fact were common knowledge. Treasures thus remained in the hands of private owners. In those days there were no local requirements to show good faith, nor international laws for the preservation of cultural heritage. Even provenance, a precaution against looting, was unknown. There was the difficulty of disseminating information back in the days before electronics. This made it easy to acquire purloined or stolen pieces and sell them afterward.[10]

Today, however, with legislative protection present at the national and international levels, added to governments' increased awareness, there are ways for an owner or a nation to claim an item of cultural heritage. Selling or loaning of such an item without official approval would hardly be allowed. Furthermore, the burden of proof is on the third party to show legitimate possession when the government alleges that an item was transferred to him in order to dodge confiscation, or in the belief that he would deliberately act without due caution. This is how repatriation has been accomplished.

There are no due diligence requirements in place for churches and temples to prevent unlawful behavior. Without due diligence requirements, churches and temples may not be liable for the further removal of an object from the victim if acting in good faith (under a doctrine of conscious avoidance or assumption of the risk). They should be required to search official and unofficial lists of stolen items, and to check with the authorities to ensure that they do not gain possession of any item that has an illegal origin. The activities of church and temple leaders are typically perceived as being performed in a good manner, and there is an honest belief that nothing suspicious is going on. This general perception should not exempt churches and temples from due diligence requirements.

When crimes (like embezzlement) are committed within churches and temples, money laundering efforts depend on the later use of the product of the crime and the attempt to hide it. Certainly, individuals and institutions that are obligated to submit Suspicious Activity Reports (banks, notaries, IRS, etc.) must disclose any suspicious financial activities related to churches and temples.

Thus, confiscation and repatriation are two stages of legal proceedings in which the assets of criminals are forfeited on behalf of victims, communities, or governments. Central to this procedure is the decision that a given asset was acquired as the proceeds of unlawful conduct, and may therefore be confiscated.

The first stage in repatriation is the tracking and identification of goods. This normally involves coordinated efforts on the part of prosecutors and government agencies (revenue authorities, the police, and private collaborators). These efforts also require substantial expertise and skill in dealing with the financial transactions

---

[10] Cf. CHARNEY, Noah. *The Mystic Lamb. The True Story of The World's Most Coveted Masterpiece*. New York: PublicAffairs, 1st ed., 2010, pp. 110–11.

that are sometimes involved. These normally involve communication among the authorities. In the United States, for example, the Asset Recovery Office (ARO) in one state will surely provide another ARO with information as to the whereabouts of goods. But once these move into international jurisdictions, court orders are necessary to block or freeze them so that they may then be permanently confiscated. Those cases require cooperation with foreign authorities so that the items may return to their countries of origin.

International legal cooperation has been essential to shed light on the activities of organized groups that invariably rely on companies that have their main offices in tax havens or elsewhere abroad. It has enabled goods to be blocked and assets to be repatriated.

One approach calls for the application of reciprocity, pursuant to which governments may cooperate with one another in the absence of some previous treaty or international agreement, acting through mutual commitments undertaken in dealing with a specific case.

The UN Convention against the Illegal Traffic in Narcotic Drugs and Psychotropic Substances (Vienna, 1988, Articles 6 and 7), Act No. 11,343 dated 08/23/2006 (the Brazilian drug law, Article 65), the Extradition Treaty to which MERCOSUL Member States are party,[11] the UN Convention against Transnational Organized Crime (Palermo, 2000, Articles 16–19), the UN Convention against Corruption (Mérida, 2003, Articles 44 and 46), the Council of Europe Convention on Laundering, Search, Seizure and Confiscation of the Proceeds from Crime (Strasbourg, 1990, Articles 7–35), the Council of Europe Convention on Laundering, Search, Seizure and Confiscation of the Proceeds from Crime and on the Financing of Terrorism (Warsaw, 2005, Articles 15–45), Brazil's Money-Laundering Act (No. 9,613, of 03/03/1998, Article 8, as amended by Law 12,683 of 07/09/2012), and the Model Regulation promulgated by the Inter-American Drug Abuse Control Commission (CICAD/OAS, Article 20), all contain such provisions of mutual reciprocity.

The Financial Action Task Force clearly emphasizes in its Recommendations the need to reinforce international cooperation through general exchange of information relating to suspicious transactions. There is the understanding that the various standards relating to the element of intent in criminal conduct should not affect the ability or the will of countries to cooperate on judicial matters. The Recommendations establish: the possibility of freezing and seizure, even when the antecedent crime was committed in some other jurisdiction (country), as well as the implementation of specialized multidisciplinary teams or task forces (Recommendation No. 30); international legal cooperation, pursuant to the UN Conventions of Vienna (international traffic, 1988), Palermo (transnational organized crime, 2000), and Mérida (corruption, 2003), by withdrawing obstacles (Recommendation No. 36); direct

[11] They specifically address International Legal Cooperation and one conclusion arrived at in Rio de Janeiro on Dec. 10, 1998 was promulgated in Brazil through Legislative Decree No. 605 of Sept. 11, 2003, which became effective internationally on Jan. 1, 2004, as a result of the Treaty of Asunción, creating the South American common market, MERCOSUL (signed Mar. 26, 1991).

mutual legal assistance toward a quick, constructive, and effective solution (Recommendation No. 37); freezing and confiscation even when there is no prior conviction (Recommendation No. 38); extradition (Recommendation No. 39); an approach favoring the repression of antecedent crimes, money laundering, and terrorism financing (Recommendation No. 40).

International cooperation, however, requires more than just legal cooperation. It also requires administrative cooperation that not contingent upon indictments. In the latter case, all communication occurs through intelligence channels. Information is exchanged by direct cooperation among Financial Intelligence Units, the Attorney-Generals' Offices, and police authorities, of various countries.

Patrícia Núñez Weber explains as follows:

> International administrative cooperation is in the strictest sense not tied to any criminal demands or occurrences, but aimed at technological improvement, exchange of information, creation and maintenance of databases, and the sharing of strategies among the agencies involved. Yet the term is also used to designate cooperation among administrative authorities quite apart from court orders.[12]

This brings us to the possibility of direct exchanges of information, through the aforementioned intelligence channels. Most of the information would originate out of legal cooperation, under the aegis of the judicial branch, and notably in cases that require measures such as seizure and lifting of bank or tax record secrecy whenever a court order is needed.

Brazil's basic institutions for judicial cooperation on criminal matters include extradition, transfer of convicts, certification of a foreign criminal sentence, rogatory letters, and direct assistance. The latter two are intrinsically bound up with investigations and information on criminal activity, and, for this reason, are given greater attention here.

International legal cooperation, generally speaking, may be viewed as active or passive depending on the relative position of each of the States involved. It is active when the requesting State formulates a petition that a measure be taken and passive when a requested State receives a request for cooperation.

International legal cooperation may also be direct or indirect. It is direct when "the Court of Examination judge is fully apprised."[13] It is indirect when it is intrinsically related to the prima-facie evaluation, as in the case of letters rogatory transmitted to Brazil.

Incoming letters rogatory are received in Brazil through diplomatic channels, most notably through the Ministry of External Relations, and all active letters rogatory in Brazil lack the *exequatur.* The bureaucratic side of processing letters rogatory

---

[12] CARLI, Carla Veríssimo De (Org.). *Lavagem de dinheiro: prevenção e controle penal.* Porto Alegre: Verbo Jurídico, 2011, p. 589.

[13] Cf. CESTRI, Virgínia Charpinel Junges; TOFFOLI, José Antonio Dias. Mecanismos de Cooperação Jurídica Internacional no Brasil. *Manual de Cooperação Jurídica Internacional e Recuperação de Ativos* – Matéria Civil. Asset Recovery and the International Legal Cooperation Council Department, National Secretariat of Justice, Ministry of Justice. 2nd Ed. Brasília: 2009. p. 24.

led to an increase in direct assistance. Direct assistance allows authorities to get around the sending and procedural delays of letters rogatory by enabling direct transmission. It has emerged as the most effective alternative in the fight against international crime.

Through this form of cooperation, authorities other than the judiciary may avail themselves of international requests, and the procedures are much simpler than those involving traditional letters rogatory, and even dispense the prima-facie evaluation in Brazil.

This brings us back to the observations of Patrícia Núñez Weber, who assures us that:

> Direct assistance is cooperation offered by national authorities and likely to satisfy the foreign request, in the performance of their legal duties as though it were a national procedure, when in fact it arises from a request by a foreign State channeled through Brazil's central authority.
>
> (…)
>
> Currently, the most widespread understanding is that direct assistance presupposes the existence of a treaty or agreement with the requesting State, or a promise of reciprocity. Our feeling is that that restriction arises from the relatively recent arrival of the institution on the international scene, compared to letters rogatory.[14]

With direct assistance, once the request is received by the central authority and forwarded to judicial authorities, the judge may examine the facts presented by the foreign nation on their merits, much as in domestic proceedings to which procedural rules would apply. This is something that does not happen with rogatory letters.

Requests for direct assistance are generally couched in terms of international treaties or agreements. One approach is through the application of reciprocity, according to which governments may cooperate with one another in the absence of some previous treaty or international agreement, acting through mutual commitments undertaken in dealing with a specific case.

For example, José Antônio Dias Toffoli and Virgínia Charpinel Junger Cestari explain as follows:

> Requests for direct assistance are, as a rule, couched in terms of bilateral treaties or agreements (the so-called Mutual Legal Assistance Treaties or MLATs). Absent any express understanding between the two States, assistance can still be provided based on the requester's assurance of reciprocity. This allows cooperation in many different tax, labor or pensions-related areas. Still, the treaties most frequently encountered in an international setting have to do with criminal and civil subject matters.[15]

---

[14] CARLI, Carla Veríssimo De (Org.). *Lavagem de dinheiro: prevenção e controle penal*. Porto Alegre: Verbo Jurídico, 2011, pp. 593–602.

[15] CESTRI, Virgínia Charpinel Junges; TOFFOLI, José Antonio Dias. Mecanismos de Cooperação Jurídica Internacional no Brasil. Manual de Cooperação Jurídica Internacional e Recuperação de Ativos – Matéria Civil. Asset Recovery and the International Legal Cooperation Council Department, National Secretariat of Justice, Ministry of Justice. 2nd Ed. Brasília: 2009. p. 27.

How to determine which acts require a granting of *exequatur* (in passive cooperation) and which require issuance of rogatory letters (for active cooperation) for their proper performance is a question that calls for a comprehensive analysis.

The Brazilian Superior Court of Justice did shed some light on how it handles cases of international legal cooperation in its Resolution No. 9 of April 5, 2005. Specifically, Article 7 addresses the direct assistance mode of cooperation, and provides that when a request calls for judicial consideration, it should be brought to the judicial notice of the court of first instance:

> Article 7. Letters rogatory may request decisional acts or non-decisional acts.
>
> Sole paragraph. Requests for international cooperation which do not involve prima-facie evaluation by the Superior Court of Justice shall—even if classified as letters rogatory—be forwarded or returned to the Ministry of Justice so that all necessary steps may be taken to comply with them by direct assistance.

One can infer from this provision that the granting of *exequatur* may be waived, allowing the central authority to take all appropriate action to provide direct assistance.

The First Panel of the Supreme Federal Court has made a declarative statement as to the need for a granting of *exequatur* by the Superior Court of Justice for acting on indictments issued by foreign judicial authorities, stating as follows:

> CRIME – INTERNATIONAL COOPERATION – ENFORCEMENT – INVESTIGATIONS – NATIONAL TERRITORY – MEANS.
>
> Engaging in law enforcement actions within Brazilian national territory to enforce orders issued by foreign judicial authorities presupposes the transmission of a letter rogatory, for purposes of enforcement, to be passed on by the Superior Court of Justice, there being no proper way to bring about international cooperation at the cost of relegating to a lesser role a formality essential to the validity of the acts to be performed.[16]

Afterward, the Special Court of the Superior Court of Justice was able to have its say in the matter, in Complaint No. 2645/SP, reported by Minister Teori Albino Zavascki, by showing that the rogatory letter procedure ought only to be followed for requests of a jurisdictional nature formulated by the foreign authority, and that all other solicitations ought to comply with the requirements set by international regulatory bodies.

[16] STF – Habeas Corpus No. 85.588/RJ, Rapporteur: Minister Marco Aurélio. First Panel. Daily Judicial Gazette, Dec. 15, 2006, p. 95

At an opportune time, amidst allegations of usurpation of jurisdiction of the Superior Court of Justice for the granting of *exequatur* for rogatory letters, the Superior Court of Justice authorized, at the request of the Office of the Federal Prosecutor, the shipment of the hard drive confiscated from the computer in possession of a defendant to the Russian Federation's Attorney-General's Office, in response to a request transmitted by the Russian Assistant Attorney General.[17]

[17] *The Office of the Federal Prosecutor in making the complaint sought to assemble an exhibit with all documents (in Russian and in English) and forward it on to the Attorney General for the Russian Federation, along with corresponding official translations (folios 163–165). In the opening statement of the acknowledgment of receipt of that exhibit (folios 167/168), this Court ordered that Attachments be compiled to include all documents alluded to, and they were named as follows: 'Attachments VII and VIII.' The following was granted on an item 'c' of the decision set forth on folios 169–214, the petition likewise formulated by the Attorney General's Office for forwarding copy of the hard drives to the Office of the Attorney General of the Russian Federation, as requested by that Authority. The devices in question were at the Federal Police Intelligence Bureau in Brasilia for forensic analysis and were apprehended in May 2006 in the possession of Boris Abramovich Berezovisk, pursuant to a search warrant, as well as a bench warrant naming the suspect, who was then taken to the Office of the Attorney General in this capital city to depose on facts being investigated in Brazil and theoretically related to the racketeering offense (Art. 288 of the Criminal Code), given the suspect's supposed association with other persons for the constant and ongoing purpose of engaging in illegal 'laundering' of money, by exploiting the partnership entered into between MSI and Sport Club Corinthians of São Paulo. At the time of the seizure, consideration was also given to the fact that the suspect had entered Brazil using the name Platon Ilyich Yelenin, and was also included in the Red Notice issued by Interpol requesting that the individual be located and arrested for extradition, even though at the time the warrant had not been through proceedings in Brazil for purposes of certification by the Supreme Federal Court (folios 932–934, 1052, 1057–1060, 1061, 1063–1064, 1065–1072, 1082–1084, 1092, 1094 and 1098 of record No. 2006.61.81.005118-0/Attachment VII, admitted in connection with the Criminal Action). The copies in question were forwarded through official communiqué No. 1040/2007-rba dated 09/28/2007 to his Excellency, Russia's Ambassador to Brazil Wladimir Turdenev, for forwarding to the Attorney General's Office in Russia (See folio 75 of the Addendum compiled pursuant to Order No. 18/2005 of this Court). The Russian Federation, like Brazil, is a signatory to the UN Convention against Corruption known as the Mérida Convention, after the Mexican city in which it was signed. It has been signed by 150 countries, 95 of which enforce it internationally, foremost among them being Argentina, Australia, Spain, the United States, China, France, and the United Kingdom. The procedure adopted by this Court in response to the request formulated by the Ministry follows the recommendations set forth in that Convention, notably in the chapter relating to International Cooperation in its Articles 43 and 46, among others, and by the 2000 UN Convention at Palermo on transnational organized crime, in particular in its Articles 18, 27, and 28. And this was accomplished with no deviation from Brazil's own legal proceedings, inasmuch as it also followed the form outlined in Article 7 of Resolution No. 09 of 05/04/2005 by the President of this Respectable Court, to wit: 'Art. 7. Letters rogatory may request decisional acts or non-decisional acts. Sole paragraph. Requests for international cooperation which do not involve prima-facie evaluation by the Superior Court of Justice shall—even if classified as letters rogatory—be forwarded or returned to the Ministry of Justice so that all necessary steps may be taken to comply with them by direct assistance.' Direct assistance, absent better options, follows from the application of the rules of procedure of the Mérida and Palermo Conventions as from the measure requested by the Office of the Federal Prosecutor, to say nothing of the policy of reciprocity which, in the absence of specific rules, underlies international relations. This is why it was unnecessary to raise the issue of the granting of exequatur as set forth in Article 105, subsection I, clause 'i' of the Federal Constitution. In fact, the Palermo Convention stipulates the duty of mutual legal assistance between the Parties when the Requesting State has reasonable grounds to suspect a transnational infraction, and hence the duty to provide all legal cooperation (Article 18, items 1 and 2), to which is added the*

recommendation that special investigative techniques be used, such as electronic eavesdropping (Article 20, item 1). It further provides an interchange of information to keep the State Parties apprised of trends in organized crime in their territory, of the circumstances in which it operates and of professional groups and technologies involved, and may, to that end, be shared among them (Article 28, items 1 and 2). Furthermore, and in particular, this cooperation is aimed toward detecting and tracking the proceeds of crime, transfer methods, and the dissimulating or disguising of these proceeds in the 'fight against money laundering and other financial crimes' (Article 29, item 1, 'd'). The international treaty in question, now duly integrated as the law of the land, provides a basis for the investigation, but in addition, urges the State Parties to effectively repress transnational criminal organizations. The UN Conventions against Organized Transnational Crime and against Corruption, it can actually be said, amount to an attempt by all sovereign states to eliminate groups rooted in a certain criminal milieu which systematically resorts to obstruction of justice—in addition to engaging in criminal behavior which affronts the rule of law, and often operates by what amounts to intimidation. What we have here are global legal guidelines. There has been no news yet of forensic analysis of the hard drives, but please note that documented proof by examination was already on the record before this Court, for it was produced on account of the search warrant issued by the Brazilian Federal Justice System in May 2006 in record of proceedings under No. 2006.61.81.005118-0/Attachment VII, as we have seen, and THIS DID NOT RESULT from any request submitted by a foreign authority, so that the prima-facie evaluation was never an issue. This is simply a case of sharing legitimate evidence produced here. In the Complaint lodged before this Honorable Court, Plaintiff also holds that the official foreign documents were neither translated into Portuguese nor stamped with diplomatic or consular certification required to make them stand up in any court of law, and further postulates renewed application of Code of Criminal Procedure Articles 780 et. seq. [Jurisdictional Relations with Foreign Authorities], as previously submitted on occasion of filing for Habeas Corpus No. 2007.03.00.091069-0. No such argumentation would apply absent additional information, at the heart of a Complaint expostulating only about jurisdiction. In any case, in the aforementioned writ, in proceedings before the Second Panel of the Hon. Regional Federal Court for Region 3, the petition was not granted by the Eminent Rapporteuse for the Habeas Corpus, Her Excellency, Federal High Court Justice Cecília Mello. The foreign language document in question is accompanied by a certified translation, in full compliance with Code of Criminal Procedure Article 236. Hence no taint of irregularity or affront to the law may be ascribed to the admission of those documents, for what we have is a true copy duly forwarded by an agency of the Russian Government. This Court also understands that the provisions contained in Articles 780 et seq. of the Code of Criminal Procedure do not apply as claimed in the Complaint, for the instant case does not involve transmittal of letters rogatory. The reasons set forth in the documents comprising the record are beyond reproach, inasmuch as all provisions of the Code of Criminal Procedure which govern the matter have been fully complied with. Observe that the Claimant, in the reasons for filing the aforesaid writ acknowledged that the '... Code of Criminal Procedure contained no specific provision on admissibility of foreign documents intended as evidence in criminal proceedings...' that only being expressly required for letters rogatory (folios 952–953). The admissibility of the foreign documents is in order, in no small part for having been obtained from a foreign authority free of any imputations of illegal behavior given the absolute lack of any grounds for indicating such a thing. There is no denying that international recommendations now seek to simplify procedures and international cooperation, provided there is not, as in this case, any reason to question authenticity, and also provided there is no infringement of our national legal system. Even absent all of the above, one could still argue that the Claimant is a Russian citizen and has resided in the United Kingdom for a considerable time, circumstances that warrant the conclusion that both Counsel and Claimant ought to be familiar with the probative material. Indeed, the aforementioned Article 236 of procedural law does not even require the translation where it is patently unnecessary. Although this Court has been unable to discern any irregularity in the documentation forwarded by the Russian Authorities, it has been previously noted that if the Defense so wishes, the Defense could produce a new translation of the documents so as to clear up its misgivings. And so it did, inasmuch as it requested the translation into Portuguese of all documents contained in folios 08, 11 and 12 of Attachment No. 12, which request was met by the order issued on 11/14/2007 (folios 1392 and 1400–1414).

By the understanding set forth in the decision, the constitutional requirement contained in Article 105, subsection I, item i, does not grant exclusivity to the Superior Court of Justice to intermediate all international legal cooperation.

Thus the request for legal cooperation formulated by a foreign authority (in this case, the Office of the Attorney General for the Russian Federation, regarding the sharing of evidence during an ongoing investigation and transmitted to its Brazilian counterpart, Brazil's Office of the Attorney General) was not contingent upon issuance of a rogatory letter by Russian judicial authorities, thereby obviating the need for an *exequatur* from the Superior Court of Justice.

For a clearer understanding I call attention to an excerpt from the vote cast by the eminent Rapporteur, Teori Albino Zavascki:

> The international system of legal cooperation clearly does not exclude cooperative measures among agents of the judiciary brought about through the use of letters rogatory, within the scope of proceedings already within the jurisdictional sphere. But in addition to these, as pointed out, mutual cooperation encompasses a host of other provisions which may even, where applicable, give rise to future criminal prosecutions. Yet insofar as their scope is restricted to prevention and investigation, they require for their performance no prior approval or judicial intermediation. There is no such requirement in Brazil's domestic law, nor is there any reason for such a requirement in the area of international law.
>
> In Brazilian law, as in most countries, the prevention and investigation of crimes, not jurisdictional by nature, is not the purview of the Judicial Branch, but rather, of police authorities or the Office of the Public Prosecutor, under the Executive Branch.
>
> Indeed, the nature of jurisdictional questions—which as a rule are submitted to formal, public, adversarial proceedings—is neither proper to nor compatible with typical police matters, such as these now under consideration, involving prevention and criminal investigation. In our system, only a few such measures require prior judicial approval, such as in the case of those requiring entry into an individual home, or wiretaps (Federal Constitution, Art. 5, XI and XII).
>
> Aside from these cases, there is no reason at all—even in the case of investigations or preventive measures undertaken during international cooperation efforts—to impose jurisdictional boundaries on these activities, thereby rendering them subject to intermediation or advance prima-facie evaluation by agencies of the corresponding Judicial Branch. Because it takes account of such circumstances, the international legal cooperation system, in which Brazil participates, reflects and honors the system of duties and assignments already in place in domestic law, and strictly and fully preserves all of the constitutional duties of the Judicial Branch, including those having to do with jurisdictional considerations affecting the standing of the agencies and authorities involved to take action.[18]

Moreover, the subject of actual standing to issue a rogatory letter to Brazil was quite recently raised by the First Supreme Federal Court Panel in the Clarification Requests on *Habeas Corpus* Declaration No. 87,759/DF, reported by Minister Marco Aurélio, in which the Clarification Requests were honored in order to state that the Italian Attorney General's Office did indeed have standing to issue them:

> APPEALS REQUESTING CLARIFICATION – OMISSION. Once an omission was found in the judgment, faced with the treaty of cooperation on criminal matters entered into

[18] Rcl. 2.645/SP, Rapporteur Minister TEORI ALBINO ZAVASCKI, Special Court, decided on Nov. 18, 2009, Gazetted on Dec. 16, 2009).

between Brazil and the Republic of Italy—as part of its national legal process—honoring the appeals for clarification would follow, albeit with no power to bring about change, it being recognized that the Italian Attorney General's office does have standing to issue letters rogatory.[19]

Initially when the *habeas corpus* petition was granted, it was understood that the rogatory letter had not been issued by a judicial authority, which would have violated the provisions of Article 202, subsection I of the Brazilian Code of Civil Procedure, which regulates the *indication of courts of origin*, so that international cooperation through letters rogatory transmitted by a foreign Attorney General's office would cease to exist.[20] In accordance with the precedent set by the Supreme Federal Court in examining the Explanatory Restatement of Decisions, account was taken of Article 784 of the Code of Criminal Procedure, which makes provisions concerning *competent foreign authorities*, inasmuch as it allows a broader interpretation of *judicial authority* for purposes of transmitting rogatory letters to Brazil to include agencies clothed in judicial powers.

Legislative Decree No. 501 of March 21, 2012,[21] published in the Federal Official Gazette on March 23, 2012, made provisions regarding the procedures for handling

[19] HC 87759 ED, Rapporteur(euse): Min. MARCO AURÉLIO, First Panel, decided 12/13/2011, UNANIMOUS PANEL RULING DJe-053 RELEASED 03/13/2012, GAZETTED 03/14/2012.

[20] However, in examining the appeals requesting clarification, the Rapporteur noted that: *There was warning of a defect, at the beginning of the voting, in that it had not been issued by a judicial authority per se, which brought up the provisions of Article 202, subsection I of the Code of Civil Procedure. It was deemed apropos to remark on not having taken proper account of the fact that Article 784 of the Code of Criminal Procedure makes reference to letters rogatory issued not from judicial authorities, but from competent foreign authorities. Moreover, consonant with item 1 of Article 1 of the Treaty on Legal Cooperation in Criminal Matters entered into between Brazil and the Republic of Italy—promulgated through Ministerial Decree No. 862 of July 9, 1993—"each of the parties shall, on request, provide to the other party, in the form set forth in this Treaty, ample cooperation for criminal proceedings conducted by the judicial authorities of the requesting party." The reference to judicial authorities by the requesting party suggests, initially, agencies clothed in judicial appointments, as in the Brazilian system. However, in Italy, the Attorney General's office is part of the judicial system, per Articles 107, 108 and 112 under the title headed "The Courts" (Italian Constitution, Part II, Title IV). The judicial branch is organized institutionally in a linear fashion, within that same Branch, its duties involving judgment or work traditionally included in the area reserved to the Office of the Public Prosecutor. Briefly, it is a blending of functions, all of them subject to the Superior Council of the Courts. As pointed out by best doctrine, the Attorney General's Office in Italy is an agency for the administration of Justice, and includes all measures that may be taken there for purposes of criminal investigations. See "O Ministério Público na Investigação Penal Preliminar," by Marcos Kac. Hence, the Supreme Court of Justice, in Letter Rogatory No. 998/IT, through a unanimous panel decision authored by Minister Humberto Gomes de Barros, concluded: "The Attorney General's Office together with the Tribunal of Parma does have standing to request Brazilian cooperation in investigations."*

[21] *Art. 1 – This Decree establishes procedures for letters rogatory and both active and passive requests for direct assistance in criminal and civil matters in the absence of any bilateral or multilateral international legal cooperation agreement, and applies only subsidiarily to this case. Art. 2 – The following considerations apply for purposes of this Decree: I. Request for passive direct assistance, the request for international legal cooperation which does not require a prima-facie evaluation by the Superior Court of Justice, pursuant to Art. 7, of Superior Court of Justice*

Resolution No. 9 of May 4, 2005; and II. Passive letter rogatory, a request for international legal cooperation which does require a prima-facie evaluation by the Superior Court of Justice. Sole Paragraph. Definition of the request for active direct support and an active letter rogatory is in accordance with the domestic legislation of the Requested State. Art. 3 – In all cases in which the request for passive international legal cooperation does not entail the granting of exequatur by the Superior Court of Justice, and may be handled through administrative channels, not requiring intervention by the Judicial Branch, the Ministry of Justice shall, together with the competent administrative authorities, see to its granting. Art. 4 – The Ministry of External Relations shall forward to the Ministry of Justice all requests for passive international legal cooperation, on criminal and civil matters, transmitted through diplomatic channels. Art. 5 – In the absence of bilateral or multilateral international legal cooperation agreements, the Ministry of Justice shall forward to the Ministry of External Relations all active requests for international legal cooperation on criminal and civil matters, to be handled through diplomatic channels. Art. 6 – The Ministry of Justice shall: I. Provide attachments and opinions to and coordinate the granting of requests for international legal cooperation in criminal and civil matters, by forwarding these to the competent judicial or administrative authority; II. Issue and publish understandings on international legal cooperation within the scope of its powers. Art. 7 – Letters rogatory must include: I. Identification of the requesting and requested courts; II. The address of the requesting judge; III. A detailed description of the measure requested; IV. The purpose to be achieved by the requested measure; V. Complete name and address of the person to be cited, notified, served a summons or questioned in the jurisdiction of the requested court, and, if possible, full particulars, specifying the mother's name, date of birth, place of birth and passport number; VI. Closure, with the judge's signature; and VII. Any other information which might be of use to the requested court for purposes of facilitating compliance with the letter rogatory. § 1 – Should a requested measure consist of interrogation of the party or questioning of a witness, it is recommended, under penalty of inability to comply with the measure, that the letters rogatory further include: a) The text of the questions to be asked by the requested court; b) Setting up a hearing, beginning with the transmittal of the letter rogatory to the Ministry of Justice, with a lead-time of at least: (i) Ninety (90) days, for criminal matters; and (ii) One hundred eighty (180) days, for civil matters. § 2 – In the event of civil cooperation, letters rogatory must also include, where appropriate, the full name and address of the person responsible, at the addressee end, for payment of court costs and procedural fees arising from performance of the letter rogatory in the requested country, except for those taken from actions: I. Handled under the auspices of free justice; II. For the sending of foodstuffs abroad, for countries bound by the New York Convention, promulgated in Brazil by Ministerial Decree No. 56826 of September 2, 1965, pursuant to Article 26 of Law No. 5478 of July 25, 1968; III. Coming under the jurisdiction of child and adolescent courts, pursuant to Law No. 8069 of June 13, 1990. Art. 8 – Letters rogatory must be accompanied by the following documents: I. Initial petition, criminal information or complaint, depending on the nature of the matter; II. Background documents; III. Court order for its transmittal; IV. Original copy of the official or certified translation of the letter rogatory and all accompanying documents; V. Two original copies of the letter rogatory, of the translation and all accompanying documents; and VI. Other documents or exhibits considered indispensable by the requesting court, in accordance with the nature of the action. Sole paragraph. Where the purpose of the letter rogatory is forensic examination of a document, it is recommended that the original be sent to the requested court, the copy remaining in the record of the requesting court, otherwise the measure may not achieve fruition. Art. 9 – All petitions for direct assistance must include: I. Indication of provision contained in an international bilateral or multilateral legal cooperation agreement or reciprocity agreement; II. Indication of the requesting authority; III. Indication of Central Authorities in both requesting and requested States; IV. Summary containing the number(s) of proceedings or lawsuits in their requesting State, to serve as the basis for the request for cooperation; V. Complete and accurate particulars on all persons to whom the request makes reference (name, last name, nationality, birthplace, address, birth date and, wherever possible, mother's name, profession and passport number); VI. A clear,

letters rogatory and requests for direct assistance, after the Ministry of Justice and Ministry of External Relations modernized their rules for handling requests for international cooperation, always trying to make the procedures move faster. Article 3 of this decree establishes that whenever the request can be granted administratively, that is, with no intervention from the Judiciary, action on the part of the Superior Court of Justice may be dispensed with, and the Ministry of Justice shall see to the performance by the competent administrative authorities.

The institution of Central Authority came about to speed up and facilitate cooperation between countries. As the name itself suggests, the primary role of the Central Authority is to function as a centralizing agency for all cooperation—requests and investigations alike—whether coming from abroad or transmitted from Brazil. All rogatory letters and requests for legal assistance, whatever their purpose, shall be handled through the intermediation of central authorities.

In Brazil, as in most countries, the Central Authority lies in the executive branch, given that it typically represents the State in international relations.[22] The Central Authority is an idea espoused in the Hague Conventions and international conventions on public international law, arising out of the need to have an agency in each country to regulate the administrative procedures for International Legal Cooperation.

Its creation was imperative given the increase in volume and complexity of mechanisms for international cooperation. It imparts uniformity of performance,

objective, concise and complete narrative couched in the actual verbiage of the request for international legal cooperation, of the events which gave rise to it, to include: a) Place and date; b) Causal nexus between the ongoing proceedings, all those involved, and measures solicited in the request for assistance; and c) All documentation attached to the request. VII. References to and full transcripts of all applicable laws and regulations, especially, on criminal matters, criminal laws; VIII. Detailed description of the assistance requested, indicating: a) In cases of tracing or freezing of bank accounts, the account number, the name of the bank, the bank location and the endpoints of the desired timeframe, along with specific instructions as to how the documents to be obtained shall be forwarded (physical or electronic media); b) In cases requiring notice, citation or summonses, full particulars on the person to be served notice, cited or issued a summons, and the corresponding address; c) In cases of interrogations and questioning, the list of questions to be asked. IX. Description of the purpose of the request for international legal cooperation; X. Any other information which might prove useful to the requested authority, for purposes of facilitating the granting of the request for international legal cooperation; XI. Other information solicited by the requested State; and XII. Signature of the requesting authority, location and date. Art. 10 – This Decree revokes Foreign Office/Justice Ministry (MRE/MJ) Interministerial Order No. 26 of August 14, 1990, and the MRE/MJ Interministerial Order of September 16, 2003, published in the Federal Official Gazette on September 19, 2003. Art. 11 – This Order shall take effect as of the date of its publication.

[22] According to Goal No. 02 of the National Strategy for the Fight Against Money Laundering Report (ENCLA, now the National Strategy for the Fight Against Corruption and Money Laundering) of 2004, requests for active international cooperation from the Judicial Branch or the Office of the Public Prosecutor and federal and state police authorities, regarding authorization for direct cooperation on operations (which require an international reciprocity agreement), all go through the Ministry of Justice Asset Recovery and International Legal Cooperation Council Department (DRCI) (Art. 13, IV, of Decree No. 4991 of February 18, 2004).

standardizes all procedures, and provides the necessary specialization for handling such matters, avoiding duplication and waste in the requests.

There are countless advantages to the institution of a single Central Authority: specialization, speed, efficiency, publicity, and affordability of proceedings. It is argued that placing Central Authority in the executive branch will also ensure neutrality, transparency, and due process, inasmuch as executive branch agencies are subject to oversight by the Office of the Public Prosecutor and their acts are subject to review by the Judicial Branch.[23]

It is important to mention that Central Authority is by no means a *sine qua non* for making international cooperation feasible. Cooperation may occur directly between the competent authorities. The institution of a Central Authority can help bring these authorities closer together to eliminate obstacles in the way of a rapid fulfillment of shared national interests. Indeed, there is no point in demanding the establishment of a Central Authority unless it is committed to achieving efficiency, simplification, and speed in transmitting information and acting on requests.

Freezing and seizure operations require significant efforts and hard work. It is not enough to simply attach a court order. One typically has to turn over convincing documents to establish a link between assets or a bank account and illegal activity. It helps if the goods in question are the proceeds from criminal activity abroad or at least flow (by action or omission) from corrupt practices. Legal assistance has allowed the freezing and repatriation of assets, but often requires an affidavit—an internally consistent sworn statement—to enable such measures as freezing assets or bank accounts.[24]

A case that had an important impact on U.S. asset forfeiture legislation is the one in which Brazil filed for freezing of assets belonging to a Brazilian defendant, and for keeping those assets in the United States. An issue was whether, based on 28

---

[23] The great challenge at this point is to further popularize the benefits of adopting a single Central Authority for all International Legal Cooperation issues, and broaden the horizon of this institution. With the assistance of the policies of Brazil's Justice Ministry, through the National Anti-Money Laundering Qualification and Training Plan (PNLD), the idea is being spread that, even in the absence of an agreement, it is possible to have requests for active or passive cooperation routed through the Central Authority.

[24] Brazilian Congressman Eduardo Valverde submitted a bill (No. 1982, dated Sept. 16, 2003) to regulate International Legal Assistance on Criminal Matters, irrespective of the transmittal of letters rogatory. The bill, which is still pending in the Brazilian Congress, would provide for temporary administrative freezing of proceeds of crime undergoing laundering. It would also provide a *Council on International Legal Assistance*, empowered to formulate directives and serving as a permanent clearinghouse for information among the various government agencies it represents (the Federal Courts, Office of the Federal Prosecutor, Ministry of External Relations, Office of the Attorney General, Brazil's Federal Revenue Secretariat, the Central Bank, the Council for Financial Activities Control (COAF), the Federal Police Department, and the Office of the Comptroller-General), all offering guidance to Brazilian authorities needing to secure international cooperation.

U.S.C. § 246(d)(3), titled Enforcement of Foreign Judgment,[25] foreign assets may only be frozen after a foreign court has definitively ruled in favor of forfeiture, or if they may be frozen before any final decision on confiscation has been rendered. The United States Court of Appeals for the District of Columbia Circuit, on review of two lower-court decisions from March and April 2009, decided that a final decision by Brazil regarding confiscation was required, according to its interpretation of 28 U.S.C. § 2467(d)(3).[26] Following this decision, the U.S. Department of Justice requested and obtained from Congress a resolution of the problem because, if upheld and followed, the decision would have compromised international cooperation efforts with other countries.

The disposal of confiscated assets is provided in the 1988 UN Vienna Convention against Illicit Traffic in Narcotic Drugs (Article 5, item 5, clause b) and in the Convention at Palermo on Transnational Organized Crime (Article 30, item 2, clause c), and can stimulate cooperation among authorities in different countries.

Pursuant to the principle of specialization, applicable to relations among States and, therefore, to international legal cooperation efforts, no information or documents obtained through legal assistance may be used to prosecute crimes for which international cooperation is excluded on account of jurisdiction being regarded as an attribute of the State. Switzerland provides such an example, with regard to exchange quota violations.[27]

Insistence on dual criminality, that is, that the alleged behavior constitutes a crime in both of the jurisdictions involved in the request for legal assistance on criminal matters is a common requirement in cooperation cases—with the proviso that the two criminal categories need not be exactly the same, but only similar. Indeed, Article 43 of the UN Convention on Corruption signed at Mérida makes it clear that "in matters of international cooperation, whenever dual criminality is considered a requirement, it shall be deemed fulfilled irrespective of whether the laws of the requested State Party place the offence within the same category of offence or denominate the offence by the same terminology as the requesting State Party, if the

[25] 28 U.S.C. § 246: *(d) Entry and Enforcement of Judgment.—(1) In general.—The district court shall enter such orders as may be necessary to enforce the judgment on behalf of the foreign nation unless the court finds that—(A) the judgment was rendered under a system that provides tribunals or procedures incompatible with the requirements of due process of law; (B) the foreign court lacked personal jurisdiction over the defendant; (C) the foreign court lacked jurisdiction over the subject matter; (D) the foreign nation did not take steps, in accordance with the principles of due process, to give notice of the proceedings to a person with an interest in the property of the proceedings in sufficient time to enable him or her to defend; or (E) the judgment was obtained by fraud.*

[26] *United States v. Opportunity Fund and Tiger Eye Investments*, Ltd. No. 1:08-mc-0087-JDB, United States District Court for the District of Columbia. Decided 07/16/2012. http://www.cadc.uscourts.gov/internet/opinions.nsf/1B9DC0B1D05DB6D585257807007OEC9C/$file/09-5065-1255619.pdf. Accessed June 14, 2012.

[27] Pursuant to ENCLA 2005 Target No. 40, the Justice Ministry's Asset Recovery and International Legal Cooperation Council Department agreed to share *information on the need to keep within limitations on the use of documents obtained through International Legal Cooperation*, and reaffirmed the principle of specialization at the international level.

conduct underlying the offence for which assistance is sought is a criminal offence under the laws of both State Parties."

The rule cannot, however, be interpreted as an absolute. The Financial Action Task Force, pursuant to the UN Conventions of Vienna (international traffic, 1988), Palermo (transnational organized crime, 2000) and Mérida (corruption, 2003), advocates withdrawing obstacles (Recommendation No. 36) and providing direct mutual assistance toward a quick, constructive, and effective solution through international legal cooperation (Recommendation No. 37). Thus, not even the FATF gives the rule significant weight with regard to money laundering. Although the principle of dual criminality is important in international public law, it must be interpreted flexibly to enable international cooperation.

Brazil's Money Laundering Act (Act No. 9,613/1998, as amended by Law 12,683/2012) contains the following provisions on assets located abroad:

> **Art. 8.** The judge shall determine, given the existence of an international treaty or convention and by request of the competent foreign authority, measures to secure assets, securities or amounts proceeding from crimes described in Article 1, and committed abroad.
>
> § 1. All provisions contained in this article shall apply, irrespective of any treaty or international convention, whenever the government of the country whose authorities make the request promise reciprocity to Brazil.
>
> § 2. Absent a treaty or convention, all goods, securities or amounts subject to security measures at the request of the competent foreign authority—or the proceeds from their alienation—shall be divided equally between the requesting States and Brazil, following proper provisions for injured or good-faith third parties.

The UN Convention signed at Mérida (corruption) made no provisions regarding the division of goods there was an understanding that there ought to be full restitution of assets to the injured-party-State in view of the legal assets affected (Articles 51–59).

Finally, with regard to the seizure or freezing of assets, there are no obstacles to international application once the universal rule of reciprocity is in effect, and it is still possible to divide up the goods confiscated or seized, and consequently repatriate them, once the decision awarding forfeiture to the government becomes final. It is extremely difficult to obtain the repatriation of assets based only on an appealable decision, even if reciprocity is invoked.

The authorities of requested States usually wish to be informed regarding: (1) evidence that all owners, agents, curators, or others involved with the assets in question are aware of the issuance of an order that they should be seized, and of its content; (2) evidence to show that the Brazilian seizure order was signed prior to the legal sale or transfer of the assets abroad; (3) proof of direct association between the asset and the fraud detected in Brazil which would demonstrate that its acquisition does indeed flow from criminal behavior; (4) unavailability of the assets (e.g., works of art) precisely because such a procedure is public knowledge and one might therefore infer that the interested parties, curators, art dealers, and such had knowledge of the illegal events involving large holdings; (5) listing of all legal events (seizure orders, forfeitures, decisions that have become final) relating to the accused, including all corresponding dates.

At the first Judicial Roundtable Meeting between federal judges from Brazil and the United States, attended by several judges from Colombia and Mexico,[28] in Washington, D.C. on October 27–31, 2011, initial conclusions were drawn that the more the evidence, the easier the seizure, and that where drug trafficking is concerned, it is easier to secure the granting of the request because the laws are not as difficult to understand. The purpose of this unprecedented meeting was to establish a framework of judicial decisions to render international legal cooperation feasible and efficient.

The following ideas were presented at the Judicial Round Table Meeting:

JUSTIFICATION FOR LEGAL DIALOGUE AIMED AT ESTABLISHING CASE LAW PRECEDENT

WHEREAS there is a need to facilitate International Cooperation;

AND WHEREAS the fight against organized crime must not be defeated by lack of understanding regarding the various international legal systems;

AND WHEREAS explanation of domestic legal systems has converged on the stripping away of assets from criminal organizations from small conceptual changes;

AND WHEREAS standardization of judicial decisions to facilitate cooperation among all countries involved in the fight against organized crime is important;

AND WHEREAS there is a need for States to unite behind the seizure, confiscation and repatriation of goods, securities and money,

BE IT RESOLVED THAT WE ESTABLISH THE FOLLOWING TO ENSURE BETTER UNDERSTANDING TOWARD PROPER INTERNATIONAL COOPERATION WITH NEEDED STANDARDIZATION OF JUDICIAL DECISIONS:

1. The fight against crime is independent of the place where the crime was committed, and confiscation is indispensable;
2. Cooperation through Letters Rogatory is not recommended because it is slow and bureaucratic, and because analysis in the requested country is limited to checks on public policy and affronts to sovereignty;
3. Cooperation by Direct Assistance is a response to be followed by States because it is faster, based on mutual trust and conveys to the requested State a proper analysis of the requests;
4. The simplified Mutual Legal Assistance Treaty (MLAT) approach is recommended, and must be objectively clear;
5. Central authorities have placed no obstacles in the way of direct contact between magistrates or competent authorities, and channels of communication must be opened up to ease unnecessary bureaucratic burdens (Article 18.13 of the UN Convention against Organized Crime at Palermo does not prohibit such understandings);
6. The regular legal systems of countries involved must be respected (requesting and requested States), and it is no bar to cooperation if the request originated with or was addressed to the police, the Office of the Public Prosecutor, or the courts;
7. If Extradition is refused, on grounds of citizenship, then the persons believed to be involved ought to be promptly submitted to authorities in their own country (Art. 16.10, Palermo). However, if extradition is accepted, it is recommended that the

[28] Two judges per country, along with U.S. federal prosecutors, attended the meeting organized by the U.S. Department of Justice.

sentence be served out in the requested State (Art. 16.11, Palermo), otherwise, require serving the sentence or part of it in the requesting State (Art. 16.12, Palermo);

8. Possibility of joint prosecution or transfer of criminal proceedings (Art. 21, Palermo) for final disposal of assets and joint measures (cooperative debriefings with effects in both countries) and to achieve better administration of Justice;
9. International Cooperation ought not to be blocked while the whereabouts of an asset are unknown. The requested State should try all available measures for tracing or seizure for future confiscation or repatriation;
10. As a condition for restitution to the interested party, the requested State should provide proof of the legality of the asset, security or pecuniary amount whenever the requesting State requires seizure with an eye to confiscation or repatriation, but which request was mooted by legal decisions setting aside the merits as to its legal origin;
11. Invocation of absence of dual criminality cannot justify failure to cite or subpoena defendants, victims, witnesses, or affected third parties once criminal proceedings have been initiated in the requesting State;
12. Information gained for criminal proceedings may be used in other such proceedings if the requested State so authorizes, even if retroactively;
13. Assets, securities, or pecuniary amounts shall be restituted for indemnification of victims or to be turned over to the United Nations Fund for technical assistance among countries or even for reimbursement of the State. A division might be arrived that to deduct only expenses, except for such crimes as corruption and the like, and also with regard to cultural goods, which should be so disposed of as to give priority to public access;
14. Reimbursement of States lies outside the reach of the statute of limitations, which does not nullify International Cooperation;
15. What does negate International Cooperation is invocation of a need for a court order for a mere citation, subpoena or copies, and it is incumbent upon States to simplify their legal system to make Direct Assistance workable;
16. Defense witnesses ought to be heard in the country filing charges or, otherwise, by teleconference from embassies or consulates, with International Cooperation not being invoked except where the evidence is accepted by the prosecution;
17. International Cooperation does not require the attachment of proof, but rather, a presentation of arguments leading to the decision to see that measures be taken abroad;
18. No specific Mutual Legal Assistance Treaty is required for each asset, security or pecuniary amount if the requesting State attaches to its request a list of assets and gives grounds.

Bibliography

BALDWIN, Fletcher. Art Theft Perfecting The Art of Money Laundering. (Jan. 2009 for the 7th Annual Hawaii International Conference on Arts & Humanities). An unpublished work, sent to the U.S. Library of Congress on April 20, 2012, by University of Florida College of Law Professor Emeritus Levin, by request of the author.

CARLI, Carla Veríssimo De (Org.). Lavagem de dinheiro: prevenção e controle penal. Porto Alegre: Verbo Jurídico, 2011.

CESTRI, Virgínia Charpinel Junger, and TOFFOLI, José Antonio Dias. Mecanismos de Cooperação Jurídica Internacional no Brasil. *Manual de Cooperação Jurídica Internacional e Recuperação de Ativos* – Matéria Civil. Asset Recovery and the International Legal Cooperation Council Department, National Secretariat of Justice, Ministry of Justice. 2nd Ed. Brasília: 2009.

CHARNEY, Noah. The Mystic Lamb. The True Story of The World's Most Coveted Masterpiece. New York: PublicAffairs, 1st ed., 2010.

CONFISCATION and Asset Recovery: Better Tools to Fight Crime. States New Service, Brussels, Mar 12, 2012, www.lexis.com, accessed May 26, 2012.

GROS, Jean-Germain. Trouble in Paradise: crime and collapsed states in the age of globalization (in The British Journal of Criminology, 2003, v. 43, pp. 63–80).

HENRIQUES, Diana B. Madoff Is Sentenced to 150 Years for Ponzi Scheme New York Times, June 29, 2009, http://www.nytimes.com/2009/06/30/business/30madoff.html?pagewanted=all&_r=0

LOULA, Maria Rosa Guimarães. Auxílio direto: novo instrumento de cooperação jurídica internacional civil. Belo Horizonte: Fórum, 2010.

MAZZUOLI, Valério de Oliveira. Curso de Direito Internacional Público. 2nd ed. São Paulo: Ed. Revista dos Tribunais, 2007.

McCAW, Catherine. Forfeiture as a Form of Punishment: A Case for Integrating Asset Forfeiture into Criminal Sentencing. 38 American Journal of Criminal Law 181, 195 (2011).

MERCED, Michael J. De la, Prosecutors Try to Claim Madoffs's Properties New York Times, Mar. 17, 2009, B6.

PINHEIRO, Luís de Lima. *Direito internacional privado*. Vol. 1. Coimbra: Almedina, 2002.

REZEK, Francisco. Direito internacional público: curso elementar. 10th ed. São Paulo: Saraiva, 2005.

THE UNITED STATES DEPARTMENT OF JUSTICE, Asset Forfeiture Program, Annual Financial Statements, Fiscal Year 2013, Audit Report No. 14-08, February 2014, http://www.justice.gov/jmd/afp/01programaudit/index.htm, accessed Nov. 2, 2014, p. 6.

UNITED States v. Bajakajian, 524 U.S. 321, 330–31 (1998).

UNITED States v. One-Sixth Share, 326 F.Wd 36, 40 (1st Cir. 2003).

Chapter 6
Payments Through Illegal and Disguised Means, and the Misuse of Churches, Temples, NGOs, Trusts, Associations, and Foundations

The movement of criminal proceeds between States through the transportation of large sums in cash or stored value instruments, or through electronic transfers between bank accounts, or even black market moneychangers, is a real problem that must be stopped.

But money laundering can also occur through the mechanism of fraudulent payments, and there have been instances of misuse of money donated to churches and temples. For example, a church may pay a broadcaster for a prime time spot when it really occupies a different time, or it may simply overpay, in order to launder money. These amounts may be paid in cash or by some other untraceable means to further disguise the amount. Then again, when prices are pegged at artificially high levels, the launderer may wish to have illicit financing of his acquisition and will thus resort to corrupt appraisers and fake documentation.

No money-laundering crime should go unpunished because such impunity will surely perpetuate the commission of the crime.

There is much intelligence work to be done, more than that involved in simply controlling one's borders. Intelligence forces need to work together, for, if they are kept apart, each one of them may, in isolation, feel that someone else is responsible for the problem. We must approach the problem from a technical angle, because in many countries there is a perspective that fosters the adoption of solutions that are ineffective, poorly coordinated, and not cohesive.

6.1 Wire Transfers and Black Market Moneychangers

When religious people (in case of embezzlement) or businesspeople (when using churches or temples to commit tax fraud and money laundering) seek to send or receive money from unlawful behavior across national borders, undetected by government institutions, they have come to rely more and more on transfers known as

F.M. De Sanctis, *Churches, Temples, and Financial Crimes*,
DOI 10.1007/978-3-319-15681-1_6

dollar wires or Euro wires, operated by agents known as clandestine dollar-changers (*doleiros*) whose activities stretch the legal envelope.

Terry Goddard informs us that the Arizona Financial Crimes Task Force searches for financial anomalies and disproportionate events unconnected with economic reality. "They immediately saw that Arizona was a huge net importer of wired funds. At the top-ten Arizona wired-funds locations, over $100 were coming in for every dollar wired out. Wire transfers into Arizona from other states, in amounts over $500, totaled more than $500 million per year. Since there was no apparent business reason for this imbalance, the investigators took a closer look."[1]

For example, to preclude the use of fake identities for structuring or fragmentation of operations by companies and individuals in order to keep below the regulatory daily limit of $10,000 which would justify reporting the operation to the authorities, the State of Arizona established Geographic Targeting Orders (GTOs). GTOs require additional identification, such as fingerprints and signatures, from all persons receiving wire transfers in excess of $500. Based on such information, twenty-five warrants were issued in 2001 through 2006 for the seizure of wire transfers supposedly made in payment for human smuggling or narcotics trafficking.[2]

The Financial Action Task Force recommends that participating nations obtain detailed information on all parties involved in wire transfers, both senders and beneficiaries, for monitoring purposes. This would enable prohibiting transactions by certain people in accordance with UN Security Council Resolutions 1269/1999 and 1373/2001 on the prevention of terrorism and its financing (Recommendation No. 16).

Brazil's foreign-exchange legislation includes several regulations that are often unheard of, even in the United States. Take, for instance, Law No. 4,131 of October 19, 1962, which requires contracts for currency exchange operations:

> Art. 23. Operations on the free exchange rate market shall be conducted through establishments licensed to conduct foreign-exchange operations, with the intervention of an official broker whenever the law or regulations provide so, both of entities being required to know the client's identity, and how to correctly classify information provided by said client, pursuant to regulations established by Brazil's Currency and Credit Authority.
>
> (...)
>
> § 2 False statements of identity on the form which, in number of copies and following the model established by the Brazilian Central Bank shall be required in each operation to be signed by the client and checked and initialed by the banking establishment and broker therein intervening, shall render the banking establishment subject to charges for infraction, which carry a penalty of a fine in the amount of fifty percent (50 %) to three hundred percent (300 %) of the amount of the operation assessed against each of the violators. (New wording given by Law No. 9069 of 1995)
>
> (...)

[1] Cf. GODDARD, Terry. How to Fix a Broken Border: FOLLOW THE MONEY. Part III of III. American Immigration Council Publication. Immigration Policy Center, May 2012, p. 3.

[2] *Id.* p. 4.

§ 7 Completion of the form referenced in § 2 of this article is not required for foreign currency purchase and sale operations of up to three thousand dollars (US$3,000) or its equivalent in other currency. (Included by Law No. 11371 of 2006)[3]

Pursuant to Brazil's currency exchange regulations, remittance companies are required to conduct all of their operations exclusively through financial institutions duly licensed by Brazil's Central Bank, and this also holds for international banking institutions. They must have agreements on file with accredited banks to engage in exchange operations in Brazil, under penalties provided by several regulations, in particular, Law No. 9069 of June 29, 1995 (the *Lei do Plano Real*),[4] which established the real as Brazil's legal tender. The real is the currency used to settle all transactions in Brazil. Article 65 of Law No. 9069/1995 provides as follows:

Art. 65. The entry into and departure from Brazil of domestic and foreign currency must be processed exclusively through bank transfers, where banking establishments are required to fully establish the identity of the customer or beneficiary.

§ 1 Excepted from the provisions contained in the heading of this article is the transportation, in cash, of the following amounts:

I – When in Brazilian currency, up to ten thousand reals (R$10,000);

II – When in foreign currency, the equivalent of ten thousand reals (R$10,000);

III – When it can be shown to have entered or left Brazil in accordance with pertinent regulations.

§ 2 The National Monetary Council shall, according to the guidelines from the President of the Republic, regulate the provisions of this article and also provide limitations and conditions for entry into and exit from Brazil of national currency.

§ 3 Failure to comply with the provisions of this article shall, in addition to sanctions provided in specific legislation and following due legal process, entail forfeiture to the National Treasury of all amounts in excess of those set forth in § 1 of this article.

Brazilian Legislative Decree No. 857 of September 11, 1969 requires the use of national legal tender in all domestic operations, rendering null and void all operations stipulated in foreign currency or which would, in effect, restrict or refuse Brazilian currency as legal tender, but does list several exceptions to the ban.[5] In this regard, it provides as follows:

Art. 1 – All contracts, securities and documents, and bonds callable in Brazil, which stipulate payment in gold, in foreign currency, or in any way serve to restrict or refuse the cruzeiro as legal tender, are null and void by law.

Art. 2 – The provisions of the preceding article do not apply to:

---

[3] In www.planalto.gov.br/ccivil_03_leis/L4131.htm. Accessed July 16, 2012. The fact that the Central Bank deals more simply with amounts of up to $3,000, dispensing with the currency exchange agreement, in no way constitutes a waiver of the requirement that all debits and credits in customer accounts or through financial instruments be recorded so as to allow tracking of assets.

[4] See www.planalto.gov.br/ccivil_03/leis/L9069.htm. Accessed July 16, 2012.

[5] In www.planalto.gov.br/ccivil_03/Decreto-Lei/Del0857.htm. Accessed July 17, 2012.

I – Contracts and paper relating to the importation and exportation of goods;

II – Contracts for financing or putting up bonds or guarantees relating to the exportation of nationally-produced goods, sold abroad on credit;

III – Foreign-exchange purchase and sale agreements in general;

IV – Loans and any other obligations in which the creditor or debtor is a person residing and domiciled abroad, excepting only contracts for the lease or rental of real property within Brazilian territory;

V – Contracts for purposes of assignment, transfer, delegation, assumption or modification of obligations referenced in the preceding item, even if both parties to the agreement are residents of and domiciled in Brazil.

Sole Paragraph – Real property lease or rental agreements stipulating payment in foreign currency must, to be enforceable, be registered in advance with the Brazilian Central Bank.

Decree No. 23258 of October 19, 1933 provides that the purchase and sale of foreign currency shall be made exclusively in institutions authorized by the Brazilian Central Bank to engage in currency exchange operations, by establishing as follows:

Art. 1. All foreign exchange operations conducted between banks, natural persons or legal persons domiciled or doing business in Brazil, with any entities abroad—whenever such operations are made other than through banks licensed to operate in foreign exchange through prior accreditation by examiners on behalf of the Brazilian Central Bank—are considered illegal exchange operations.[6]

This set of codes (Law No. 4,131/1962, Article 23; Law No. 9,069/1995, Article 65, *caput*, and Legislative Decree No. 23,258/1933, Article 1) makes foreign exchange agreements mandatory (or, for operations of up to US$3,000, more simplified forms), establishes Brazilian currency (the real) as legal tender, requires identification of customers, and voids all foreign exchange operations not conducted through banks accredited by the Brazilian Federal Reserve ("Banco Central").[7]

By the rules of Brazil's Financial Intelligence Unit (COAF), the term "cash transfers" includes remittances but only applies to the mail and Brazilian postal money orders, both domestic and international, because everything coming from abroad and involving currency exchange operations comes under Central Bank supervision.

There are operators and currency brokers in the United States who make use of the gray market to allow transfers of money belonging to uninformed foreigners residing in Brazil. To stock its operations, Brazilian currency (reals), usually in cash and acquired from illegal conduct in Brazil, is deposited by the currency exchange into the accounts of beneficiaries of wire transfers coming from abroad, while the dollars or euros received from the senders (who are easy prey) are diverted to

[6] In www.planalto.gov.br/ccivil_03/decreto-1930-1949/D23258.htm. Accessed July 17, 2012.

[7] The International Capital and Foreign Exchange Market Regulations (RMCCI). www.bcb.gov.br/?RMCCI. Accessed July 18, 2012. Consolidate Brazil's currency-exchange regulations. Resolution No. 3568 of May 29, 2008 is the primary regulation http://www.bcb.gov.br/pre/normativos/busca/normativo.asp?tipo=Res&ano=2008&numero=3568. Accessed July 20, 2012.

redeem and deposit money as part of this bartering in funds. This is the so-called wire operation.

One should bear in mind that whenever the number of immigrants in a given location increases, there is a proportional increase in the gray-market transfer of money. Similarly, wherever there is an increase in illegal immigration, it becomes easier to commit financial crimes and go undetected.[8]

Another topic of concern is factoring companies that pump money into the accounts of wire transfer beneficiaries in the receiving country, thereby contributing to the offsetting of amounts in furtherance of an illegal black market of unauthorized financial dealings. Quite apart from their main purpose, which is short-term business financing of creditors' claims for goods and services provided on credit, the factor, or invoicer, is only required to keep a record of sales and perform administrative work relating to accounts receivable, receiving no sums and guarding against debtor insolvency.

According to the 1988 Convention on International Factoring held in Ottawa,[9] a factoring contract is a contract between two parties, the client (supplier) and the factor, and the factoring company should perform at least two of the following functions: (1) provide financing for the supplier, including loans and advances on payments; (2) maintain accounts related to the receivables; (3) collect of receivables; and (4) protect against default in payment by debtors. Nothing is said, therefore, about assisting remittance companies or currency brokers so as to obtain financial compensation on their balances.

According to Resolution No. 13 of the Council for Financial Activities Control (COAF), factoring companies are required to report to the council, even if not accredited as financial institutions by the Central Bank, which is why they do not apply for licenses or registration. The COAF code is intended, however, to make it possible to identify their owners and directors, perform due diligence on customers, and check whether internal controls are in place.

Something similar to the Peso Exchange Black Market, which has long served international drug trafficking, also occurs Brazil, with the establishment of the black market in reals.

Central Bank Circular No. 3542 of March 12, 2012 establishes in its Article 1, Part XI, a requirement for notifying the Financial Intelligence Unit if: the customer does not provide justification for the origin of the money, or if the amount is incompatible with the customer's financial strength (item f); there is financial incompatibility or absence of proper grounds for when resources originate abroad (item g); or payments occur abroad after deposit of credit in reals into accounts held by persons named in the currency exchange operations, absent any business or financial links (item j). The U.S. Financial Crimes Enforcement Network (FinCEN)

---

[8] For more on the influx of new immigrants who wire money back to their countries of origin, and their profiles, see *Briefing explores the factors that have influenced increases in remitting*, a publication of the Inter-American Dialogue, March 20, 2012, p. 1.

[9] See http://unidroit.org/english/conventions/1988/factoring/main.htm. Accessed July 10, 2012.

requires banks to perform due diligence on wire transfers to foreign agents or counterparties (31 CFR § 103).

This is why deposits are flagged as "irregular" when they originate from wire transfers with no identification of the depositor or when they are cash transfers to a beneficiary account from a company not authorized by the Central Bank to operate in the currency exchange market. An occasional such operation may be deemed acceptable if it has, in addition to an investigation as to the origin of funds, proof of deposit through a financial institution accredited by the Central Bank (such as a letter from the bank responsible for settling the operation). But as the general rule, only financial institutions are eligible to receive Central Bank authorization to operate in currency exchange markets.

Cases have been observed of payments for drugs through the use of remittances from the United States in a triangle involving Colombia, the United States, and Europe. Euros were brought in by mules (or smurfs) to Colombian currency exchanges, which shipped them to the United States, where they were bundled and sent to Europe, where the receiving company exchanged them for dollars which were then wired to the United States. These operations usually involve immigrants. With the arrival of greater numbers of immigrants in many, the number of transfers from one person to another increases annually.

It is common for churches and temples to handle cash. Especially if they are international institutions, however, they must manage this cash in a proper way to avoid its use by criminals. Also, many cases show that some of these religious organizations were conceived for embezzlement and to make their members wealthy. That is why it is important to carefully monitor and verify these actors who are becoming tools to disguise illegal cash flows.

6.2 The Misuse of Churches, Temples, NGOs, Trusts, Associations, and Foundations for Illegal Ends

The work of beneficent and religious entities is indeed important and significant, but unfortunately, scandals have stained some of their images and have opened the door to an increase in judicial actions against their directors and leaders. Because their work is philanthropic, and they are generally motivated by altruism, divinity, and compassion, charities, churches, and temples have historically been immune to legal proceedings. But more and more often, they are being made to answer to a variety suits—everything from labor suits to fraud, and even money laundering by reason of insolvency, negligence, or poor practices. A church's entire board of directors or leaders might be held liable for some failure of accounting or diversion of funds.

Churches, temples, nongovernmental organizations, trusts, associations, and foundations tend to be as diverse as a country's population. People are increasingly getting involved in some kind of social or charity effort, and donations to these entities can be considerably large.

Recent disclosures have tarnished the images of certain entities and brought the glare of publicity onto the conduct of some of their managers. A backlash of skepticism has brought about a proportional reaction affecting the volume of donations and volunteer work.

Because philanthropic and religious work is normally motivated by feelings of generosity and empathy, charitable organizations, churches, and temples often imagine themselves immune to legal proceedings. Liability could surface based on some poorly-handled internal activity, or some other cause occurring outside the organization. This is why the role of managers (priests, chaplains, reverends, pastors) is so important.

By the simple fact that they operate with personal and institutional donations, charity organizations, temples, churches, mosques, NGOs, educational associations, etc., often believe that they are not required to reveal the source of their funds, nor to be examined for the large financial transactions they conduct.

The U.S. Congress has, since 1917, allowed tax deductions for donations to charitable, religious, educational, and other such entities organized as nonprofit NGOs. A 1938 report from the House Committee on Ways and Means explains that tax revenue losses due to charitable donations are offset by easing the financial burden, which, through the resulting benefits, promotes the general welfare.[10]

According to Andrew Cuomo, philanthropic organizations "contribute substantially to our society. They educate our children, care for the sick, preserve our literature, art and music for us and for future generations, house the homeless, protect the environment and much more."[11]

The correctness of granting large tax deductions has been the subject of frequent debates assessing the law's effectiveness, purpose, and potential for abuse. These debates have led to changes in statutes and regulations governing charitable deductions.

Thus, a philanthropic donation in the United States must satisfy a complex set of rules to qualify as a tax deduction. These rules are grouped into three main requirements. First, the transfer must be sent to a qualified addressee.[12] Second, it must clearly state the purpose of the donation, that is, not be an exchange of goods or services.[13] And third, it must consist of a payment or other allowable goods.[14]

In the state of New York, for instance, in order for a foundation or NGO[15] to qualify for tax exemption, a license must be obtained and returns must be filed to the State tax authorities, under penalty of being closed down, by means of Form No. 990, which must be dated, properly signed under penalty of perjury, and contain

[10] THOMPSON, Erin. *The Relationship between Tax Deductions and the Market for Unprovenanced Antiquities*. 33 Colum. J.L. & Arts 241 (2010).

[11] Cf. Internal Controls and Financial Accountability for Not-for-Profit Boards. *Charities Bureau*. In http://www.oag.state.ny/bureaus/charities/about.html, p. 1. Accessed June 20, 2012.

[12] Cf. I.R.C. § 170 (c) (2006).

[13] See *Mcleman v. United States* (24 Cl. Ct. 109, 91–2 USTC 50, 447, 1991).

[14] In I.R.C. § 170 (e) (3) (2006).

[15] Provided they are also recognized as such in the U.S. tax code, also known as the Internal Revenue Code, Section 501 (c); 527; 4947 (a) (1).

the name and telephone number of the person who keeps books and records for the organization. A detailed list of all of the organization's activities, management, revenue, overhead, and liquid assets must be included on the form. It must also state the name and purpose of the institution; number of members; whether it has more than 25 % of its liquid assets on hand; number of voting members listed within or outside of the entity; number of employees; number of volunteers; revenues from unrelated businesses and taxes paid; contributions and donations; resources invested; benefits paid by and for members; total assets and obligations; basic description of all assistance programs; whether any loans or benefits are granted to or for employees, directors, trustees, or any other persons; the names, hours worked, and job descriptions of all employees and former employees (including directors, trustees, and key personnel); earnings made by these individuals, and expenses paid (including travel and leisure).

For gross revenues of up to $100,000, no external audits are required. From $100,000-$250,000, the information must be entered by an outside auditor (and documentation reviewed by that professional). This auditor, however, is not required to check the truthfulness of information obtained. In other words, it is not the auditor's job to check donor transactions or conduct the due diligence. But NGOs with gross annual revenues in excess of $250,000 are required to turn in an outside auditor's report, and that auditor must perform the due diligence.[16]

The Foundation Center, a U.S. center for information on foundations, has published some 29 standards. Brazil, meanwhile, has six unpublished standards (a true case of living in a glass house).[17]

Regarding churches and temples there are no similar requirements or standards, except the acknowledgment of the Internal Revenue Service.

Managers and employees of nongovernmental organizations must be answerable for their management and for the protection of the goods and services that benefit us all. A primary responsibility is to ensure proper accounting of funding received from their supporters (public or otherwise) and of expenses for social programs. This means they must strictly comply with the law and ethical standards, be committed to the mission of the NGO they represent, protect the rights of their members and, indirectly, of those assisted, and prepare annual reports for their country's federal revenue service and regulatory authorities having jurisdiction—reports that should be available to all interested parties. The organizations should therefore have ready access to technical resources to enable them to monitor and record all assets and amounts received, spent, and entrusted to their care.

The website of the National Association of State Charity Officials (NASCO) contains important information on recording and reporting required of NGOs.[18] NASCO members are employees of U.S. government agencies charged with regulating NGOs and their funds.

---

[16] Cf. www.charitiesnys.com/pdfs/statute_booklet.pdf. Accessed May 29, 2012.

[17] Information is provided by Patricia Lobaccaro on May 16, 2012. Ms. Lobaccaro is president and CEO of BrazilFoundation, with offices at 345 7th Ave., Suite 1401, New York City.

[18] www.nasconet.com. Accessed June 2, 2014.

Marion R. Fremont-Smith, who teaches Public Policy at the John F. Kennedy School of Government, produced an important comparison for Harvard University on the bookkeeping requirements for such organizations. She revealed that most U.S. states (for example, NY, CA, AK, MO, and NJ) require NGOs to have at least three directors.[19]

FATF Recommendation No. 8, in the spirit of clearly delimiting the rights and responsibilities of directors and employees of NGOs, encourages countries to establish good policy whereby information on their activities, size, and other important characteristics such as transparency, integrity, openness, and best practices can be had in real time for purposes of supervision and monitoring.

Terrorism financing through NGOs is a real danger. In Pakistan, the Central Bank has placed much stricter controls on NGOs and beneficent societies, ordering a complete review of all of their accounting, on pain of making them subject to penalties. The purpose was to establish a policy and a set of rules for compliance (to strengthen due diligence) and to protect them from the risk of money laundering and terrorism financing. All of the country's financial institutions are required to open accounts in the name of NGOs that match the documents submitted to them. In the event of an organization publicly soliciting donations or the like, accompanied by a bank account number, those financial institutions must promptly take note of and report that account in the event that the account owner of record does not match that of the publication.[20]

Pakistan has also adopted strict measures to curb money laundering and financing of terrorism by NGOs by putting in place a very broad know-your-customer policy. It requires photocopies of customer photo IDs (identification card or passport), and a copy of the assignment, if done through power of attorney. Companies must produce their charter, bylaws, and a list of directors. Similar documentation is required of individuals, as well as audit documents from clubs, associations, and nonprofit organizations.

In neighboring India, two government intelligence agencies were created to detect sources of funding used to finance terrorist activity. Analysts there believe that terrorist attacks in India are funded by neighboring countries through NGOs and nonprofits. Until recently, they had no way of checking on how funds from abroad, purportedly intended for health and education, would actually be used.[21] In 2010, there were some two million NGOs in India, but of that number, only 71 had requested any reimbursement for taxes paid. In 2009, there were 38,600 registered with the government to receive donations from abroad. Some are suspected of being

---

[19] *The Search for Greater Accountability of Nonprofit Organizations. Summary Charts: State Nonprofit Corporation Act Requirements and Audit Requirements for Charitable Organizations* (document obtained 05/16/2012 from Patricia Lobaccaro, president and CEO of the BrazilFoundation Foundation).

[20] Cf. Terror outfit-turned 'charity' JuD set to come under Pak Central Bank scanner. In *Asian News International*, Mar 13, 2012. www.lexis.com. Accessed June 19, 2014.

[21] In Prafulla Marpakwar. State forms cells to detect source of terror funds. *Times of India*. www.westlaw.com. Accessed June 19, 2014.

money laundering channels for the return of illegal cash received from Indian politicians or for terrorism financing.[22]

NGOs, associations, and foundations that lack proper controls are recognized today as channels for money laundering for organized crime. In fact, the Financial Action Task Force (FATF) has found that sums transferred from NGOs abroad have provided funding for the financing of terrorism on a par with counterfeiting, drug trafficking, extortion, and corruption. This has prompted India, for example, to assemble an umbrella database listing all NGOs in its jurisdiction.[23]

Thus, there are efforts underway in India to publicize the names of organizations (religious NGOs and trusts) requesting tax exemptions. One of India's wealthiest trusts collects huge sums of cash. At the time of writing, there are a number of laws and several states seeking to monitor the activities of these entities. Yet Parul Soni (of Ernst & Young Pvt. Ltd.) believes that federal legislation will be required to achieve bookkeeping transparency and to strengthen the reporting of suspicious activity in that sector.[24] It is important to note that money laundering is usually carried out using a layered structure to give the appearance of legality. One such method is to establish trust companies through which the company manages business for its clients, the beneficiary being one or more holding companies, or a series of companies in several tax havens, to create a separation between the aforesaid holding companies and their ultimate beneficiary. Moreover, the discovery of the real beneficiary requires considerable cooperation on the part of authorities in those tax havens. Some means would have to be established to require the trust to provide its beneficiaries' names whenever requested by the authorities. It is not even easy to establish who is in charge of the trust, for there is no obligation that that name be revealed. Hence, being its legal beneficiary is an enviable business—which may explain the rather timid recovery of illegal assets.

In India, trusts, temples, churches, mosques, nongovernmental organizations, and educational institutions registered as NGOs are now to reveal the sources of their funds and have their financial transactions closely scrutinized. This is because of new requirements set forth in the jurisprudence under India's Prevention of Money Laundering Act of 2002.

Indian attorney Bhusham Bahal tells us that the laundering of illegal money has been largely made possible by NGOs operated by powerful businessmen and top

[22] For more on this, see John Samuel Raja, in Ten means to put an end to black money issue. Economic Times (India). Copyright 2011 Bennett, Coleman & Co., Ltd., *The Financial Times Limited*, Nov. 18, 2011.

[23] Cf. Most recent FATF report in www.gafi-fatf.org, June 22, 2012; Government plans 'umbrella law' to tighten scrutiny and regulation of religious trusts and NGOs. *Economic Times* (India). Copyright 2011. Bennett, Coleman & Co. Ltd. May 3, 2011. www.westlaw.com. Accessed June 22, 2014.

[24] Cf. Government plans 'umbrella law' to tighten scrutiny and regulation of religious trusts and NGOs. *Economic Times* (India). Copyright 2011. Bennett, Coleman & Co. Ltd. 05/03/2011. www.westlaw.com. Accessed June 22, 2014.

politicians, so that this new instrument should prove to be of valuable assistance to authorities.[25]

The trump card in the Indian case is the requirement that sources of funds be revealed, so that know-your-customer policies have to be in place for donations received by the NGOs, as is already the case for financial institutions. They must also provide detailed information on investments and donations received, and anonymous donations are henceforth barred.[26]

In Canada, nongovernmental organizations are as diverse as the population. Many Canadians are involved in charity work, with estimates running to some 36 % of the population. Economically, the sector is a major player, inasmuch as two million people are employed within it, with another two billion hours voluntarily contributed. There are over 160,000 NGOs operating nationwide and 85 % of the population makes financial contributions to Canadian social entities.[27]

In conclusion, considerable customer due diligence should be required for churches and temples that accept donations. The donor's name or job title is no longer enough. The donor's purposes and actual financial position must be known (preferably face-to-face), a photo ID must be provided, and a signature or the signatures of those acting on his behalf must be submitted. The source of funding must also be disclosed and supported by documentation. In the case of a donor company, a copy of the bylaws should be acquired from the civil or deed registry having jurisdiction in order to check the list of directors. The true directors of the NGO or religious institutions must be known, again with photo ID, along with the scope of their authority, and all of this backed by documentation to properly support the information provided.

Bibliography

ANISTIA poderá coibir o 'esquema Daslu'. Colecionadores afirmam que sonegação continuará sendo praxe no meio enquanto carga tributária não diminuir. Folha de São Paulo, Jan. 1, 2012, Ilustrada supplement, p. E5.

BICKERTON, Rob. Good Cause. *Canadian Underwriter.* 01/25/2010. 2009 WLNR 26429376. www.westlaw.com. Accessed on June 23, 2014.

BRIEFING explores the factors that have influenced increases in remitting. *Inter-American Dialogue*, Mar 20, 2012.

CHRISTIE'S. http://christies.com/features/guides/buying/pay-ship.aspx. Accessed 06 May 2012.

CINTRA, Marcos Antônio. O Acordo de Basiléia e os bancos públicos. *Folha de São. Paulo*, São Paulo, Jan. 4, 2006.

COELHO, Fábio Ulhoa. *Curso de direito comercial*. 4th ed., vol. 1. São Paulo: Saraiva, 2000.

______. *O empresário e os direitos do consumidor.* São Paulo: Saraiva, 1994.

______ et al. *Comentários ao Código de Proteção ao Consumidor.* São Paulo: Saraiva, 1991.

[25] See Palak Shah. Trusts, NGOs under ambit of money-laundering law. *Business Recorder.* Recorder Report, 09/12/2009. WLNR 17872644. www.westlaw.com. Accessed on June 23, 2014.

[26] *Id.*

[27] For more on this, see Rob Bickerton Good Cause. *Canadian Underwriter.* 01/25/2010. 2009 WLNR 26429376. www.westlaw.com. Accessed on June 23, 2014.

CORREIA, Eduardo. A responsabilidade jurídico-penal da empresa e dos seus órgãos (ou uma reflexão sobre a alteridade nas pessoas colectivas à luz do direito penal). In: CORREIA, Eduardo et al. *Direito penal econômico e europeu: textos doutrinários*. Vol. 1. Coimbra: Coimbra Ed. 1998.

______, and PEDRAZZI, Cesare. *Direito Penal Societário*. 2nd ed. São Paulo: Malheiros, 1996.

______. Direito penal das sociedades anônimas. In: ANTUNES, Eduardo Muylaert (Coord.). *Direito penal dos negócios*: crimes do colarinho branco. São Paulo: Associação dos Advogados de São Paulo, 1990.

CUOMO, Andrew M. Internal Controls and Financial Accountability for Not-for-Profit Boards. *Charities Bureau*. http://www.oag.state.ny/bureaus/charities/about.html.

______. Right From the Start – Responsibilities of Directors and Officers of Not-for-Profit Corporations. http://www.oag.state.ny.us/bureau/charities/guide_advice.html.

DENICOLA, Robert. C. Access Controls, Rights Protection, and Circumvention: Interpreting the Digital Millennium. 31 Colum. J.L. & Arts 209 (Winter 2008).

DE SANCTIS, Fausto Martin. *Responsabilidade Penal das Corporações e Criminalidade Moderna*. São Paulo: Saraiva, 2009.

______. *Combate à Lavagem de Dinheiro. Teoria e Prática*. Millennium: Campinas, 2008.

______. *Punibilidade no Sistema Financeiro Nacional*. Campinas: Millennium, 2003.

______. *Responsabilidade penal das pessoas jurídicas*. São Paulo: Saraiva, 1999.

EIZIRIK, Nelson. *Instituições financeiras e mercado de capitais – jurisprudência*. Vol. 1–2. Rio de Janeiro: Renovar, 1996.

FERRARA, Francesco. *Le persone giuridiche*. Con note di Francesco Ferrara Junior. 2nd ed. Torino: UTET, 1958. (Trattato di diritto civile italiano, dir. Filippo Vassali, 2).

FOLEY, Rita Elizabeth. *Bulk Cash Smuggling. United States Attorney's Bulletin*. Washington, DC, vol. 55, no. 5, Sept 2007.

FREMONT-SMITH, Marion R. *The Search for Greater Accountability of Nonprofit Organizations. Summary Charts: State Nonprofit Corporation Act Requirements and Audit Requirements for Charitable Organizations* (document obtained from Patrícia Lobaccaro, president and CEO of Brazil Foundation).

GIORGI, Giorgio. *La dottrina delle persone giuridiche o corpi morali*. 3rd ed., vol. 1. Firenze: Fratelli Cammelli, 1913.

GODDARD, Terry. How to Fix a Broken Border: FOLLOW THE MONEY. Part III of III. American Immigration Council Publication. Immigration Policy Center, May 2012.

GOVERNMENT plans 'umbrella law' to tighten scrutiny and regulation of religious trusts and NGOs. *Economic Times* (India). Copyright 2011. Bennett, Coleman & Co. Ltd. May 3, 2011. www.westlaw.com. Accessed June 22, 2014.

HIDALGO, Rudolph et al. *Entreprise et responsabilité pénale*. Paris: LGDJ, 1994.

LEONARDO Jr., Maurício Fernandes. Transferências Financeiras de Pessoas Físicas entre Estados Unidos e o Brasil. Delivered to the author in June 2012. Article undergoing publication.

LINN, Courtney J. One-Hour Money Laundering: Prosecuting Unlicensed Money Transmitting Businesses Using Section 1960. *United States Attorney's Bulletin*. Vol. 55, No. 5. Washington, DC, Sept 2007.

LOBO, Jorge. Curso de Direito Comercial. Rio de Janeiro: Forense, 2002

MARPAKWAR, Prafulla. State forms cells to detect source of terror funds. *Times of India*. www.westlaw.com. Accessed June 19, 2014.

MARTINS, Fran. Curso de Direito Comercial. 28th ed. Rio de Janeiro: Forense, 2002.

MATONIS, Jon. The Monetary Future At The Intersection of Free Banking, Cryptography, and Digital Currency. Thoughts on Bitcoin Laundering. May 13, 2011. http://themonetaryfuture.blogspot.com/2011/05/thoughts-on-bitcoin-laundering.html.

MEXICO proposes to limit cash purchases of certain goods to 100,000 pesos. 2010 Fintrac Report.

PALAK, Shah. Trusts, NGOs under ambit of money-laundering law. *Business Standard*, Mumbai. 2009 WLNR 23270783, Nov. 18, 2009.

PALLANTE, Maria. Symposium: Digital Archives: Navigating the Legal Shoals Orphan Works, Extended Collective Licensing and Other Current Issues. 34 Colum. J.L. & Arts 23 (2010).

PARIENTE, Maggy et al. Les groupes de sociétés et la responsabilité pénale des personnes morales. In: *La responsabilité pénale des personnes morales*. Paris: Dalloz, 1993.

PEDRAZZI, Cesare. O Direito Penal das Sociedades e o Direito Penal comum. *Revista Brasileira de Criminologia e Direito Penal*. Vol. 9. Rio de Janeiro: Instituto de Criminologia do Estado da Guanabara, 1965.

RAJA D, John Samuel. Ten means to put an end to black money issue. Economic Times (India). Copyright 2011 Bennett, Coleman & Co., Ltd., *The Financial Times Limited*. Nov. 18, 2011.

ROCHA, Fernando A. N. Galvão da. Responsabilidade penal da pessoa jurídica. *Revista da Associação Paulista do Ministério Público*, São Paulo, no. 18, May 1998.

ROCHA, Manuel Antônio Lopes. A responsabilidade penal das pessoas colectivas – novas perspectivas. In: CORREIA, Eduardo et al. *Direito penal econômico e europeu*: textos doutrinários. Vol. 1. Coimbra: Coimbra Ed., 1998.

ROTHENBURG, Walter Claudius. *A pessoa jurídica criminosa*. Curitiba: Ed. Juruá, 1997.

SEXER, Ives. Les conditions de la responsabilité pénale des personnes morales. *Droit et patrimoine*, [S.l.], pp. 38–46, Jan. 1996.

SHAH, Palak. Trusts, NGOs under ambit of money-laundering law. *Business Standard*, 11/19/2009, 2009 WLNR17872644. www.westlaw.com. Accessed June 23, 2014.

SHECAIRA, Sérgio Salomão. A responsabilidade das pessoas jurídicas e os delitos ambientais. *Boletim do IBCCrim*, São Paulo, ed. esp. no. 65, Apr. 1998.

SIKARWAR, Deepshikha. Religious trusts, non-profit organisations to face greater scrutiny. *Economic Times* (India). 2011 WLNR 19624448. Sept. 27, 2011.

SIRVINSKAS, Luís Paulo. Questões polêmicas atinentes à responsabilidade penal da pessoa jurídica nos crimes ambientais. *Revista da Associação Paulista do Ministério Público*, São Paulo, no. 17, Apr. 1998.

SNELL-PYM, Alaric. Bitcoin Security. http://www.snell-pym.org.uk/archives/2011/05/12/bitcoin-security/. Accessed Aug. 3, 2012.

TERROR outfit-turned 'charity' JuD set to come under Pak Central Bank scanner. In *Asian News International*, Mar. 13, 2012. www.lexis.com. Accessed June 19, 2014.

THOMPSON, Erin. The Relationship between Tax Deductions and the Market for Unprovenanced Antiquities. 33 Colum. J.L. & Arts 241 (2010).

TIEDEMANN, Klaus. Responsabilidad penal de personas jurídicas y empresas en derecho comparado. *Revista Brasileira de Ciências Criminais*, São Paulo, no. 11, pp. 21–35, Jul/Sept 1995.

______. *Poder económico y delito* (Introducción al derecho penal económico y de la empresa). Barcelona: Ariel, 1985.

______. *Delitos contra el orden económico*: la reforma penal. Madrid: Instituto Alemão, 1982.

VAROTO, Renato Luiz Mello. Da responsabilidade penal dos sócios. *Repertório IOB de Jurisprudência*, São Paulo, no. 2, Jan 1996.

Chapter 7
Conclusions

It is very easy to commit fraud on behalf of God because creating a religious entity does not require theological or doctrinal evidence, nor a minimum number of followers.[1]

A review of the resounding cases in which religious entities conducted illegal businesses, taking advantage of the pious image that their activities naturally exudes, raises the following question: Could the writers of the constitution, intending to guarantee freedom of religion, have imagined such abuse of their intentions?

Religion plays an important role in ensuring and maintaining conformity to social norms.[2] The stronger an individual's connection to conventional others and to conventional institutions, the less likely it is that the individual will commit a delinquent act. This is the expectation, at least. Churches and temples, as highly conventional institutions, should provide people with a stake in divine conformity to reduce the likelihood of their engagement in delinquent behavior.

The Penal Code of the Old Testament, unlike the New Testament, identifies in Exodus seven categories of crimes: crimes against God and religion (foreign cults and usages, blasphemy, violations of religious institutions), homicide, sexual offences, insubordination and treason, perjury and defamation, crimes against the person (kidnapping and bodily injury), and crimes against property (damage, theft, misappropriation, and robbery).

Whoever acquires the property of someone without his consent and knowledge is considered a thief. In the Old Testament Penal Code, it is irrelevant whether the

[1] See DALLARI, Dalmo. Fraudes em nome de Deus. *Observatório da Imprensa, caderno da cidadania,* http://observatoriodaimprensa.com.br/news/view/fraudes_em_nome_de_deus, Mar. 16, 2010, accessed Sept. 3, 2014.

[2] In this sense, it is worth mentioning Hirschi and Stark, who believe that the role of religion should be viewed through its belief system and rituals which legitimate and reinforce conventional values, and through its "system of eternal rewards and punishment (which help) to ensure the embodiment of values in actual behaviour" (in LINDEN, Rick, and CURRIE, Raymond. Religiosity and Drug Use: A Test of Social Control Theory. Department of Sociology of University of Manitoba, 19 Canadian J. Criminology & Corrections, 346, 1977).

F.M. De Sanctis, *Churches, Temples, and Financial Crimes*,
DOI 10.1007/978-3-319-15681-1_7

property came into the culprit's possession legally or illegally. A bailee who misappropriates goods entrusted to him is treated the same as a burglar: both pay double damages (Exodus 22; 4, 7, 9). Theft of beasts is aggravated by subsequent slaughter or sale; there is a fourfold penalty for sheep, and a fivefold for oxen whose absence prevented the farmer from ploughing (Exodus 22:1). If the thief cannot pay, he is sold into slavery and the value paid for him goes to the injured party. Regarding robbery, the Old Testament Penal Code forbids the taking of property by force or intimidation (Lev 19:13; Deut. 24: 14–15), but it is remarkable that no penalty is prescribed for convicted offenders (Lev. 6: 1–7). For voluntary restitution of property taken by robbery or fraud, the property must be returned with the addition of a fifth of its value to its rightful owner plus a guilt offering for atonement. Here the emphasis seems to be on voluntary surrender.[3]

Teaching moral values and respect for conventional authority is one of the roles of churches and temples, which have a strong influence over their members. Deviant behavior of parishioners, then, can surprise people because of the belief church attendance decreases delinquency involvement. In fact, Rick Linden and Raymond Currie concluded that those who attend church have the lowest degree of illicit drug use.[4]

If religious ties can be a factor in reducing the likelihood of involvement in illicit acts, then that means that religiosity has some effect in society. It means that the effectiveness of churches and temples as an agent of social control is limited but important, especially when the social situation is less restrictive. This role, although it is a limited one, can be neutralized if there is no constraint on the deviant behavior of churches and temples.

Yet we must challenge the usual role of churches and temples, and the legal protections afforded to them, in light of illegal conduct perpetuated by and through religious organizations. The usual role of and protection of rights for churches and temples must be challenged by a new reflection due to some ill-gotten gains and illegal activities carried out under the cloak of "religious purpose."

Within churches and temples, it is possible to find abuses, negligence, and other unlawful acts relating to financial crimes, including the deviation of money through overpayments (overvaluing a good's price), such as payments for primetime TV spots when non-primetime spots are actually used. This causes considerable damage that is often difficult to even imagine. For example, a church may pay for a primetime spot on television when it really occupies a regular spot, thus overpaying to disguise the transfer of money as seemingly legal. A broad range of misconduct by churches and temples occurs at an international level. Cash is the common way

[3] In Medieval times, the Church Courts were particularly concerned about both action and intention in their administration of punishment to criminal offenders. In other words, the Ecclesiastical Courts were concerned with the relative degree of guilt of each offender. The Penal Code expresses a similar concern. See SANDS, Fr. Kirkley C. The Christian Church and the Penal Code. A Christian Response to Crime in the Bahamas, L. Th. B.D., A.K.C., 1983, pp. 3–5.

[4] LINDEN, Rick, and CURRIE, Raymond. Religiosity and Drug Use: A Test of Social Control Theory. Department of Sociology of University of Manitoba, 19 Canadian J. Criminology & Corrections, 346, 349 (1977).

for churches and temples to receive donations, and it is not uncommon for these cash donations to be smuggled, deposited, or transferred outside of the country in places with less rigorous rules.

The religious freedom and tax immunity rights granted to religious institutions create a unique complexity and difficulty in dealing with these crimes, especially because of the sacredness and mystery that conceals the conduct of churches and temples.

Many countries, like the United States and Brazil, have constitutionally guaranteed liberties that include religious freedom, which is expressed in the forms of freedom of belief, freedom of worship, and freedom of religious organization. To effectively grant this freedom, it is necessary to grant tax immunity to those entities to avoid any possibility of the State thwarting such freedom by means of undue tax collection. The interpretation given by the Brazilian Supreme Federal Court, for instance, affirms that this immunity must be broad to achieve its goal, and therefore extends to income, property, and services of these organizations, as long as these are used for the religious purposes.

In the Brazilian legal order, religious institutions, in spite of being ontologically very similar in nature to civil associations, enjoy a separate regime of rights because they are denominated "religious organizations" in the Civil Code. Legal regulations grant these religious organizations special benefits conditioned upon the recognition of public utility of these organizations or institutions linked to them. These matters are subject to legislator discretion, but, nevertheless, can still benefit religious organizations.

Although the guarantees, assistance, and prestige given to those entities exist to ensure religious freedom and to encourage their charitable actions in society, they may be used as tools by some people to increase their own personal wealth and to hide illegal activities. Among the crimes possibly practiced within religious institutions, money laundering, larceny, and tax evasion stand out from the rest. With their eagerness for justice and to condemn those who commit these crimes, some government agents may confuse legal judgments with moral and even judgments, promoting a trial about questions that enter the field of the divine and the unknowable, going beyond the reaches of a secular State. Dealing with such delicate themes demands calm, yet firm action from authorities.

A review of the notorious cases of financial scandals involving religious institutions allows us to identify two basic modes of criminal action: first, the use of the legal status of religious institutions to hide illegal activities from authorities; and second, religious leaders' personal misappropriation of funds collected for charitable work. In both cases, the issue of transparency raises difficulties. If an institution's actual use of resources for religious activities could be easily identified—that is, if the institution is regulated by a unified system of practices and beliefs directed towards something sacred—then it would be possible for the state to fulfill its regulation role. Thus, the promotion of measures and policies that grant access to the financial activity of these organizations would allow a greater supervision by state bodies, by society and, most importantly, by the contributing members of the religious community.

Although religions are considered sacred, there must be a space to discuss issues concerning the use of religion for immoral and illegal purposes, particularly by leaders who explicitly take advantage of faith. For example, there could be a religion that preaches the sacredness of a religious leader who, as consequence of this divinity, demands donations without disclosing the destination of the money donated. It is important to preserve a secular and plural state which allows all forms of religiosity and does not adopt an official system of beliefs. The state should still grant the freedom to not adhere to such religions, as well as the freedom to express, peacefully, against a belief of this kind. The promotion of transparency would subject these institutions to the scrutiny of society and of its members, mitigating the possible harmful side effects of the subsistence of religions such as the one hypothetically presented.

The basic characteristics of money laundering (anonymity, speed, complexity, and secrecy) allow individuals to disguise the illicit source of income. Money launderers use offshore destinations (fictitious implantations of companies, simply used as a mailbox, in places where currency exchange control is lax and there is great freedom from taxes[5]) to protect their fund. Money launderers also use shell companies, which essentially exist only on paper permit money launderers to open valid bank accounts, using the name or address of a lawyer or agent, and proxy (if any) shareholders.

Churches and temples, as non-profit organizations, collect large sums of money annually from donors and distribute this money to beneficiaries according to alleged religious purposes. Both their administrative expenses and the amount of beneficiaries' expenses may be exaggerated and their usefulness may be difficult to assess.

Besides that, the synchronization of money laundering techniques with technological developments enables criminals to easily avoid being detected. Money launderers are increasingly resorting to the use of virtual platforms and electronic payment systems (transferring funds from commercial or non-commercial activities).[6]

Also, the use of religious organizations by third parties is a method of earning income and withholding taxes because it is difficult to track money, making money laundering one of the most common types of financial crimes.

One of the solutions to the problem of money laundering by and through religious organizations is to find a way to track and monitor money flows. Another solution is finding a way to verify accurately the merit to have tax immunity in a way that respects religious freedom and constitutional rights.

A big issue regarding crimes committed by and through churches and temples is a better approach to dealing with mega-churches. It is important to accurately verify the appropriate legal state of mega-churches, as well as the nature of the organizations' activities (whether they are entirely ancillary to their eleemosynary purpose

[5] NEDELCU, Constantin. Money Laundering Techniques Commonly Used. General Approaches. Challenges of the Knowledge Society. Law, p. 37.

[6] See DUMITRACHE, Ana Alina, and MODIGA, Georgeta. New Trends and Perspectives in The Money Laundering Process. Challenges of the Knowledge Society. Law, p. 54.

or in competition with commercial companies). They should not be granted statutory protection from involuntary bankruptcy as an eleemosynary institution if their activities are commercial.

Mega-churches and mega-temples are larger, more intrusive, and retain greater abilities to influence religious accommodations than their predecessors. Most significantly, mega-churches often operate amenities that are not inherently religious in nature and that occupy a great deal of land.[7] This raises innumerable challenges associated with religious land use in a modern religious society.

In other words, the presumption of eleemosynary status should be rebutted by different aspects, especially commercial activities outweigh eleemosynary presumption. This is a way to avoid fraud and abuse.

Lawmakers must also clarify the extent to which churches and temples may engage in lobbying efforts and what activities constitute attempts to influence legislation. "The purpose of applying the lobbying restrictions to churches has never been to prevent religious beliefs from influencing public policy, but rather to ferret out those organizations that would abuse their tax-exempt status to promote a purely nonreligious political agenda under the guise of religion. Accordingly, the law must recognize the rights of churches or temples and church/temple leaders to teach members about important policy issues and urge members to apply their religious beliefs by participating in the political process."[8]

Tensions between religious institutions and government regulations are at an all-time high and are especially evident in tax-exempt lobbying restrictions and disputes over land use.

The charitable nature of an institution is not sufficient reason in and of itself to be considered tax free or free from government supervision. When adjudicating crimes related to religious institutions, judges must consider the nature and purpose of the crime, the character of the offender, the circumstances in which the crime was committed, as well as the need to preserve churches' or temples' rights. Magistrates must also take into account the seriousness of the offence and the need to protect the public and its values. The purpose of sentencing is not only to punish the wrongdoer and to protect the public by deterring others of like mind from breaking the law.

When religious leaders remit large sums of cash to foreign countries without properly notifying authorities, it becomes necessary to inquire into the existence of profitable activity that will eventually collide with the institution of tax immunity.

Citing Reverend Dr. Urban T. Holmes III, late Dean of the School of Theology at the University of the South, Tennessee, Fr. Kirkley C. Sands deems that "human action is a product of the manner in which we construct our world in our heads and hearts. Human action is not merely a result of how we have been programmed by society. Therefore what we make of our religion (its orientation) and how we think

[7] In WELCH, Heather M. The Religious Land Use and Institutionalized Persons Act and Mega-Churches: Demonstrating the Limits of Religious Land Use Exemptions in Federal Legislation. 39 University of Baltimore Law Rev. 255 (2010).

[8] See ANDERSEN, David M. Political Silence at Church: The Empty Threat of Removing Tax-Exempt Status for Insubstantial Attempts To Influence Legislation. 2006 B. Y. U. L. Rev 115.

about our experience (its articulation) have a great deal to do with how we behave as people and as Christians."[9] What could we say, in this sense, of those who talk "on behalf" of God?

The European Court of Human Rights, which is commonly regarded as part of the most advanced and effective of the international human rights enforcement systems, decided on July 1, 2014, that the 2010 French law prohibiting women from using the burka and veil in public areas is valid. The Court considered that the prohibition was a society decision to enhance security. It did not believe that the law offended religious freedom.[10] Religion has several attributes that should not distract from the point that religion can be a determinative element in the construction of an inferior or superior racial or gender category. It cannot oblige or restrict people to the right of decision to live free of it. It is not possible to force a religious conversion under punishment. There are limits to it as there are to the States.[11]

When religious leaders trick worshippers (though false statements) to donate money, this could be considered the crime of larceny. The improper use of the status of a religious organization to evade taxes could also be considered larceny.

Although it is important to cast some light on the necessity of the neutrality and secular religious purpose, the freedom of thought and conscience is an important value linked to freedom of religious belief. Any attempt to violate this freedom cannot be based on the grounds of illegal activity. However, states can legitimately ban all criminal activity, even criminal activity committed on behalf of "promoting religion."

The task of reconciling competing traditional values and public interest is difficult. The next chapter will discuss some proposals to work towards a solution.

Bibliography

ANDERSEN, David M. Political Silence at Church: The Empty Threat of Removing Tax-Exempt Status for Insubstantial Attempts to Influence Legislation. 2006 B.Y.U.L. Rev. 115.

CORTE Europeia confirma lei francesa que proíbe burca em locais públicos. Folha de São Paulo, July 1, 2014, http://tools.folha.com.br/print?site=emcimadahora&url=http://www1.folha.uol.com.br/mundo/2014/07/1479127-corte-europeia-confirma-lei-francesa-que-proibe-burca-em-locais-publicos.shtml, accessed Aug. 10, 2014.

DALLARI, Dalmo. Fraudes em nome de Deus. Observatório da Imprensa, caderno da cidadania, http://observatoriodaimprensa.com.br/news/view/fraudes_em_nome_de_deus, Mar. 16, 2010.

[9] See SANDS, Fr. Kirkley C. The Christian Church and The Penal Code. A Christian Response to Crime in the Bahamas, L. Th. B.D., A.K.C., 1983, p. 35.

[10] CORTE Europeia confirma lei francesa que proíbe burca em locais públicos. Folha de São Paulo, July 1, 2014, http://tools.folha.com.br/print?site=emcimadahora&url=http://www1.folha.uol.com.br/mundo/2014/07/1479127-corte-europeia-confirma-lei-francesa-que-proibe-burca-em-locais-publicos.shtml, accessed Aug. 10, 2014.

[11] See similar thoughts in JENKINS, Laura Dudley. Legal Limits on Religious Conversion in India, 71 Law & Contemporary Problems 109 (2008).

DUMITRACHE, Ana Alina, and MODIGA, Georgeta. New Trends And Perspectives In The Money Laundering Process. In Challenges of the Knowledge Society. Law.

JENKINS, Laura Dudley. Legal Limits on Religious Conversion in India, 71 Law & Contemporary Problems 109 (2008).

LINDEN, Rick, and CURRIE, Raymond. Religiosity and Drug Use: A Test of Social Control Theory. Department of Sociology of University of Manitoba, 19 Canadian J. Criminology & Corrections, 346 (1977).

NEDELCU, Constantin. Money Laundering Techniques Commonly Used. General Approaches. Challenges of the Knowledge Society. Law.

SANDS, Fr. Kirkley C. The Christian Church and The Penal Code. A Christian Response to Crime in the Bahamas, L. Th. B.D., A.K.C., 1983.

TIDEMAN, Sander G. Tibetans and Other Minorities in China's Legal System, 14 Review of Socialist Law 1888, No.1.

WELCH, Heather M. The Religious Land Use and Institutionalized Persons Act and Mega-Churches: Demonstrating the Limits of Religious Land Use Exemptions in Federal Legislation. 39 University of Baltimore Law Rev. 255 (2010).

Chapter 8
Proposals to Improve the War Against Financial Crimes Within Temples and Churches

A number of different international and national initiatives are being put forth in the war against money laundering and the financing of terrorism. International treaties, supplemented by recommendations from foreign multilateral organizations, along with recurring discussion meetings, have all sought to improve the global system of enforcement to curb these serious crimes. Now we turn to effective enforcement in the sectors under study: *temples and churches*.

The subject is one of constant concern, for much is said about the need to improve financial regulation and crime prevention in these sectors, yet in practice, not much has been done toward the prevention of crime. There should be a more significant reporting record on the part of those sectors which are in charge of supervising accounts from temples and churches. The real work ahead is to get all government agencies to put some teeth into the prevention and punishment of money laundering through the recovery of dirty money in this delicate field surrounded by important beliefs and guarantees.

There is no word of important advances in this area, and that may explain the fact that organized crime finds an extraordinary array of techniques to put a legal face on the proceeds of crime using temples and churches. It is hard not to notice that priests, pastors, and businessmen, among other criminals, use religion as a way to illegally profit.

What is called for it is an immediate rereading of all mechanisms of enforcement and prevention of money laundering as a general proposition, and all of its myriad forms of expression, but notably in this very important area where enforcement is the reaffirmation of cultural, religious, and social traits.

This chapter presents proposals to reflect upon, but is not meant to serve as the last word, but rather as the beginning of a new debate. It is hoped that these proposals

F.M. De Sanctis, *Churches, Temples, and Financial Crimes*,
DOI 10.1007/978-3-319-15681-1_8

will prove useful to the mentioned sectors, but also, as a means of better handling prevention and enforcement in the war on financial crimes, especially money laundering and even the financing of terrorism.

8.1 An International Perspective

8.1.1 The Financial Action Task Force (FATF)

Explanation The FATF has not yet expressed particular concern regarding religious institutions aside from the general mention of non-profit organizations (Recommendation No. 8[1]), in spite of the significant number of cases discovered so far.

01. Clearly include all forms of churches and temples as subject to the Suspicious Transaction Reporting Recommendation for financial or non-financial companies when there is no doubt that religion is being used as an excuse for committing crimes.

8.1.2 Law Enforcement Agencies and Financial Intelligence Units (FIUs)

Explanation The FATF recommends that all countries identify, evaluate, and understand the hazards they face from money laundering and the financing of terrorism, and that they take coordinated action to mitigate these hazards (Risk-Based Approach, Recommendation No. 1). This entails the cooperation and national coordination of prevention and enforcement policies, as well as proper action by Financial Intelligence Units (FIUs) (Recommendation No. 2). All countries should do as follows:

02. Require financial institutions to conduct *Customer Due Diligence* (CDD) on companies, religious institutions, and individuals; ban anonymous accounts and accounts bearing fictitious names; require account holders to show identification and prove that they are the beneficial owners (i.e., broaden the Recommendation No. 10 to include religious institutions);

[1] Recommendation 8. "Non-profit organisations. Countries should review the adequacy of laws and regulations that relate to entities that can be abused for the financing of terrorism. Non-profit organisations are particularly vulnerable, and countries should ensure that they cannot be misused: (a) by terrorist organisations posing as legitimate entities; (b) to exploit legitimate entities as conduits for terrorist financing, including for the purpose of escaping asset-freezing measures; and (c) to conceal or obscure the clandestine diversion of funds intended for legitimate purposes to terrorist organizations." See site of Financial Action Task Force—FATF (in http://www.fatf-gafi.org/media/fatf/documents/recommendations/pdfs/FATF_Recommendations.pdf, accessed Oct. 1, 2014).

03. Require religious organizations to keep records for at least five years (i.e., extend Recommendation No. 11 to religious organizations);

04. Broaden the definition of "politically exposed persons," that is, persons more readily able to launder money, such as politicians (in prominent positions) and their relatives, priests, pastors, cardinals, bishops, archbishops, monks, reverends and so on to include both nationals and foreigners, and even international institutions (i.e., extend Recommendation No. 12 to members of churches and temples);

05. Require designated non-financial businesses and professions (DNFBPs), such as casinos, real estate offices, dealers in precious metals or stones, and even attorneys, notaries, and accountants with a specific eye to religious institutions, to report suspicious operations. Internal controls must be established along with protection for whistleblowers from civil or criminal liability (Recommendation No. 22, in combination with Nos. 18–21). Religious people in charge of receiving donations must be monitored. Moreover, transparency ought to be required of the beneficiaries of companies, and countries should obtain sufficient information in real time (Recommendation No. 24), including information about trusts, settlors, and trustees or beneficiaries (Recommendation No. 25). FIUs need to have timely access, direct or indirect, to financial and administrative information in the hands of law enforcement authorities in order to fully perform their functions. This includes analysis of suspicious activity reports (Recommendations Nos. 26, 27, 29, and 31). In fact, the existence of money laundering depends on the later use of the money laundered, and thus individuals and institutions are in a position to detect the crime and report it through Suspicious Activity Reports;

06. Properly regulate the financial administration of religious organizations, with effective supervision and rules to prevent money laundering (Recommendation No. 28). Although the FATF did not publish recommendations similar to those for churches and temples to cover the misuse of donations, this does not mean that the FIUs cannot engage in this oversight;

07. Broaden the concept of religious institutions to include those people who are in charge of financial administration or act on behalf of the financial administration or administrators, besides their religious leaders. These people, regardless their faith, rituals, or doctrine, must be supervised to verify if there is a correspondence between their living expenses – economic status and assets – and what they believe and express;

08. Establish regulations, irrespective of any legal obligation, that require suspicious activity reports to be filed by individuals, companies, and religious institutions that sell, import, export, or intermediate sales—whether on a permanent or temporary basis, in a principal or accessory role, and cumulatively or otherwise—to prevent money laundering. The rules should make it clear that churches and temples are included in this requirement. In the absence of a regulatory agency, oversight shall be performed by the FIUs;

09. Require suspicious activity reports on the part of deed registries or by agencies in charge of regulating real estate brokers, most notably when cash payments or attempted cash payments occur, or when payments are made through overseas accounts. There are frequent reports of people acquiring real estate and paying for it entirely or in large part in cash, which has caused unprecedented inflation in the real estate market.

8.1.3 Tax Havens, Offshore Accounts, and Trusts

Explanation The best way to combat illegal activities is transparency, which permits the collection and sharing of more information.[2] The Financial Action Task Force (FATF, or *Groupe d'Action Financière sur le blanchiment des capitaux*—GAFI) established 40 Recommendations that highlight the importance of transparency to avoid money laundering. These Recommendations should apply to religious institutions. Thus, it should be mandatory to record the true beneficial owners of companies, to keep records up-to-date, and to make records readily available to investigators in cases of suspected wrongdoing. The costs of openness will be outweighed by the benefits of shining light on the shady corners of finance. There is much intelligence work to be done, more than that involved in simply controlling one's borders. Intelligence forces need to work together because, if they are kept apart, each one of them may, in isolation, feel that someone else is responsible for the problem. Transparency will also help curb the more aggressive forms of corporate tax avoidance. The advantage of offshore accounts is that they enable the free movement of capital, which is only taxed in negotiations taking place in-country, with exemptions for transfers to other offshore or nonresident accounts, corporate income taxes, and income tax withholding on payments made to nonresidents. Arnaldo Sampaio de Moraes Godoy has apropos observations on this point, especially concerning Barbados, Panama, the Bahamas, and Vanuatu.[3]

Moreover, there are treaties to avoid double taxation that allow governments to establish unilateral domestic measures (such as exemptions for fiscal credits at a reduced proportional rate, and deduction of taxes paid abroad from domestic taxable income), which is why they are referred to as tax havens. Arnaldo Sampaio de Moraes Godoy also adduces that there is a draft being circulated by the Organization for Economic Cooperation and Development (OECD), called the *Model Tax Convention on Income and on Capital* (comprising of 31 articles distributed over seven sections) aimed at eliminating obstacles related to double taxation. It provides,

---

[2] According to an article in *The Economist*, "not all these havens are in sunny climes; indeed not all are technically offshore. Mr. Obama likes to cite Ugland House, a building in the Cayman Islands that is officially home to 18,000 companies, as the epitome of a rigged system. But Ugland House is not a patch on Delaware (population 917,092), which is home to 945,000 companies, many of which are dodgy shells. Miami is a massive offshore banking centre, offering depositors from emerging markets the sort of protection from prying eyes that their home countries can no longer get away with. The City of London, which pioneered offshore currency trading in the 1950s, still specialises in helping non-residents get around the rules. British shell companies and limited-liability partnerships regularly crop up in criminal cases. London is no better than the Cayman Islands when it comes to controls against money laundering. Other European Union countries are global hubs for a different sort of tax avoidance: companies divert profits to brass-plate subsidiaries in low-tax Luxembourg, Ireland and the Netherlands." In The Missing $20 Trillion. How to Stop Companies and People Dodging Tax, in Delaware as well as Grand Cayman. The Economist, Feb. 16, 2013, http://www.economist.com/news/leaders/21571873-how-stop-companies-and-people-dodging-tax-delaware-well-grand-cayman-missing-20.

[3] In *Direito tributário comparado e tratados internacionais fiscais*. Porto Alegre: Sergio Antonio Fabris, 2005, pp. 83–84.

for example, that dividends paid by a company having its home office in one State Party to someone living in another State Party to the Convention will be taxed by the latter, and their remuneration taxed by the State in which the services are rendered.[4] It is true, as they say, that offshore accounts facilitate the circulation of goods, services and capital, but they are also an effective instrument for evading taxes with considerable legitimacy. They lend themselves to legal uses, of arguable utility, but also to illegal practices. There are considerable advantages to be had by using them as conduits, especially by those interested in laundering ill-gotten money, on account of defective or nonexistent government control, but also because they make it easy to generate false trails and international wire transfers. Offshore bank accounts make it possible to disguise their real controllers, since ownership is—according to the legislation in the countries in which they are located—evidenced by bearer paper, and partners or officers are simply proxies, often proxies for hundreds of companies of the same pattern. All of this amounts to creating a veil for the actual owners to hide behind. Their paper cannot be traded on the domestic market, nor cashed in without considerable expense and questions about possible complicity in money laundering directed at anyone who converts it.

It is argued that offshore accounts are advantageous in that owning one does not involve liability to taxes, unless one were to actually invest in the country. Loan agreements are often written so as to lay hold of funds from offshore accounts without exposing them to tax liability. There are transparency requirements for beneficiaries of companies, with countries required to obtain reliable real-time information (FATF Recommendation No. 24), including information on trusts, settlors, and trustees or beneficiaries (Recommendation No. 25), which would preclude anonymous accounts. This is why the customer and actual beneficiary must be identified (i.e., know-your-customer duties, often called Customer Due Diligence) along with a requirement to collect enough information about the institution to which service is rendered, so that the trustee, who administers the assets, is accountable for turning in suspicious transaction reports. Observe that the FATF takes a clear stand against the invocation of banking secrecy or professional privilege as a means of obstructing its recommendations (Recommendation No. 9).

10. Countries should establish policies to supervise and monitor financial transactions from tax havens, offshores, and trusts, even if they are related to a religious purpose, so as to obtain real-time information on their activities, size, and other important features such as transparency, integrity, and best practices (i.e., extend Recommendation No. 8 such that it clearly applies to religious institutions);

11. Financial institution secrecy laws, professional privilege, and First Amendment concerns (freedom of speech and freedom of religion) should not inhibit the implementation of the FATF Recommendations (i.e., broaden the scope of Recommendation No. 9);

12. Financial institutions should be required to undertake customer due diligence and verify the identity of beneficial owners, and should be prohibited from keeping anonymous accounts or those bearing fictitious names (Recommendation No. 10);

[4] Cf. *id.* pp. 166–70.

13. Financial institutions should be required to maintain records for at least five years (Recommendation No. 11);

14. Financial institutions should closely monitor "politically exposed persons" (PEPs), that is, persons who have greater facility to launder money, such as politicians (in high posts) and their relatives (Recommendation No. 12), but also priests, pastors, cardinals, bishops, archbishops, monks, reverends, and so on, who are in charge of financial activities within religious organizations, including both nationals and foreigners;

15. Financial institutions should monitor wire transfers, ensure that detailed information is obtained on the sender and the beneficiary, and prohibit transactions by certain people pursuant to UN Security Council resolutions, such as Resolution 1267 of 1999 and Resolution 1373 of 2001, for the prevention and suppression of terrorism and its financing (Recommendation No. 16);

16. Designated non-financial businesses and professions (DNFBPs), such as casinos, real estate offices, dealers in precious metals or stones, and even attorneys, notaries, and accountants, must report suspicious operations, including transactions taken on behalf of religion, and those who report suspicious activity must be protected from civil and criminal liability (Recommendation No. 22, in combination with Nos. 18 through 21).

17. Countries should take measures to ensure transparency and obtain reliable and timely information on the beneficial ownership and control of legal entities (Recommendation No. 24), including information on trusts—settlors, trustees, and beneficiaries (Recommendation No. 25);

18. Require tax havens to comply with all provisions whereby information must be provided to proper international authorities and cannot be denied by invoking religious freedom or freedom of speech. This amounts to placing ethical and legal considerations above financial considerations, all the way down to obtaining information about the ownership (beneficial or ultimate beneficial ownership) and identifying the controllers. Indeed, the controllers merit special attention, and their very existence ought to be looked into to check whether they might be providing services to criminal enterprises. The hurdles in the way of their suppression are closely related to the Janus-faced discourse of many States which rely on tax havens to conduct non-transparent transactions purportedly having connections to "reasons of State" or for the management of assets belonging to their political elite.

8.1.4 International Legal Cooperation, Repatriation, and Extraterritoriality: Conflict of Laws

Explanation International cooperation must be improved to lend substance to the administration of justice and provide repatriation of assets through the following measures and national policies, mindful that the fight against crime is independent of where the crime occurred, and that confiscation is essential. As already established by the FATF, freezing and seizure of assets is essential, even if the antecedent crime occurred in another jurisdiction (country). There is also a need for deployment of specialized multidisciplinary teams, task forces if you will (Recommendation

No. 30). The FATF also recommends International Legal Cooperation, pursuant to the UN Conventions of Vienna (international traffic, 1988), Palermo (transnational organized crime, 2000), and Mérida (corruption, 2003), by withdrawing obstacles (Recommendation No. 37) and enabling direct mutual assistance toward a quick, constructive, and effective solution (Recommendation No. 38). The fight against organized crime must not be defeated by a lack of understanding regarding the various international legal systems. Regarding conflict of laws and extraterritoriality, issues can arise when different legal jurisdictions disagree on the legality of the acts concerned. For instance, some countries criminalize online gambling activities while such activities are legal in other countries.

19. Cooperation through Letters Rogatory is not recommended because it is slow and bureaucratic, and because analysis in the requested country is limited to checks on public policy and affronts to sovereignty;

20. Prioritize State to State cooperation by direct assistance because it is faster, is based on mutual trust, and conveys to the requested State a proper analysis of the request;

21. Give preference, if possible at all, to the clear, simplified standard of the Mutual Legal Assistance Treaty format. Specific, separate MLATs should not be required for each asset, security, or pecuniary amount if the requesting State attaches to its request a list of assets and gives grounds;

22. Consider that central authorities have facilitated matters, for they placed no obstacles in the way of direct contact between magistrates or competent authorities, and channels of communication must be opened up to ease unnecessary bureaucratic burdens (Article 18.13 of the UN Convention Against Organized Crime at Palermo does not prohibit such understandings);

23. The legal systems of countries involved must be respected and should not bar cooperation if a mutual legal assistance request originates with or is addressed to the police, the Office of the Public Prosecutor, or the courts;

24. If extradition is refused on the grounds of citizenship, then the case against the person believed to be involved ought to be promptly submitted over to authorities in their own country (Art. 16.10, Palermo);

25. States should consider the possibility of joint prosecution or transfer of criminal proceedings (Art. 21, Palermo) for final disposal of assets and joint measures (cooperative debriefings with effects in both countries) to achieve better administration of justice;

26. International Cooperation ought not to be blocked while the whereabouts of an asset are unknown. The requested State should try all available means to trace, seize, confiscate, and repatriate the assets;

27. As a condition for restitution, the requested State should require proof of the legality of the asset, security, or pecuniary amount whenever the requesting State requests seizure with an eye to confiscation or repatriation, mooted by court decisions that did not rule on the merits as to the illegality of its origin;

28. Invocation of the absence of dual criminality or of freedom of religion cannot justify failure to cite or subpoena defendants, victims, witnesses, or affected third parties once criminal proceedings have been initiated in the requesting State;

29. Information gained for criminal proceedings may be used in other such proceedings if the requested State so authorizes, even if retroactively;

30. Assets, securities, and pecuniary amounts shall be restituted for indemnification of victims or turned over to the United Nations Fund for technical assistance among countries—or even for reimbursement of the State. A division might be arrived at to deduct only expenses, except for such crimes as corruption and the like, and also with regard to cultural goods, which should be so disposed of as to give priority to public access;

31. Reimbursement of States should lie outside the reach of the statute of limitations, which does not affect international cooperation;

32. Denying the request of a court order due to a lack of a citation, a subpoena, or copies undermines international cooperation. It is incumbent upon States to simplify their legal systems to make direct assistance workable;

33. Defense witnesses ought to be heard in the country filing charges, or else by teleconference from embassies or consulates, with international cooperation not being invoked except in cases of evidence being disguised by the charges;

34. International cooperation does not require the attachment of proof, but rather, a presentation of arguments leading to the decision to see that measures be taken abroad;

35. Give weight to the primary bases of jurisdiction of nationality and territoriality to consider a violation of a crime adopting the method called "the test of reasonableness," which weighs the links between a state and its conduct against the links between its conduct and another state, allowing some flexibility.[5]

8.2 A National Perspective

8.2.1 Institutional Measures (Executive, Legislative, and Judicial Branches)

Explanation The hazards of globalization may be minimized if with globalization, our notions of law draw authority from social and philosophical—as opposed to just economic—considerations. The subject cannot be dealt with from a purely economic view. Criminal organizations must be curbed by denying what gives them their mobility and power, continuous and unprecedented illegal wealth. The subjective

[5]BANA, Anurag. Online Gambling: An Appreciation of Legal Issues. 12 Bus. L. Int'l 335, 342 (2011).

collective degradation afoot in the world today, which regards economics as the standard of value, can never so bind our numbers together as to gloss over such indispensable critical thinking. Legitimate social movements and individuals ought to assume a stance for ethical values to compel obedience to basic rules of coexistence. Standing these rules at defiance by parallel paths amounts to the real breakdown of rights both *de facto* and *de jure*. There is a duty to perform Customer Due Diligence for all financial and non-financial activity, whether with natural or artificial persons, to ban anonymous accounts or those bearing fictitious names, and require identification of their beneficial owners, with records to be kept for at least 5 years (FATF Recommendations Nos. 10 and 11). There are, at times, requirements to make suspicious transaction reports on non-financial companies engaged in domestic or international cash transfer services, obliging them to record the amounts transferred, form of payment, transaction date, purpose of the wire transfer, name, individual or corporate taxpayer ID, where applicable, of both sender and receiver, and addresses for both.[6] These requirements give a false impression that any money laundering occurring in that sector could actually be detected.

8.2.2 Money Laundering as a Crime

Explanation The communications system for reporting suspicious transactions is the key to effective suppression of money laundering. It reveals a number of suspicious deals. Many others go unnoticed when there is no cooperation from those whose who have a legal duty to report transactions. Certainly the failure of one of the methods of control held to be essential in the fight against money laundering, namely, reporting, can give rise to misleading statistics. Moreover, making one liable to criminal charges for incorrect notices of suspicious transactions is clearly aimed at protecting privacy and image, on the one hand, and the effectiveness of early investigations on the other, for the danger is that future freezes on accounts and other confidential security measures might be rendered inoperative. The FATF noted three characteristics of the Internet that make it potentially susceptible to money laundering: ease of access, depersonalization of contact between the customer and the institution, and the speed of electronic transactions.[7]

36. People who do the following should be liable to criminal prosecution: (1) fail to report suspicious operations, (2) delay in reporting suspicious operations, (3) make incomplete or false reporting, (4) make public the required reporting, or (5) structure transactions or operations to circumvent reporting requirements;

---

[6] See, for example, the Resolution by the Brazilian Financial Intelligence Unit, the Council for Financial Activities Control, COAF Resolution No. 10 of Nov. 19, 2001.

[7] FATF, Vulnerabilities of Casinos and Gaming Sector, March 2009, available at http://www.fatf-gafi.org/media/fatf/documents/reports/Vulnerabilities%20of%20Casinos%20and%20Gaming%20Sector.pdf.

37. Require suspicious activity reports by individuals, companies, and religious institutions that sell, import, export, or intermediate a transaction—whether on a permanent or temporary basis, in a principal or accessory role, and cumulatively or otherwise, to prevent the laundering of money through churches and temples;

8.2.3 The Role of Jurisprudence

Explanation Defining what constitutes a church is a difficult legal question. Churches are protected by law as eleemosynary institutions. But if they are commercial organizations, churches, mega or not, should not be warranted the same protection as traditional churches if, for example, they offer gym memberships, bookstores, and franchises. This does not fit the definition of eleemosynary and should not have the same level of protection that is granted to the church itself. The numerous complex actions involved demand considerable specific knowledge and may entail huge setbacks to criminal jurisdiction for failure to act at the proper time. With respect to punishment, if there is indeed any reasoning behind unlawful conduct involving cost–benefit analyses of the outcomes to the perpetrator, a given crime will be committed if and only if the expected penalty is outweighed by the advantages to be had from committing the act.[8]

38. Courts must develop an understanding of religion to be applied in cases presented before them. They cannot avoid defining religion and the definition should be express, even though it will never be perfect. A stricter and clearer definition may be required in order to avoid the adoption of a "Temple of Marijuana" as a church, for example. The evolution of the U.S. Supreme Court's jurisprudence in religious matters reveals that courts do not have access to a settled definition of "religion" to determine whether a set of beliefs and practices constitutes a religion. A court should classify an entity as religious by analogizing it to traditional religions, with consideration given to at least three fundamental indicia of traditional religions: the belief proclaims the underlying theories of man's nature and the fundamental problems of human existence; such a belief is the ultimate concern of the group and is subordinate to no other idea; and there are formal, external signs, such as ceremonies, services, clergy, and efforts to propagate;

39. Courts should not make judgments about the divine because this would open a dangerous precedent to legitimize the State as acting as a censor, choosing conceptions about what is and what is not acceptable in the religious field, compromising the secularism of the State. Nevertheless, one should question in what measure the character of larceny by fraud could be attributed to the donations given by worshippers. As immoral—and even against some religious principles—as the collection of donations based on promises may be, it probably should not be the subject of criminal law, since the error in which the victim is supposedly induced does not consist of a false statement about a situation of facts, but rather is a conception about the supernatural, something quite impossible to prove;

[8] SILVA SÁNCHEZ, Jesús-María (in *Eficiência e direito penal.* Coleção Estudos de Direito Penal. São Paulo: Manole, 2004, No. 11, p. 11); MIRANDA RODRIGUES, Anabela (in Contributo para a fundamentação de um discurso punitivo em matéria fiscal. *Direito Penal Económico e Europeu: textos doutrinários.* Coimbra: Coimbra ed., 1999, pp. 484–85).

40. The presumption of eleemosynary status should be allowed to be rebutted by different facts, especially in case of commercial activities outweighing eleemosynary purposes. This is a way to avoid fraud and abuse;

41. Establish courts that specialize in money laundering, with criteria established for recommending, appointing, and replacing judges, in addition to specialized criminal teams at the courthouses;

42. Pecuniary penalties ought not to be so freely applied, and should perhaps even be restricted, and the same goes for incarceration (even in plea bargaining), when there is a clear lack of intimidating effect. The requirements of proportionality (gravity of the crime plus guilt) and the need for overall prevention require a response that is a better fit for serious financial crimes.

8.2.4 Freezing, Seizure, Confiscation, and Repatriation of Assets

Explanation States must improve their efforts to engage in international cooperation toward the seizure and forfeiture of ill-gotten assets. The system as a whole works best when confiscation is kept as one of the solutions among the several outcomes of sentencing.

43. Governments ought therefore to allow the freezing, seizure, confiscation, and repatriation of assets in order to facilitate the fight against organized crime, itself a global business, in such a manner as to force the criminals to change their ways. With churches and temples, the theory does not change in the case of crimes committed within or through them;

44. For a state to fulfill its regulatory role, it must verify whether practices promoted by religious organization are the same as the ones preached or if there are others that are not consistent with the faith system of the religious institution;

45. Allow administrative freezing and seizure to be accomplished quickly, so as to prevent the assets from disappearing or being used for acts of terrorism;

46. Allow confiscation of assets when transferred to an outside party which may have been aware that the assets were illegal, or that they were transferred solely to avoid confiscation;

47. Allow confiscation of illegal assets when a conviction cannot be obtained on account of death, statutory limitations, or grant of immunity. Adopt civil actions to terminate ownership;

48. Even after a decision has become final, allow further financial investigations to enforce prior confiscation orders covering all of the proceeds of crime;

49. Once criminal proceedings are instituted, the statute of limitations ought to stop running, for there is no reason to count government inertia, nor lack of interest in criminal prosecution;

8.2.5 *Payments in Cash, in Stored Value Cards, Through Remittance Companies, and via the Internet*

50. Require that all churches and temples keep detailed records of loans, profit-sharing, or other benefits to avoid substantial losses;

51. Cash payments are practically untraceable and therefore facilitate tax evasion and illegal financial transactions. Cash donations to churches and temples is a common practice and cannot be prohibited, unlike cash payments for purchases of vehicles, boats, airplanes, real property, and shares of stock, which should be banned;

52. Payments by third parties should also be illegal, so as to preclude their use for purposes of masking real ownership of the goods and resources, which creates the potential for tax fraud;

53. When acting in private businesses, churches and temples should refuse payments on behalf of outside parties or trustees, or which involve offshore accounts that mask their true identity. The use of third parties may be an instrument for concealing the actual ownership of the asset or resources, and possibly for tax fraud;

54. Credit card payments should also be subject to stricter controls. Lax controls have been exercised by card issuers, often with no prior relationship, exacerbated by failure to disclose credit limits, changes of address, name, date of issue, and expiration date. "Know your client" or due diligence rules must be enforced;

55. Ban all wire transfer payments which do not allow the money to be tracked. There is always a separation between the non-financial remittance company and the financial institution receiving the investor's money whenever these come from individuals or companies unrelated to the negotiations (cash deals negotiated by factoring companies or companies having home offices in tax havens). Currency brokers or *hawala* systems are often resorted to, as are wire transfers from and to secret banks or banks in tax havens—often by people with no connection whatsoever to the institution receiving the resources. Either they are not account holders, or are unconnected with the account holder receiving the wire transfer, or even transfer the amount which is actually the sum of many small deposits. Allowing this sort of practice would amount to having no preventive measures whatsoever. In wire transfers, detailed information should be obtained on the sender, as well as the beneficiary, with monitoring made possible, and there should be an option to prohibit transactions by certain people pursuant to UN Security Council Resolutions 1269 of 1999 and 1373 of 2001, for the prevention and suppression of terrorism and its financing (FATF Recommendation No. 16);

56. Establish clearly-defined categories for stored value cards so as to make it easier for government agencies to identify suspicious cards, given that it is not easy to distinguish between traditional debit cards and prepaid access cards. Identification should be demanded of their customers, so as to enable comparison of identities of those individuals with wanted criminals. A top-down compliance program is needed, which should include customer identification, storage of records, and reporting of suspicious operations. Prepaid stored value cards have, with their explosive growth, become a perfect tool for money laundering whereby illegal money may be moved, with no documentation, identification, suspicion, or seizure. They are poorly (or sloppily) regulated, which ensures their anonymity, even when purchased or reloaded. Their daily limits are the same as the face value. They offer advantages over physical transfers because they are easy to carry and may be sent through the mail, and hence even replace the cross-border transportation of cash. Regulations alone will not suffice if they are issued by non-financial institutions. Their issuers' obligations must therefore be clearly established. They ought to be classified as monetary instruments and, therefore, be subject to declaration when going through customs. These cards, then, possibly in combination with cash or other monetary instruments, once aggregating the $10,000 limit, ought to be subject to customs declaration;

57. Tighten controls on remittance companies, so as to have real knowledge of situations which might allow clandestine wires or wires not subject to suspicious operation reporting requirements (poor or borderline tracking by authorities). One example would be requiring a declaration by a bank accredited by the Central Bank to handle the conversion whenever called upon by the national government to appear for settlement of the currency exchange operation. Detailed information should be obtained on the sender and beneficiary of the wire transfer, with monitoring made possible, and the option of prohibiting transactions by certain people pursuant to UN Security Council Resolutions 1269 of 1999 and 1373 of 2001, for the prevention and suppression of terrorism and its financing (FATF Recommendation No. 16);

58. There has to be some form of electronic tracking of payments over the Internet. Tracking such payments has the potential to be easier than tracking cash that passes from hand to hand. Electronic tracking should enable detection of payments made using electronic methods (like Bitcoins), even when such payments are considered a transparent method of conducting transactions inasmuch as the system allows nicknames and aliases to identify users. To monitor traffickers, the electronic tracking system should record data on individuals transferring money, including a list of parties with whom traffickers have dealings. Although mediums like Bitcoin are not as anonymous as would appear at first blush, there is no denying the possibility of someone setting up channels on the Bitcoin system to conceal transactions anonymously. As more services like this come online, the more complex the transactions, and the greater the opportunity for apparently disguised, off-the-grid transactions.

8.2.6 Offshore Accounts and Trusts

Explanation According to Susan Ormand, "Some large banks and credit card companies, including Visa and Mastercard, have refused to transfer money to offshore betting accounts because of the potential for fraud, but bookmakers circumvented these efforts by encouraging bettors to use debit cards or payment services like PayPal."[9] Obtaining information has been hampered considerably by a lack of channels of communication with the competent authorities—to say nothing of

[9] In Pending U.S. Legislation to Prohibit Offshore Internet Gambling May Proliferate Money Laundering, 10 Law & Bus. Rev. Am. 447, 451 (2004).

timely notice—in the conduct of international legal cooperation. Moreover, investors may have committed antecedent crimes and wish to launder the proceeds.[10]

59. Full particulars absolutely must be obtained on all actual investors, even if they belong to companies chartered abroad, provided they do business and are represented within a given country. A simple listing of proxies or stockholders is not enough. Complete identification must also be required of partners and administrators concealed within offshore accounts or trusts domiciled in tax havens. A listing of all partners and administrators ought to be required for being listed or removed from the tax rolls (which in Brazil is the Treasury Ministry's National Corporate Register or CNPJ).

8.2.7 NGOs, NPOs, and Foundations

Explanation NGOs, including churches and temples, should be required to keep records on all transactions entered into within the country and/or abroad. This would comply with FATF Recommendation No. 8, in the spirit of clearly delimiting the rights and responsibilities of directors and employees of NGOs. It would encourage countries to establish good policies whereby information on NGO activities, size, and other important characteristics such as transparency, integrity, openness, and best practices are supervised and monitored in real-time monitoring (FATF Recommendation No. 8). There is evidence that such organizations have even been used for the financing of terrorism. Government policies have been initiated to curb the practice, most notably in Pakistan.[11] Cases of NGO involvement in terrorism and its financing have also been reported in India.[12]

60. A primary responsibility is to ensure proper accounting for social programs that NGOs run, and for funding received from their supporters (public or otherwise). This means they must strictly comply with the law and ethical standards, be committed to the mission of the NGO they represent, protect the rights of their members and, indirectly, of those assisted, and prepare annual reports for their country's federal revenue service and regulatory authorities having jurisdiction—reports that should be available to all interested parties;

[10] In Brazil, the Internal Revenue Service Regulatory Directive No. 748/RFB of June 28, 2007, does not require offshore accounts or trusts to completely identify stockholders and administrators as it requires of companies domiciled in Brazil. All that is required for enrollment in the Corporate Taxpayer Register (CNPJ) is a copy of the company charter. This means they might be satisfied with a simple declaration issued by a tax haven's public agency (bearing the company name, date chartered, type, purpose, and address).

[11] Cf. Terror outfit-turned 'charity' JuD set to come under Pak Central Bank scanner. In *Asian News International,* March 13, 2012, www.lexis.com, accessed June 19, 2012; BUTT, Naveed. Insurance/takaful companies: SECP enforces compliance with AML Act. *The Financial Times Limited.* NPO 3/25/2012, 2012 WLNR 6308356.

[12] See Prafulla MARPAKWAR. State forms cells to detect source of terror funds. *Times of India.* Copyright 2011 Bennett, Coleman & Co. Ltd. Dec. 24, 2011. www.westlaw.com. Accessed June 19, 2012.

61. NGOs should have ready access to technical information to enable them to monitor and record all assets and amounts received, spent, and entrusted to their care;

62. Licensing should be required for operation under tax exempt status, and continuation of this status ought to be contingent upon regular reporting to revenue authorities of all relevant information, in an official document duly dated and signed under penalty of perjury, listing the name and telephone number of the person in charge of the books and records of the organization or foundation;

63. The organization's books and records ought to include a detailed list of its activities and management, revenue, expenses, and liquid assets, to include: the name and purpose of the institution; number of members; whether they have on hand more than 25 % of their liquid assets; number of voting members listed within and outside of the organization; number of employees; number of volunteers; unrelated business revenue and amount paid in taxes; contributions and donations; resources invested; benefits paid to and for members; total assets and liabilities; basic description of all assistance programs; whether any loans or benefits were granted to employees, directors, a trustee, or any other person; name, number of hours worked, and job description of all employees and former employees (including directors, trustees, and key personnel); earnings had by these individuals; expenses claimed (including travel and entertainment); and names and particulars of all donors;

64. An external audit should be required above a given gross revenue ceiling (more than $100,000, for example), as the state of New York so capably provides[13];

65. Organizations should include in their bylaws requirements for distribution of financial reports and outside audit reports for all directors and management personnel (president, manager, and financial department), for easy review;

66. Universal access to the bank account transactions, records, and reporting requirements of all NGOs, associations, and foundations;

67. In the case of a temple, church, mosque, educational institution, or trust, even if registered as an NGO, association, or foundation, all sources of funding must be provided in sufficient detail to the authorities, including the IRS;

68. There should be a bar on receiving cash donations, or at least a cap above a certain amount (say, $3,000), which would, above that amount, restrict donations to banking instruments;

69. Accounts of all such entities should be reviewed to reinforce due diligence and check whether they actually perform the purposes for which they are organized. Accounts should be allowed to be opened only in the organization's own name and in accordance with the documentation submitted;

70. If announcements are made that a given account will be receiving donations or something similar, banking institutions must check on the beneficiary of wire transfers made from that account, and promptly submit a suspicious activity report to the Financial Intelligence Unit if the published account is different from the account owned by the NGO or foundation;

---

[13] Cf. www.chariries nys.com/pdfs/statute_booklet.pdf, accessed June 29, 2014.

71. Check that all donations and contributions received for specific purposes are properly recorded and faithfully accounted for;

72. Provide clear procedures for board membership, thus ensuring diversity among the members;

73. See to it that all board members act in good faith to avoid any conflict of interest between the entity, its purposes, and themselves;

74. Secure independent and exempt financial evaluation

8.2.8 Regulatory Agencies, Financial Institutions, and the Internal Revenue Service

Explanation Given the extreme ease with which a church can be legally formed, the proliferation of mega-churches and mega-temples, and the occurrence of numerous abuses, it is important to reflect critically on the extent of the phenomenon and its consequences. It is unfortunate that some pseudo churches operate under the cloak of faith in order to carry out fraudulent acts. States must be able to identify, disrupt, and dismantle hypocritical religiosity networks that engage in money laundering and terrorist financing. The international Financial Action Task Force (FATF) compels states to seek to fight money laundering through various fronts, including an aggressive policy to allow its discovery and eradication. The inviolable freedom of conscience and religion, the free exercise of religious activities, and the guarantee of the protection of places of worship and their rites must be assured. No one can be deprived of rights on the grounds of religious, philosophical, or political belief unless the individual invokes those beliefs to exempt himself or herself from all legal liability and refuses to perform an obligation established by law. New religious movements may claim the right to enjoy the privileges accorded to churches and temples in non-separationist societies and have the right to not be seen with suspicion.

75. Public financing of education constitutes a violation of the constitutional separation of church and state; nevertheless, secular and sacred subjects in education must be distinguished such that aid to religious schools should not be considered the same as aid to the church or temple itself. The educational curriculum of religious schools can be verified by the state in the name of the principle of separation[14];

76. Establish a regulatory agency, if it is not feasible for Financial Intelligence Units to provide proper oversight so as to timely obtain direct or indirect access to financial and

---

[14] See KONVITZ, Milton R. in a similar perspective, but defending the refusal of public aid to parochial schools. Separation of Church and State: The First Freedom, 14 Law & Contemporary Problems 44 (1949).

administrative information, and information from law enforcement authorities in order to fully perform their functions, including analysis of suspicious transaction reports (thereby fully complying with FATF Recommendations Nos. 26, 27, 29, and 31);

77. The regulatory agency should be empowered to demand secure records of individuals (photo ID, proof of domicile, employment information), and of religious institutions for constant review—for many entities are deterred when they believe that full compliance is being enforced upon companies similar to their own;

78. Compare records with the contents of other databases to determine whether the underwriters demanded complete documentation before the transaction. Whenever a third party is involved, check whether guarantees are accepted without proper appraisal;

79. Consider board members of churches and temples as Politically Exposed Persons, that is, persons in prominent positions, such as priests, pastors, cardinals, bishops, archbishops, monks, rabbi, and reverends (both nationals and foreigners);

80. Require that churches and temples conduct Customer Due Diligence (CDD) on donors. Prohibit companies, nonprofit organizations, churches, temples, and individuals from maintaining anonymous accounts. Make identification requirements, with records kept for at least five years. If donors are found to be Politically Exposed Persons, they ought to be more closely monitored. This brings us to the need for churches and temples to hire compliance employees who can monitor and verify donations. These employees should look for forged documents, unconvincing or nonexistent identification, negotiations made in the name of outside parties or trustees, and the involvement of offshore accounts to conceal the true identity of buyer or seller;

81. Religious organizations should be freely created (unless they have a clear illegal intent), internally structured, and able to function freely without the government denying their recognition or the registration of their acts necessary for operation. Leaders who profess religion must be monitored if they engage in profitable activity that could eventually collide with the institution of tax immunity;

82. The government must accommodate religious interests by granting immunity from intrusive regulation, unless a state interest of the "highest order" is present. If a church or temple seeks exemption from a government regulation, it must demonstrate that the regulation, directly or indirectly, compels the church to perform an act that the religion forbids, or proscribes an act that the religion commands. Although tax immunity has been a well-established and constitutionally guaranteed way for achieving religious freedom, there is a need for discussing borderline issues, such as the contrast between the wealth of temples and the lack of resources of its followers, the financing by people who profess no religion, discriminatory conduct of many cults, and a lack of control over their earnings, facilitating unlawful practices;

83. As commercial organizations, churches and temples, mega or not, must not be granted the same protection as traditional churches and temples if, for example, they offer gym memberships, bookstores, and franchises. The presumption is still that they have eleemosynary status since the religious benefits can be associated with typical churches or temples. In this case, the protection of the law should be granted as it is granted to any church or charitable organization;

8.2.9 Violation of Parishioners' Rights (Consumers' Rights) and Antitrust Laws

Explanation Breach of trust violates consumer rights and compromises fair competition in the market. Good faith or loyalty contracts should be a rule of conduct submitting to administrative penalty in order to prevent fraudulent business practices. Misconduct is unacceptable.[15] On the other hand, it is important to provide a minimum level of protection for all parishioners regardless of their host country's position. Consumer protection and interest must ensure that church and temple management is conducted in a fair and open way. According to Charles E. Brown, "antitrust laws are designed to maximize consumer welfare by minimizing excessively large combinations of economic power."[16]

84. Penalize business practices that violate good faith or loyalty contracts that are designed to protect parishioners' rights. These contracts are supervised by the National Consumer Protection System in Brazil, and by the Federal Trade Commission and the U.S. Department of Justice in the United States. Employment arrangements within churches and temples should follow certain procedures in order to avoid conflict of interest;

85. Prohibit contracting services from companies owned by officers or persons related to churches and temples (priests, pastors, cardinals, bishops, archbishops, monks, reverends and so on, both nationals and foreigners) in order to avoid unethical negotiations that allow all sorts of illicit gains and interests.

8.2.10 Churches, Temples, Mega-Churches, and Mega-Temples

Explanation The number of cases involving embezzlement, fraud, capital flight, and money laundering within religious organizations should spark serious concern on the part of authorities and church parishioners. Religious institutions are centers for faith and cultural diffusion, intended to draw people in, educate them, and diffuse relevant values. Such a role should strengthen their primary objectives and commitments as eminently social institutions.

86. In principle, regardless of the amount of money that these institutions make, mega-churches and mega-temples might be considered religious institutions and as such, deserve the protection of the law. It is important for the law to indicate how much of a church's or

---

[15] See Humberto THEODORO JÚNIOR. *Consumer Rights* (*Direitos do Consumidor: a busca de um ponto de equilíbrio entre as garantias do Código de Defesa do Consumidor e os princípios gerais do direito civil e do direito processual civil*). Rio de Janeiro: Forense, 2009, p. 25.

[16] In Professional Football and the Antitrust Laws: Impact of *United States Football League V. National Football League* and a Proposal for Change. 31 St. Louis U.L.J. 1057, 1058 (1986–1987).

temple's activities, labor, and funds can be devoted to influencing legislation and to what extent churches and temples may engage in—and encourage their members to engage in—the direct lobbying of policy makers and what are the legal implications of a church taking a particular stance on a public policy;

87. Churches and temples should review their codes of conduct, with proper supervision, to ensure that there are no conflicts of interest or that there are measures in place to detect fraudulent behavior and illegal activity. All sensitive information ought to be analyzed and duly reported to the directors of these institutions;

88. Directors and board members of international churches and temples must follow procedures regarding the need to prevent money laundering. There have been cases where these individuals, instead of adhering to the faith and doctrine that they profess, instead acquire luxury automobiles, horse farms, and other luxury products. The value of religious knowledge needs to be made clear, avoiding cases like this will ensure them the continued respect of the public;

89. Being such complex and dynamic organizations, churches and temples must have the ability to control and shape changes in their religious doctrine free of substantial government interference. Their general right of autonomy might be recognized, but it must also be consistent with the common standard rules about the best administration of churches and temples;

90. Mega-churches and mega-temples can accumulate vast amounts of wealth. If they cannot pay creditors, the massive nonpayment could cause serious financial strain for both the creditors and the surrounding community. If there is fraud or abuse of the eleemosynary status, the corporate veil of the mega-church or mega-temple should be pierced and this presumption should be revoked;

91. Payments or donations in cash, prepaid access cards, or through electronic transfers cannot be prohibited. However, institutions should cancel negotiations with or donations from businesses that cannot provide enough financial justification to make it possible to check on the investor's financial strength since they can be the result of some sort of tax evasion or illegal act. All cash payments must be received in an envelope that identifies the donor, and should be duly registered in the church or temple accounting books;

92. Churches and temples should provide information to Federal Revenue Authorities in their countries, or, whenever required, and to the Financial Intelligence Unit, including detailed records on clients (name, address, identity, profession, fingerprints, profits or losses, deals made) when the services provided are not completely associated with faith (private businesses).

Bibliography

ABOVITZ, Ian. Why the United States Should Rethink Its Legal Approach to Internet Gambling: A Comparative Analysis of Regulatory Models that Have Been Successfully Implemented in Foreign Jurisdictions. 22 Temp. Int'l & Comp. L. J. 437 (2008).

BANA, Anurag. Online Gambling: An Appreciation of Legal Issues. 12 Bus. L. Int'l 335, 2011.

BLANKENSHIP, Michael. The Unlawful Internet Gambling Enforcement Act: A Bad Gambling Act? You Betcha! 60 Rutgers L. Rev. 485 (Winter 2008).
DE SANCTIS, Fausto Martin. Responsabilidade penal das Corporações e Criminalidade Moderna ou Responsabilida da pessoa jurídica e Criminalidade Moderna. São Paulo: Saraiva, 2009
EZABELLA, Felipe Legrazie. Agente FIFA e o Direito Civil Brasileiro. São Paulo: Quartier Latin, 2010.
FATF, Vulnerabilities of Casinos and Gaming Sector, March 2009, available at http://www.fatf-gafi.org/media/fatf/documents/reports/Vulnerabilities%20of%20Casinos%20and%20Gaming%20Sector.pdf
FEDERAL Bureau of Investigation—FBI, http://www.fbi.gov/about-us/investigate/vc_majorthefts/arttheft. Accessed May 21, 2012.
FIFA exigiu mudanças na justiça da África do Sul. Jornal da Globo, TV Globo June 23, 2010, http://g1.globo.com/jornal-da-globo/. Accessed June 24, 2010.
GODDARD, Terry. How to Fix a Broken Border: FOLLOW THE MONEY. Part III of III. American Immigration Council Publication. Immigration Policy Center, May 2012
GODOY, Arnaldo Sampaio de Moraes. *Direito tributário comparado e tratados internacionais fiscais*. Porto Alegre: Sergio Antonio Fabris, 2005.
KOBOR, Emery. *Money Laundering Trends. United States Attorney's Bulletin*. Washington, DC, vol. 55, no. 5, Sept 2007.
KONVITZ, Milton R. Separation of Church and State: The First Freedom, 14 Law & Contemporary Problems 44 (1949).
MACKENZIE, S.R.M. *Going, Going, Gone: Regulating the Market in Illicit Antiquities*. London: Institute of Art and Law – IAL, Jan 1, 2005.
MAGEE, Jonathan. When is a Contract More Than a Contract? Professional Football Contracts and the Pendulum of Power. 4 ESLJ xxvi, 2006–2007.
MARPAKWAR, Prafulla. State forms cells to detect source of terror funds. *Times of India*. Copyright 2011 Bennett, Coleman & Co. Ltd. December 24, 2011. www.westlaw.com. Accessed June 19, 2012.
MCELROY, Meghaan Cecilia. Possessions is Nine Tenths of The Law: But Who Really Owns a Church's Property in the Wake of a Religious Split Within a Hierarchical Church?. 50 William and Mary Law Review 311 (October 2008).
MEXICO proposes to limit cash purchases of certain goods to 100,000 pesos. 2010 Fintrac Report.
MILLS, Jon. Internet Casinos: A Sure Bet for Money Laundering. 19 Dick. J. Int'l L. 77 (2000–2001).
MIRANDA RODRIGUES, Anabela. Contributo para a fundamentação de um discurso punitivo em matéria fiscal. Direito Penal Económico e Europeu: textos doutrinários. Coimbra: Coimbra ed., 1999
OLSON, Eric L. Considering New Strategies for Confronting Organized Crime in Mexico. Washington, DC: Woodrow Wilson International Center for Scholars. Mexico Institute. Mar 2012
ORMAND, Susan. Pending U.S. Legislation to Prohibit Offshore Internet Gambling May Proliferate Money Laundering. 10 Law & Bus. Rev. Am. 447, 2004.
SILVA SÁNCHEZ, Jesús-María. Eficiência e direito penal. Coleção Estudos de Direito Penal. São Paulo: Manole, 2004, No. 11.
STERNAL, Patrick. *The Business of Religion. Current Legal Issues Facing Religious Organizations*. 18 Business Law Today 47 (2008–2009).
TERROR outfit-turned 'charity' JuD set to come under Pak Central Bank scanner. In *Asian News International*, Mar. 13, 2012. www.lexis.com. Reporter, Naveed Butt.
THEODORO JÚNIOR, Humberto. Consumers Rights (Direitos do Consumidor: a busca de um ponto de equilíbrio entre as garantias do Código de Defesa do Consumidor e os princípios gerais do direito civil e do direito processual civil). Rio de Janeiro: Forense, 2009.

Index

F.M. De Sanctis, *Churches, Temples, and Financial Crimes*,
DOI 10.1007/978-3-319-15681-1

The manufacturer's authorised representative in the EU is Springer Nature Customer Service Centre GmbH, Europaplatz 3, 69115 Heidelberg, Germany. If you have any concerns regarding our products, please contact ProductSafety@springernature.com

Printed and bound by CPI Group (UK) Ltd, Croydon, CR0 4YY
30/09/2026
02225513-0012